DISCRIMINATION
WITHOUT VIOLENCE

Discrimination
Without Violence

. . . .

MISCEGENATION AND RACIAL
CONFLICT IN LATIN AMERICA

MAURICIO SOLAÚN and SIDNEY KRONUS

A WILEY-INTERSCIENCE PUBLICATION

JOHN WILEY & SONS, New York · London · Sydney · Toronto

Library of Congress Cataloging in Publication Data:

Solaún, Mauricio.
    Discrimination without violence.

    "A Wiley-Interscience publication."
    Bibliography: p.
    1. Cartagena, Colombia—Race question.   2. Latin
America—Race question.   3. Social conflict.
4. Miscegenation.   I. Kronus, Sidney, joint author.
II. Title

HN310.C37S64   301.6′36′098   73-8606
ISBN 0-471-81100-9

Printed in the United States of America

10 9 8 7 6 5 4 3 2 1

To our wives *Joan* and *Carol,*
and, of course, *Nurse Ann*

PREFACE

. . . .

This book attempts to explain why racial discrimination has not been accompanied by substantial racial violence in Latin America. Although Latin American societies have been stratified along racial lines, *latinos* of color have predominantly expressed their grievances about their position of subordination in terms of class rather than race conflict. Our study focuses on white-black relations in a large Latin American city. It is the first major exploration of this subject in urban Colombia. As such, it provides grounds for a more solid comparative Latin American sociology on racial matters. By contrasting our findings with materials of other Latin American nations, we show some of the basic racial similarities that are found in Negroid-Iberian America, similarities that account for a common historical experience of low levels of overt racial conflict amidst substantial levels of other forms of political conflict.

Several reasons led us to embark on this investigation. Above all, the conspicuous contrast between current racial conditions in the United States and Latin America and the magnitude of the racial problem in the former suggested the need for a systematic treatment of those adaptive mechanisms that have permitted the prevalence of racial cordiality in Latin America. Our interest in Latin American race relations was furthered by the fact that although black-white relations had a similar origin in slavery in both areas, only in the United States have racial tensions acquired major societal proportions. Our curiosity in the topic was also aroused by another factor. Most Latin American nations, Colombia in particular, are now in a state of flux, the product of high levels of class conflict. That is, these societies are not currently under conditions of a "traditional equilibrium" characterized by a paternalistic control and the apathy of subordinated individuals. Yet, the rising expectations of colored persons has not led to the overt manifestation of substantial racial conflict. In this respect, in terms of their low levels of racial conflict and violence, Latin American societies have experienced "successful" race relations. Of course, a much different picture appears in the areas of political intra- and interclass relations that have been characterized by substantial strife and violence.

The previous facts notwithstanding, the literature has registered the opinion that low levels of racial strife in Latin America can be explained historically in terms of the lack of awakening of the *negro* masses—the absence of social mobilization and change. Interestingly, most of the political literature accounts for the present state of political and class rather than racial turmoil in the area precisely in terms of current high rates of social mobilization and change. Actually, two contrasting themes prevail in the study of Latin American race relations: the pessimistic and optimistic interpretations. As suggested, pessimists forsee the escalation of racial conflict in the future as blacks become increasingly aware of their condition of deprivation. Awareness is generally tied to processes of social change, such as urbanization and increased educational attainment. Optimists, on the other hand, consider that Latin Americans have been relatively tolerant in racial matters since the colonial period and that social change has and will lead to increased racial homogeneity through extensive miscegenation. Consequently, they forsee future increases in racial assimilation rather than conflict. This controversy is the main problem to be dealt with in our monograph. By placing within a comparative sociohistorical context the current sources of interracial stress and adaptation in Cartagena, Colombia, we hope to clarify the controversy and contribute to systematize the implications of critical racial patterns for strife and violence.

Discrimination without substantial societal violence has been historically associated in Latin America with the emergence of the "infused racial system." Briefly, this system is characterized by the relative acceptance of the miscegenated by whites and their infusion with equal status throughout all levels of the class structure. Paradoxically, the system is also characterized by a direct discriminatory relationship between class and race. The empirical analysis of this dialectic quality of the infused racial system whose origins can be traced to the colonial period permits us to account for the adaptive historical interaction of class and race in Negroid-Iberian America.

We wish to acknowledge the financial support given to the project by the Center for Latin American Studies, Center for International Comparative Studies, and the Graduate Research Board, of the University of Illinois, Urbana. We also express our appreciation to Robert E. Scott for his leadership as director of the overall research project of which this book is a part. Our thanks also to Dr. Germán García Restrepo of the Fulbright Commission, Bogota, for two travel grants to the area. In addition to Jerome Gagerman, three students participated in different stages of the project: Madeline Gates, Inés Elvira Mayoral, and Ann Wendell. Their contribution was invaluable. We wish to acknowledge the most helpful suggestions and criticisms of Fernando Cepeda, Norman K. Denzin, Joseph L. Love, Pierre van den Berghe, and Norman E. Whitten, Jr. Finally, the hospitality given to us in Cartagena made our work both possible and most enjoyable. To our friends in Cartagena we extend our deepest appreciation.

MAURICIO SOLAÚN
SIDNEY KRONUS

The University of Illinois
Urbana, Illinois
April 1973

CONTENTS

. . . .

DISCRIMINATION
WITHOUT VIOLENCE

. . . .

Chapter One

INTRODUCTION

THE PROBLEM

Although Latin American societies have been characterized by recurrently high levels of political and interclass violence, they have evolved institutional structures capable of producing highly adaptive relationships among racial groups; that is, groups defined according to differences in physical characteristics. Specifically, Latin American societies have experienced comparatively low levels of overt racial strife and violence. For instance, since the turn of the century Colombia has had substantial levels of political-party and class-related violence in which the lower classes have been actively involved, with a net result of several hundred thousand deaths. Although the literature has questioned the extent to which Colombian violence constitutes a case of class conflict or of a strictly political conflict void of any ideological implications, neither the participants themselves nor the social scientists who have studied the phenomenon have defined it as a case of interracial violence (1). Low levels of race conflict, however, have been accompanied by the presence of racial discrimination in the society. Not only are the bulk of the blacks found in the lower class echelons, but access to intimate elite circles is barred on

1

racial grounds. Although racial patterns have experienced changes through time in the area (2), there is some evidence that critical racial configurations were established and stabilized in Latin America during early historical periods. These configurations began in the colonial period (3), and they have permitted the maintenance of low levels of racial strife amidst much more violent political and socioeconomic changes. The basic problem, then, in this study is to explain the structural characteristics and processes that permit discrimination to coexist with interracial adaptation in Colombia. We concentrate our attention on those patterns that have a predominantly Negro-white basis, as opposed to an Indian-white foundation, and we place a priority on comparing United States and Latin American experiences in race relations. Our aim is to contribute to the analysis of alternatives to racial equality.

BASIC LATIN AMERICAN RACIAL PATTERNS

As we proceed we discuss those racial patterns that are significant to our investigation, but at this stage it is pertinent to make some preliminary statements concerning the key characteristics of Colombian race relations, placing them in the context of the overall Latin American racial patterns. There are variations in interracial relations among Latin American countries and within national regions (4). The first difference can be traced to racial composition. Some countries, such as Argentina, are mainly European; in others the predominant racial composition is a combination of Caucasian and Amerindian types (5). In still others, such as Brazil, the prevalent combination is Caucasian and Negroid. Regional variations within countries are also found, and the predominance of a particular racial combination does not always preclude the conspicuous presence of other racial types. Thus in Brazil, Amerindian elements are also found. The heterogeneity that has accompanied high levels of miscegenation has led the

Mexican philosopher José Vasconcelos to talk about a Latin American "cosmic race" (6).

The second difference in racial patterns can be traced to the nature of the composition itself. In Latin America there is a differentiation between the social definition given to Indians and Negroes. In contrast to blacks, in Latin America Indians are mainly differentiated from the rest of the population on ethnic (language and patterns of dress) as opposed to racial (visible physical) characteristics (7). In effect, if an Indian changes his cultural patterns to conform with the dominant group's standards, he is defined as a *mestizo* or mixed blood. In contrast, although there is some evidence to support the assertion that "money whitens," there is a tendency to define highly Negroid individuals, regardless of cultural patterns, as belonging to the polar racial type or *negro* (8). Thus in Latin America *racial* discrimination is centered against blacks. A reason for the relative prevalence of racial discrimination in Afro-, as opposed to Indo-Latin America that has been noted by such authors as Pierre van den Berghe can be traced to the wider physical differences found between Iberian and Negroid individuals (9).

In terms of the interracial mosaic of Latin America, as a nation Colombia is predominantly Caucasian and Amerindian (10). However, substantial pockets of Negroid populations are found in coastal areas. Cartagena, the site of our study, is located in such an area where there are significant proportions of whites and blacks.

Despite the diversity of racial patterns found in Latin America, there are sufficient similarities, particularly between areas with similar racial compositions, to warrant generalization. This is why Hoetink has conceptualized an Iberian American system of white-Negroid race relations and contrasts the Iberian variant to that of the Northwest European type (11). In doing so, the very similar Spanish and Portuguese American racial patterns are distinguished from other European types, including the French, thus we can make some broad generalizations from our data.

In our analysis of the racial patterns of the "infused system" characterized by the presence of significant proportions of whites, blacks, and miscegenated individuals with various combinations of genes (12), Iberian Negro–white relationships are discriminatory. Race inhibits the upward movements of individuals within the class structure, and the bulk of the blacks are members of the lower class. In particular, Negroid racial characteristics are deliberately employed by gatekeepers to exclude persons from membership in the socioeconomic elite or "society" circles (13). Furthermore, Negroid physical characteristics are widely considered as "ugly" (14). In Cartagena, this esthetic preference is apparent even among some predominantly Negroid slum settings, where sales of products destined to "whiten" their users are common. Racial discrimination notwithstanding, the crucial characteristics of the "infused" variant of race relations can be derived from an analysis of the particularly ambiguous position of the miscegenated in the society (15). In contrast to the United States, in Iberian America persons are neither entirely white nor black. Although the Northwest European variant of race relations in the Caribbean recognizes an intermediate racial group—the mulattoes or colored—it is in Latin America that the miscegenated experience more-fluid or less-discriminatory boundaries (16). It is in Iberian America that a significant proportion of the dominant "white" segment can recognize its miscegenated background, while at the same time exercising racial discrimination to block the access to its ranks of nonwhites.

In the Iberian American infused system there is substantial relativism in racial matters. Persons are viewed as falling within a continuum of racial types and as being "more or less" white or black (17). That is, not all miscegenated individuals receive a nonwhite *social* definition. Let us be more specific. Although Iberian Americans are aware of the presence of Negroid racial characteristics in individuals (18), there is a range in which these characteristics are dealt with purely as physical traits or qualities devoid of basic prejudicial or racist considerations. Pierson presents the case of a "white" educator in Bahia, Brazil—an example that could have been drawn from Cartagena, Havana, or Puerto Rico—who considered that one of his boys was white but that his girl was "you might say, a bit of a *mulata*" (19). According to him, "the sense of this remark seemed similar to that of a father in the United States saying, 'Look at my little blue-eyed girl,' or 'Here's a real brunette' " (20). Thus, although particularly under "experimental" conditions or probing, *latinos* are aware of racial differences; given their relative tolerance toward the miscegenated, an awareness of Negroid blood does not necessarily lead to a nonwhite *social* definition. That is, Pierson's girl most probably would be able to marry freely with phenotypic whites of her own class. This does not imply, of course, that a zealous parent might not employ the argument of "blackness" as one among other instruments used to attempt to block the liaison. (Other arguments could be personality traits, wealth, etc.) This is why Wagley has considered race as "but one criterion" to determine social status in the area (21). In contrast, it is well known that in the United States there has been the opposite rule of "hypo-descent" (22) by which persons are either "pure" white or black. Although in the Northwest European Caribbean variant an intermediate racial group has been recognized, this phenomenon did not accompany the practice of the Iberian infused system by which a significant proportion of miscegenated individuals has been capable of intermarrying freely with an elite that essentially defined itself as white or *blanco*.

The fact that racial characteristics can assume the definition of simple physical qualities in Iberian America and that intermarriages are frequent between phenotypic whites and miscegenated persons of the same social class (23) has lead to the interpretation that Latins are prejudiced according to class, not race. For example, according to Pierson, "prejudice exists in Brazil; but it is *class* rather than *race* prejudice. It is the kind of prejudice which one finds inside the ranks of the Negro in the United States" (24). There is a need to refine this conceptualization. Racial prejudice is concentrated in Negroid Iberian America against the polar racial type, the *negro*. (Throughout the text we will employ the term *negro,* Negro, and black to indicate the polar racial type). In effect, it is a well-acknowledged fact that intermarriage is highly infrequent among the racial extremes, and it must be accepted that despite the rhetorical outbursts of some *latinos* Negroes are deliberately barred on racial grounds from elite circles. The fundamental characteristic of the infused racial pattern is the relatively high acceptance of the miscegenated by phenotypic whites. There are three important corollaries to this proposition: (a) the greater the range of the racial disparity between individuals, the greater the probability that physical characteristics will operate as criteria for racial discrimination among them; (b) among physically close or similar persons, racial traits tend to describe physical characteristics, not racist sentiments; and (c) as a consequence of their acceptance and relative freedom to intermarry with whites, the miscegenated have not been prone to constitute a separate social group segregated from whites (or blacks) (25). Indeed, as noted by Harris, a fundamental characteristic of the infused racial system is that despite prejudice "there are no racial groups" (26).

The case to be stressed here is that the relatively low racism of white Iberian Americans consists of their relatively tolerant sentiments toward the miscegenated, particularly the lighter types. It is misleading to overestimate the extent to which prejudice against *negros* is of a class, rather than a racial nature in the area, for, as indicated by our data, among the lighter segments of the society racial prejudice is extensive (27). The lighter the miscegenated type, the greater the possibility of negotiating the race in relationship to whites. To return to a previously mentioned point, the selected number of nonwhites who penetrate "white" elite circles consist of miscegenated persons who have been capable of transforming their racial characteristics into physical traits.

The penetrability of some miscegenated types into white elite circles to the point of being capable of marrying freely within these sectors suggests another characteristic of the infused Iberian American racial system—extensive miscegenation and the tendency to reduce the number of individuals found in the discriminated polar racial type. Although the extent of miscegenation has varied according to several factors, such as the proportions of racial groups and the extent of their physical mobility (28), it seems that, *ceteris paribus*, Iberians have been prone to miscegenate. In any case, it appears that the Iberian modality of race relations in the Western Hemisphere has been accompanied by a greater acceptance of miscegenation than the Northwest European variant.

The volume of miscegenation for various societies is a subject of great controversy. For example, no one can reliably estimate what proportion of the United States population is genetically "pure" black. However, it is not the volume of biological miscegenation *per se* that mainly distinguishes the infused racial system, rather it is the cultural ethos toward the miscegenated. Despite the propensity in relatively racist nations like the United States and South Africa for interracial sexual relations, the cultural ideology supports the myth of racial purity, endogamy rules, or caste relations. In contrast, in the Iberian infused variant, regardless of the biological dimension, there has been a culturally supported tendency toward miscegenation. For instance, as already noted, "pure" Indians who change their cultural patterns become "miscegenated" *mestizos* or *ladinos*. In addition, in the Iberian modality instead of a two- or three-way racial categorization that distinguishes "pure" whites from persons of black ancestry, there exists a multiterm racial categorization system that obscures Negroid ancestry while accepting the fact of miscegenation. Indeed, there is a tendency to "lighten" the population.

Many sources have singled out the process of racial "upgrading" or assimilation—the bleaching process—by which miscegenation occurs at the expense of the black, not white, population (29). This is logical. In sharp contrast to the Northwest European variant, the complex and ambiguous Iberian racial terminology with racially "neutral" terms (30) creates situations in which the offsprings of interracial sexual unions can diminish or lose their "degrading" racial identity. Of course, the tendency is to employ racial terms other than the polar discriminating ones to define the self (31). These terminological variations are necessary for the coexistence of racial discrimination and the full acceptance of some miscegenated individuals in white circles because they neutralize the "shameful" background of the miscegenated.

Although the process of racial "upgrading" concomitant to miscegenation is unquestionable, it must be noted that there is evidence that migratory interracial contacts have often resulted in the subordination and occupational displacement of blacks (32). Indeed, Latin America is not a racial utopia. As we shall see, Iberian adaptive mechanisms have often contributed to produce social integration at the expense of the black population. For example, high levels of European immigration to Argentina led to the "Europeanization" of its population (33), and to the emergence of a nationalistic pride vis-à-vis adjacent lesser European nations. The mechanism of racial "upgrading" permitted rendering into oblivion the racial antecedents and the presence of a racially mixed population in this country. Nevertheless, despite subordination and displacement, processes that are not new in Latin America, the fact that discrimination has not been accompanied by substantial racial violence suggests the presence of fairly enduring structural characteristics and processes that are conducive to racial adaptation. In anticipation of our conclusions, there is evidence that the previously described characteristics of the infused racial system—which can be considered to lead toward racial adaption—were already present in Iberian America prior to independence. For example, despite discrimination, during the colonial period racial boundaries were ill defined. It is well documented that licenses that made persons of some color legally white were purchased during this period (34). Not only did mescegenated persons penetrate the national elites, but several national heroes had nonwhite ancestry. In addition, the racial terminology of colonial Latin America was already characterized by its complexity and ambiguity, factors that facilitated racial "upgrading" and assimilation. Finally, by the time of independence miscegenation had achieved substantial levels. For instance, it has been estimated that in 1789, 53.6 percent of the population was miscegenated in an area where four-fifths of the slave population of Colombia lived (35). In terms of our analysis, then, we must explore the determinants of race relations in the area during early historical periods. Nevertheless, given the persistence of some of these patterns, we can extrapolate some of our data on current Colombian racial patterns to explain the reasons for the historical duality of low racial strife amidst intense political-class conflict.

THE SETTING

Cartagena, a city of approximately 300,000 inhabitants (36), was chosen as the base for our research because it met certain criteria we felt to be important. First, our concern with current racial problems in the United States led us to select a site where blacks, as opposed to Indians, constituted the prevalent subordinate racial group. This seemed particularly important to us because previous studies of Latin America indicate that racial discrimination in the area is concentrated against the Negroid population—*negros* and *mulatos* as opposed to *indios* and *mestizos* (37).

There were other reasons for the selection of Cartagena. Of the largest Colombian cities with a high percentage of blacks, Cartagena has the most aristocratic tradition (38). This led us to expect the presence of a dominant group defining itself as *blanco* and to patterns of relatively pronounced racial discrimination (39), which in the case of Cartagena, given the high proportion of blacks, would be centered against Negroid persons.

In addition to the previous factors, Cartagena was selected because of its relatively high rates of social change. Although the Department (province) of Bolivar where it is located has been experiencing an average rate of population growth comparable to the national rate, Cartagena is among the most rapidly urbanizing cities of Colombia (40).

The combination of racial discrimination, exacerbated by the alleged dominance of a traditional aristocratic elite, and rapid social change that seemed to characterize Cartagena was particularly appealing to us because, as suggested, a theme in the literature interprets the absence of racial strife in Latin America as being partly the product of a static traditional equilibrium in which paternalistic, economically noncompetitive, quasi-feudal relationship of dependency among the races are highly institutionalized and accepted. (41). Although such consideration seems to be an overstatement, the combination of both aristocratic, *Gemeinschaft* type of relations and social change seemed to us a fertile ground to explore the dynamics of discriminatory mechanisms and processes for interracial integration. The setting was propitious to survey the survivals of traditional discriminatory patterns, and even to study incipient increases in racial conflict impinging upon a traditional order that was starting to crumble vis-a-vis the economic competition brought about by rapid social change. There was yet another possibility. The particular nature of traditional race relations in the area might have produced some basis for obtaining a durable interracial peace in a society experiencing rapid social change and mobilization (42), mechanisms that deserve systematic consideration. A major effort has been placed in this study to the answering of these general questions.

NOTES

1. For an analysis of recent patterns of violence see Mauricio Solaún, *Political Violence in Colombia*, unpublished Ph.D. dissertation, Department of Sociology, University of Chicago, 1971. Also see Mons. Germán Guzmán Campos et al., *La Violencia en Colombia*, Ediciones Tercer Mundo, Bogota, 1962. For the most comprehensive interpretation of Colombia's twentieth century political history, see Robert H. Dix, *Colombia: The Political·Dimensions of Change*, Yale University Press, New Haven, 1967. The case for the strictly political or intraclass nature of the violence is made in James L. Payne, *Patterns of Conflict in Colombia*, Yale University Press, New Haven, 1968. For an analysis of both types of escalated conflict in Latin America see Mauricio Solaún and Michael A. Quinn, *Sinners and Heretics: The Politics of Military Intervention in Latin America*, University of Illinois Press, Urbana, 1973.

2. For example, Mörner considers that prejudice increased during the eighteenth century in Latin America as the middle groups increased their wealth, and Whitten has traced increases in discrimination to migrations in contemporary Ecuador. See Magnus Mörner, *Race Mixture in the History of Latin America*, Little, Brown and Company, Boston, 1967, pp. 66–67 and Norman E. Whitten, Jr., "The Ecology of Race Relations in Northwest Ecuador," paper presented in the annual meeting of the American Anthropological Association, New Orleans, Louisiana, 1969.

3. Blumer has made a similar case for the United States. According to him, once patterns of acute racial segregation are well established, as in the United States, they tend to survive even in the presence of rapid socioeconomic change (industrialization). See Herbert Blumer, "Industrialization and Race Relations," in Guy Hunter, Ed., *Industrialization and Race Relations*, Oxford University Press, London, 1965, pp. 220–254.

4. See, for instance, van den Berghe's considerations of Brazil's greater racial discrimination over that of Mexico and of regional differences within Brazil itself in Pierre L. van den Berghe, *Race and Racism, A Comparative Perspective*, Wiley, New York, 1967, pp. 37 and 74–75.

5. For a more detailed description of the racial types found in Latin America see Marvin Harris, *Patterns of Race in the Americas*, Walker and Company, New York, 1964.

6. José Vasconcelos, *La Raza Cósmica,* Agencia Mundial de Librería, Paris, 1925.

7. In this sense, see John P. Gillin, "Some Signposts for Policy," in *Social Change in Latin America Today,* Richard N. Adams, et al., Vintage Books, New York, 1960, p. 19. According to Mörner, in Indo-Latin America, the criterion for distinguishing groups is "sociocultural," whereas in Afro-Latin America it is "physical appearance, the phenotype," that is, racial. See Mörner, *op. cit.,* p. 136.

8. For a fuller discussion see Chapter 6.

9. This proposition is predicted by the theory of H. Hoetink, *The Two Variants in Caribbean Race Relations, A Contribution to the Sociology of Segmented Societies,* Institute of Race Relations, Oxford University Press, London, 1967.

10. After 1918, Colombian censuses have avoided any racial or color classification. T. Lynn Smith has made the following racial estimate for Colombia as a whole: whites, 25 percent; Indians, 5 percent; Negroes, 8 percent; *mestizos,* 42 percent; and mulattoes, 20 percent. See T. Lynn Smith, "The Racial Composition of the Population of Colombia," in *Studies of Latin American Societies,* T. Lynn Smith, Ed., Anchor Books, New York, 1970, pp. 56–83. For a similar estimate, see Ernesto Camacho Leyva, *Quick Colombian Facts,* Editoral Argra, Bogota, 1962, p. 174.

11. Hoetink, *op. cit.*

12. The Iberian American infused racial system includes the presence of individuals with Amerindian traits, the poles being Caucasian and Negroid characteristics. In the absence of racial demographic data we cannot give a numerical racial categorization to the different racial types.

13. The criterion of deliberate exclusion from elite membership on racial grounds is a better indicator of discrimination than the concentration of blacks in the lower classes that characterizes Latin American societies because, assuming low levels of upward mobility in the society and given the historical fact of slavery, it is feasible to interpret black overrepresentation in the lower classes as a historical class phenomenon, not a deliberate racial discriminatory one. Kottak has made this case for differences in landownership in a Brazilian village. See Conrad Phillip Kottak, "Race Relations in a Bahian Fishing Village," *Luso-Brazilian Review, 4,* 1967, pp. 35–52. The case that discrimination is highest

among aristocratic elite groups is made in Charles Wagley, Ed., *Race and Class in Rural Brazil,* Unesco, Paris, 1952, p. 153.
14. *Idem* and Hoetink, *op. cit.,* p. 165.
15. This very important point is forcefully presented by Hoetink, *op. cit.*
16. Eugene D. Genovese, *The World the Slaveholders Made,* Vintage Books, New York, 1971, p. 107.
17. Marvin Harris, "Race Relations in Minas Velhas, A Community in the Mountain Region of Central Brazil," in *Race and Class in Rural Brazil, op. cit.,* p. 61.
18. For the opposite interpretation see Hoetink, *op. cit.,* pp. 167–168.
19. Donald Pierson, *Negroes in Brazil, A Study of Race Contact at Bahia,* University of Chicago Press, Chicago, 1942, p. 134.
20. *Idem.* The case that racial characteristics are but a quality of individuals is also suggested by Harris, "Race in Minas Velhas," *op. cit.,* pp. 64–65, and Wagley, *op. cit.,* p. 154.
21. Wagley, *op. cit.,* p. 9.
22. Harris, *Patterns of Race, op. cit.,* p. 37.
23. Pierson, *op. cit.,* p. 340.
24. *Ibid.,* p. 349. Emphasis in original text.
25. See Pierson, *op. cit.,* p. 172. According to him, mixed bloods advance socially "not as a group but as individuals." Also see Florestan Fernandes, "Relaciones de Raza en Brasil: Realidad y Mito" in *Brasil: Hoy,* Celso Furtado et al., Siglo XXI Editores, S.A., Mexico, 1968, p. 134.
26. Harris, *Patterns of Race, op. cit.,* p. 61.
27. See Chapters 5 and 6.
28. For instance, low levels of Portuguese immigration in Africa, although accompanied by relative tolerant attitudes toward the miscegenated, have not produced substantial miscegenation. See David M. Abshire, "The Portuguese Racial Legacy," in David M. Abshire and Michael A. Samuels, Eds., *Portuguese Africa, A Handbook,* Praeger, New York, 1969, pp. 91–106. For the role of physical mobility in miscegenation in colonial Latin America, see Mörner, *op. cit.,* p. 75.
29. See, for instance, T. Lynn Smith, *Brazil: People and Institutions,* Louisiana State University Press, Baton Rouge, 1946 and Her-

bert S. Klein, *Slavery in the Americas, A Comparative Study of Virginia and Cuba,* University of Chicago Press, Chicago, 1967, pp. 254–260. For Puerto Rico, see David Lowenthal, "Race and Color in the West Indies," in *Comparative Perspectives on Race Relations,* Melvin M. Tumin, Ed., Little, Brown and Company, Boston, p. 305.

30. *Trigueño* and *moreno* are examples of these terms. Both of them can denote white and nonwhite individuals. For the usage of the former term to define miscegenated persons in Puerto Rico, see Melvin M. Tumin with Arnold Feldman, "Social Class and Skin Color in Puerto Rico," in *Comparative Perspectives on Race Relations, op. cit.,* pp. 197–214. For the two meanings of *moreno* in Brazil, see Harry W. Hutchinson, "Race Relations in a Rural Community of the Bahian Recôncavo," in *Race and Class in Rural Brazil, op. cit.,* pp. 28 and 30. A fuller discussion of racial terminology appears in Chapter 6.

31. See, for instance, Tumin with Feldman, *op. cit.,* p. 200. Only a small majority of the highly Negroid slum dwellers of Cartagena call themselves *negro.* See Chapter 5.

32. See Fernandes, *op. cit.,* and Whitten, *op. cit.* For a discussion of some effects of migrations, see Chapter 7. Actually, the pace of miscegenation in the area has been questioned. For example, it has been considered that miscegenation is less common today than in earlier periods. For Brazil see van den Berghe, *op. cit.,* p. 70. Also, according to Hutchinson, "lightened areas seem to continue to lighten, while the darker areas retain their dark characteristics." Hutchinson, *op. cit.,* p. 37.

33. Ralph L. Beals, "Indian-Mestizo-White Relations in Spanish America," in *Comparative Perspectives on Race Relations, op. cit.,* pp. 239–257.

34. See, for instance, Mörner, *op. cit.,* p. 45.

35. See Jaime Jaramillo Uribe, *Ensayos Sobre Historia Social Colombiana,* Universidad Nacional de Colombia, Bogota, 1968, pp. 10–11.

36. According to the latest census, July 15, 1964, it had 242,085 inhabitants. See Departamento Administrativo Nacional de Estadística, *XIII Censo Nacional de Población (1964), Resumen General,* Imprenta Nacional, Bogota, 1967, p. 30.

37. *Mestizos* originally meant the offsprings of Caucasians and Indians; *mulatos,* the offsprings of Caucasians and Negroes. *Mestizo* is derived from the popular Latin term *mixticius* or mixed,

and *mulato*, from mule. Although as we show later, current racial terminology in Colombia has lost some of its biological connotations and is affected by factors such as class, among the educated both terms have maintained a meaning close to their origins. That is, a *mestizo* is a person who cannot be considered to be "pure" white and has Indian racial characteristics. *Mulato*, on the other hand, is a person with salient Negroid characteristics but who is neither a *negro* (i.e., Negro) nor a *blanco* (i.e., white).

38. For the particularly aristocratic background of the Cartagena elite, see Dix, *op. cit.*, p. 46 and Rodolfo Segovia, "Teoría de Cartagena: Por qué se Pierde un Siglo," in Donald Bossa Herazo, *Cartagena Independiente: Tradición y Desarrollo*, Tercer Mundo, Bogota, 1967, p. 32.

39. For Brazil, Wagley had established the relation between aristocratic background and attachments to racial discrimination. Wagley, *op. cit.*, p. 153. For Puerto Rico, see Tumin with Feldman, *op. cit.*, p. 202.

40. Departamento Administrativo Nacional de Estadística, *op. cit.*, p. 30.

41. See, for instance, Harris, "Race in Minas Velhas," *op. cit.*, pp. 80–81.

42. Klein, *op. cit., passim.*

. . . : . . . .

Chapter Two

FRAMEWORK FOR THE STUDY
OF RACIAL VIOLENCE

In their attempts to interpret the causes of strife among racial and ethnic groups within national boundaries, social scientists have conceptualized several patterns of intergroup relationships. In this chapter we first discuss two polar systems of race relations—the open and the closed systems. We then discuss the infused system of race relations, a system we consider to typify racial patterns in Cartagena. But before proceeding, a few introductory words are pertinent. This study is not concerned with explaining the isolated cases of racial tension that are apparent in the history of Colombia (1). Our objective is to interpret for both Cartagena and Latin America the historical absence of socially important national racial movements, and the strife that accompanies them, such as those currently in operation in the United States (2). Secondly, we are concerned mainly with the study of interracial conflict and equilibrium in situations of racial subordination that were originated by slavery. That is, we are basically interested in the analysis of hierarchical relationships among the races, not in pluralistic arrangements by which racial or ethnic communities achieve an equilibrium by sharing sociopolitical power within a national state, such as is the case of Switzerland.

THE OPEN AND THE CLOSED RACIAL SYSTEMS

There are two ideal polar concepts to typify racial (or ethnic) relationships: total integration and complete segregation. The condition of total integration is embodied in what has been called the open system of race relations, where race has no effect on the stratification system (3). Logically speaking, the purest form of this system occurs in the presence of a complete racial homogenization. That is, in the face of total racial uniformity, race cannot logically become a discriminatory device because racial *groups* cannot be formed. For example, a society of white Anglo-Saxon Protestants cannot differentiate or discriminate persons possessing the same racial or ethnic characteristics on these grounds (4). Total segregation occurs in closed systems. Here, racial *groups* are deliberately separated and differentiated from each other in a rigid fashion. Because the underlying principle of planned segregation is one of superiority-inferiority, segregation leads to a structure of occupational domination and deprivation. This is likely to occur even when avoidance is a major mechanism for the separation of the groups (5). For instance, blacks have an ascribed and highly circumscribed niche in the lower levels of the occupational structure. There is a logical prerequisite for a closed occupational structure: racially segregated family groups. The theory of family structure is of great importance for the understanding of race relations. Indeed, if persons do not discriminate in the more sacred and intimate sphere of family relations, they will not do so in impersonal business or occupational ties. There is empirical evidence that a cultural ideal or myth of endogamy is a necessary condition for a closed society. To wit, contemporary South African and historical United States antimiscegenation legislation and the relatively low incidence of mixed marriages in these countries. Perfectly closed systems require caste systems or *"endogamous and hierarchized group* [s] *in which one is born and out of which one cannot move"* (6). The ideology of segregation requires the cultural myth of endogamy and leads to hierarchical relationships among racial groups. The internal contradictions of policies of deliberate separation, such as separate but equal, are obvious. Pierre van den Berghe makes the following case:

> The proponents of "positive" apartheid claim that "parallel development" will eliminate white domination, and establish an equitable geographical partition, but Strydom, the second post-war Nationalist Prime Minister, stated categorically: "Our policy is that Europeans must stand their ground and must remain boss in South Africa." Verwoerd now speaks of "independent Bantustans," but in 1951 he said in Parliament: "Now a Senator wants to know whether the series of self-governing areas would be sovereign. The answer is obvious. . . . It stands to reason that White South Africa must remain their guardian." (7)

Next we relate in a brief fashion the two outlined types of race relations to competition, for several sources have attempted to explain the degree of racial discrimination and conflict in the society in terms of this factor (8). (See Table 2.1.)

TABLE 2.1   Race Relations and Competition

	Racial Group Competition	Racial Group Noncompetition
Racial integration or homogeneity	(1) (Logically impossible)	(2) (Logically necessary) Stable equilibrium
Racial segregation	(3) Conflict or violence	(4) Unstable equilibrium

As has been noted, under conditions of total racial integration—a condition obtained in its purest form when total racial homogeneity or uniformity materializes—groups can not engage in racial competition (cell 1); there is only one racial group. Noncompetitive race relations necessarily prevail in this open system (cell 2). The end result is a situation of a racially stable or long-run equilibrium. Although under this condition groups cannot be formed along race lines, this open system is characterized by a keen competition of *individuals,* not groups, of the same racial stock but with different physical characteristics. For example, blonds compete with brunettes for jobs and, we may add, they "miscegenate" freely. Of course, such a competitive situation cannot lead to racial conflict or violence (cell 3). Under these conditions only other types of conflicts, such as family feuds or interclass strife, will materialize. The ideal situation is approximated in the United States by relationships among assimilated, nonethnic whites.

Optimists have typified Latin American race relationships in these terms. For instance, according to Pierson,

> Whereas in the United States the rise of the Negro and of the mixed-blood has been principally within the limits of the Negro world, in Brazil the rise has been with reference to *the total community;* that is, *the Negro* in Bahia not only *competes freely* with all others of his own color but can and does compete with all aspirants to the same class; and, if he has ability and gives evidence of definite personal worth, he will be accepted for what he is *as an individual,* and his racial antecedents will, at least to a considerable degree, be overlooked (9).

High levels of miscegenation—the eventual achievement of total racial homogeneity—(cell 2) has been a corollary to this interpretation that high levels of personal, not group, competition, among individuals with different racial characteristics characterizes Latin American race relations (10).

As discussed in Chapter 1, to some extent Iberian American race relations conform to the pattern of racial integration or homogeneity, for racial movements are rarely formed in the area, and racial characteristics among racially close persons (of the same class) tend to be considered as physical, not "racial," qualities of individuals. However, a perfect equilibrium or integration has not materialized (cell 2) because total racial homogeneity has not been achieved. Polar racial types still exist. Actually, racial tensions in the area have been linked to the upward mobility of highly Negroid individuals into white society (11). Before proceeding with the specification of the racial system of Cartagena, let us continue with a discussion of Table 2.1.

It is also feasible to conceptualize ideal-type, noncompetitive situations among segregated groups. Racial slavery is a case in point. Under a *closed* and *effective* system of slavery everyone is in "his place" and "knows it." There is total subordination in a situation characterized by virtually no mobility and a division of labor along racial lines. In this division of labor there is little overlap among masters and slaves, and the society is highly segregated—each racial group has distinct ways of life. The lack of intergroup competitiveness that characterizes this type of society can be inferred from the institution of slavery itself. Its logic establishes fixed, noncompetitive boundaries between masters and slaves. In an ideal of the system, a traditional noncompetitive equilibrium (cell 4) materializes in which masters are paternalistic or benevolent despots and slaves internalize their subordinate status. Nevertheless, in reality the equilibrium is usually unstable, and the system tends to break down or move toward open competition and conflict among racial groups (cell 3). As indicated by slave history, the combination of exploitation and the absence of a cultural or religious justification (12) for the existing subordinated segregation produces revolts, which if successful, as in Haiti at the end of the eighteenth century, move the society toward an increased racial homogeneity or toward cell 2 by eliminating the master racial class (13).

We are still confronted with the intellectual problem of the relationships between segregation, conflict, and competition, a central theme of the literature. Obviously, as epitomized by slavery, segregation aims at curtailing the competition between individuals belonging to the dominant and subordinated groups, but in the long run, it tends to create conflict among racial groups; that is, there is a tendency to move from cell 4 to cell 3. Nevertheless, segregation itself has been directly tied to intergroup competition. That is, it has been considered that real or potential competition between individuals of different racial stocks increases prejudice, discrimination, and conflict (14) and that it can ultimately lead to extremely segregated systems, or to *de jure* segregation, as in South Africa (15). In terms of Table 2.1, this interpretation contends that segregation (cell 4) is most probable when racial groups are likely to place themselves in competition (cell 3). Of course, the history of slavery in the Western Hemisphere follows the opposite sequence. Racial subordination was established and avoided effective competition from the outset. In contrast to black-white relations, white ethnic immigrants to the United States have received higher levels of education and have competed more successfully with other whites than is the case of the Negro (16). As already noted, it appears that the segregation that accompanied slavery in the United States has tended to survive processes of rapid socioeconomic change.

Analysts who consider competition as the independent or determinant factor of racial segregation have argued that the harsher Northwest European racial systems are, paradoxically, the product of the greater competitiveness and equalitarianism that characterizes these societies, as opposed to their Iberian American counterparts. The argument must logically follow that in Latin America there is no race problem because of the traditional acceptance by nonwhites of their subordinated position, an opinion that reflects the pessimistic interpretation of Latin American race relations. Although we do not deny a plausible impact on race relation of the greater paternalism that in general terms characterizes Iberian American social relations, it is incorrect to categorize race relations in Cartagena as being integrated by a feudalistic equilibrium of subordination, for as we show, the adaptive mechanisms that prevail in the area are of a different nature. In Cartagena, some segments of the nonwhite population are integrated on equal terms with whites to the point of intermarrying freely with them. Persons who receive different racial designations locally compete freely with each other for economic positions at different layers of the stratification system (17). The Cartagena racial system is not characterized by a rigidly ascribed division of labor along racial lines.

Let us recapitulate and clarify the analysis. The closed system of race relations is characterized by a myth of endogamy and hierarchical relations among racial groups. Consequently it is prone toward group conflict and violence when social change leads to competitive situations. The open system, on the other hand, consists of nonendogamous and nonhierarchical race relations. It is characterized by individual, not group, competition among persons with different physical characteristics. As we show, the Latin American infused racial system is eclectic. On the one hand, endogamy and hierarchical ties are predominant characteristics of relationships among the polar racial types (the discrimination principle). On the other hand, many individuals defined locally as belonging to different races intermarry and compete on equal terms with each other for scarce resources (the integration principle). This eclectic system does not appear to be the product of a situation in which nonwhites have not threatened whites by competing for scarce resources but of a propensity on the part of Iberian Americans to assimilate the miscegenated. Indeed, it has been asserted that Brazil experienced a higher frequency of slave uprisings than the United States (18); a central political preoccupation of nineteenth century Cuba was the fear of a repetition of the Haitian experience in the Island; and, of course, Colombia experienced numerous slave revolts (19). The paternalism toward nonwhites that may exist in Latin America should be interpreted not in terms of fixed racial boundaries but in the light of the ambiguous usage that is given to some racial terms in the area. This includes the term *negro,* which is employed (with its variations) to express endearment by whites to other whites and as an affectionate nickname (20). That is, Iberians are relativists in racial matters. They do not have an ideology that views race as an "all or nothing" condition.

In the foregoing analysis we have suggested that the basic differences between United States and Latin American racial patterns cannot be explained in terms of a greater competitiveness among the races in the former, because black-white relations in both societies were initiated under conditions of noncompetitive subordination, and because nonwhites have actually competed more with whites in Latin America (21). This does not mean to imply that competition does not have an independent effect on race relations, for it does, even in Latin America. In effect, it appears that the competition between individuals of different racial stock tends to increase discrimination in all latitudes. Fernandes' case can be complemented with the Cuban experience of the first two decades of this century, when substantial Spanish immigration was accompanied by a preference to hire whites, not blacks, even as domestic servants. Furthermore, it is logical that, *ceteris paribus,* the probability of *de jure* segregation increases with the size of the minority as it becomes politically more competitive and threatening (22). The point to be stressed here is that *substantial* differences in racial systems, as those between the United States and Latin America, must be explained in terms of the lower social distance and the less disgust that white Iberians feel toward nonwhites, the miscegenated in particular, and that such attitudes cannot be explained mechanistically in terms of competition. Indeed, returning to the latter example, substantial proportions of blacks have not been accompanied by *de jure* segregation in Iberian America. The *ceteris paribus* condition has not held because of the greater racial tolerance of the *latinos.*

THE INFUSED RACIAL SYSTEM

Characteristics of the System

The infused racial system found in Cartagena is characterized by the infusion of persons considered locally as being misce- genated, that is, neither *blanco* or *negro*, throughout the entire stratification system (23). In this system we find a significant proportion of miscegenated individuals at the elite level and among the middle and lower classes as well. The system is not characterized by a structural bifurcation along racial lines (cell 4) because the miscegenated that are found at the elite level intermarry *freely* with the phenotypic whites who also belong to this group. Furthermore, the infused system is not characterized by an identity between class and race. That is, in Cartagena the upper class is not phenotypically white, the middle class, mulatto, and the lower class, black. A signif- icant number of whites do not belong to the upper class, and a number of mixed bloods do. In terms of the discussed ideal racial systems, then, the Cartagena system is open in that non- white physical traits have not impeded the access of a signifi- cant number of individuals into exclusivist, predominantly white, elite circles (24). Actually, our interviews indicated that the Cartagena elite is aware of substantial miscegenation, of racial homogenization—cell 2, if you will—in its midst (25). The infused system, however, is not fully open. Indeed, it is impossible, or virtually so, for a *negro* to enter into the social elite realm, and Negroid characteristics can be a critical factor to block the access of newcomers into these circles. Finally, blackness is inversely related to position in the class structure. To be black is a definite handicap in Cartagena.

The characteristics that we consider typify the Cartagena racial system are also found in other Latin American socie- ties. For instance, Pierson talks about the *brancos da Bahia* (Brazil), that is, miscegenated persons who intermarry freely with whites. As an upper-class white woman remarked to him: "It's different with the lighter shades. You can't easily draw the line between the pure whites and those with only *um pouco da raça*. Race mixture has now become so extensive that there wouldn't be many left to choose among" (26). Pierson concludes that "very light mixed bloods often marry whites without any question whatever arising" (27). In Hoetink's terms, "the 'old white families' in these societies [the Spanish Caribbean and Brazil] almost without exception have some amongst their *legitimate* relations who cannot be classed in the white segment" (28).

The infusion of the miscegenated throughout the entire class pyramid and the imperfect relations between class and race are also suggested by secondary sources in their references to other Latin American societies characterized by the infused system. For instance, according to Harris, in Minas Velhas, Brazil, nonwhites are admitted in the local elite social club, and "approximately 90 percent of the Negroes, 50 percent of the mulattoes, and 10 percent of the whites cannot dance in the Clube" (29). That is, as in Cartagena, there are mixed bloods who are accepted by the elite and whites who are not. In his study of the Sertão, Zimmerman considers that "with the exception of the Negro, people of all racial types may be found in all classes" (30). Later on he considers that "of the white families, only one is felt by the people of Monte Serrat to be *sem mistura* (without mixture)" (31). Finally, Tumin has made a case for the infusion of persons of color throughout the Puerto Rican class structure (32).

Although the infused racial system that characterizes Cartagena appears in many Latin American communities, it is by no means the only one. This point is important because, as we show, the structural characteristics—and their accompanying sociopsychological mechanisms—of this system are particularly conducive to racial, not class, adaptation, that is, to the absence of racial conflict. The question, then, is under what conditions is this system most probable to appear (33)? It seems that the infused system is most likely to be present in communities—large and small—in which there is a substantial proportion of miscegenated persons, blacks, and a significant minority of whites. In this respect it typifies the Iberian Caribbean as a whole. Let us be more specific. In Colombia it appears that the model does not apply to those regions which can be considered to be virtually all black, such as the Choco. Here, even highly Negroid individuals belong to the local elites, and we may add, there appears to be a greater racial consciousness in these areas (34). Conversely, in those sections, as in Bogota where there is a very small proportion of blacks, the model is also absent. In this case, Negroid individuals are not found at the elite level.

Our propositions suggest a direct relationship between the density of Negros and the presence of black blood at the elite level. As the proportion of whites increases, the probability of white hegemony increases. The analysis also suggests that the infused system is most likely to appear where substantial segments of different racial stocks are present—whites, blacks, and miscegenated.

The implications for racial conflict of our hypotheses are clear. In sharp contrast to the United States, in Iberian America substantial proportions of blacks have led to a significant Negroid penetration at the elite level. Although in the extremely Negroid regions, as the Choco, there appears to be relatively higher levels of racial awareness, these regions are economically underdeveloped and highly isolated from the national society. The concentration of blacks in these areas, coupled with their isolation and underdevelopment, particularly when compared with the lesser Negroid regions, tend to transform racial awareness into regionalistic feelings. Those conflictive manifestations that might be vocalized by the local black elites, consequently, tend to acquire regionalistic ("secessionist") characteristics (35). In a parallel fashion the low density of whites and miscegenated individuals in Portuguese Africa has led to the manifestation of racial awareness in movements for independence. In contrast, the presence of significant proportions of whites, blacks, and miscegenated persons in colonial Latin American societies produced wars of independence led by the elites that typify the infused system, that is, *blancos* and mixed bloods.

In those areas with the smallest proportions of blacks racial discrimination seems heightened, at least when measured with regard to Negroid penetration of the elite. In those few countries that are predominantly European and where there is only a remote trace of Negroid blood, one commonly finds a conspicuous pride in whiteness. In terms of race conflict, however, the potentiality for strife here is small because of the size of the minority. Indeed, the processes of increases in white domination that have accompanied white migrations in Latin America have tended to reduce the size of the Negro population (36).

We are left with the analysis of Latin American regions found in the middle of the continuum, that is, areas that have substantial proportions of white, black, and miscegenated individuals—the infused system. For the reasons expressed, these areas appear as crucial to the generation of a national racial movement because toward one end of the continuum there are very few Negroes to effectively threaten the system and toward the other end, blacks have historically been very isolated from the national society in these uncommon areas. An important national racial movement requires a coalition between black areas and cities with a large proportion of *negros* and *blancos,* such as Cartagena. The study of the predominantly adaptive mechanisms that characterize the infused racial system are presented later in the text. At this stage we introduce a brief historical statement on the origin and development of this racial system in Latin America.

Origin and Development of the Infused System

The road toward increased racial integration or homogeneity (cell 2) cannot follow only the abrupt elimination or cessation of segments (i.e., political breakdown) as was the Haitian case, where there were rapid movements from cell 4 to cell 3 and toward cell 2 (37). There is an alternative path—the gradual homogenization of the population through miscegenation and its fundamental corollary, the acceptance of a significant proportion of mixed bloods at the apex of the class pyramid. As already noted, in a more or less explicit manner several sources have considered that this has been the Iberian American pattern. Yet this system had an origin in slavery, in a "pigmentocracy" with legally established racial privileges (38).

In the colonial period, particularly in Spanish America, a legally formalized racially discriminatory society known as the Society of Castes, *Sociedad*, or *Régimen de Castas*, materialized. In Mörner's terms, the *casta* system "was created by transferring to the New World the hierarchical, estate-based, corporative society of late medieval Castile and imposing that society upon a multiracial, colonial situation" (39). The *Régimen de Castas* was similar to the feudal European system of estates in that the society was formally divided into groups differentiated in their legal status (i.e., racial groups with different rights and obligations) which were invested with corporate privileges and duties by the Crown. As with the traditional, ideal-type equilibrium of slavery (cell 4), the *casta* system was devised as a deliberately planned noncompetitive racial organization. Its ideal was to construct a static, paternalistic, discriminatory racial order in which every racial group had its place. The static aspects of the corporatist philosophy consisted of a belief that justice was the product of the achievement of a "natural" order. Justice was not conceived of as emanating from competition. The prevalent idea was that the society could be organized into an equilibrium through the creation of especial "natural" niches for racial groups (40). Of course, there was, nonetheless, ambiguity of status partly because of the overlapping of castes, corporations, and estates.

Although discriminatory, the *Régimen de Castas* does not entirely fit the closed system described in Table 2.1. Although noncompetitive in intent and formally "segregated," the regime did not close the door to racial (and cultural) homogenization and mobility. Indeed, in 1514, the liberty to marry Indians was definitely decreed (41). Although it was as late as 1806 when total freedom to marry persons of Negro origin was decreed (42), and marriages normally occurred between persons with close racial characteristics, the acceptance of extensive miscegenation characterized the colonial period. The term caste was a misnomer, for the society was not divided into religiously sanctioned, hierarchically endogamous groups. In contrast to the previously described closed slave system, all groups had a place in this order. Medieval corporatism was not universalistic in that it formally recognized human inequalities. However, it sought to include all groups in its distribution of justice, and as has been stated, groups were not seen as totally closed. Negro slaves, who received some legal "privileges" (43) were included in the system. Although at this stage it would be unproductive to digress into the nature and causes of the different slave systems in the New World, for our purposes we can, by contrast, establish that the Iberian slave systems were relatively more open, as witnessed by higher percentages of free blacks and the social acceptance of the miscegenated (44).

Mörner recounts vividly the processes of upward mobility among the Spanish American *castas* within the framework of this highly formalized society:

The Society of Castes was being undermined by the very process that had helped to bring it into being, miscegenation. Once a multiracial terminology had been adopted, it simply became impossible to apply any universally valid and strict criteria for classifying an increasingly mixed population. As early as 1646, Chilean Chronicler Alonso de Ovalle observed that there was no mark 'to distinguish (the mestizo) from the pure Spaniard, except the hair which is not modified for two or three generations' . . . (45).

Given the legally reinforced racial discriminatory practices during the colonial period, the tendency was to try "to pass from a more modest and 'obscure' category to a more 'bright' and superior one" (46). However, extensive miscegenation and the legal discriminatory system induced complex patterns of passing. According to a source:

> A Mulatto, for instance, whose color helps him somewhat to hide in another 'casta,' says, according to his whims, that he is an Indian to enjoy the privileges as such and pay less tribute, though this seldom occurs, or, more frequently, that he is Spaniard, Castizo or Mestizo, and then he does not pay any (tribute) at all . . . (47).

Of course, prior to independence, particularly in the Negro-white variant, the road toward total racial homogenization (cell 2) was far from complete (48). As exemplified by contemporary Cartagena, the racially homogeneous and open society is not yet a reality in Negroid Latin America. The majority of the *negros* still are lower class, and the mingling between the bulk of this group and the lighter classes is infrequent. The point that must be stressed here is that, facilitated by a complex and ambiguous racial terminology, processes of racial "upgrading" and assimilation, of losses in racial identity were in operation during the colonial period, and, interestingly, these processes coexisted with the continuation of slavery, even in the presence of slave uprisings (49). As established by Mörner, "the Society of Castes was . . . undermined by the very process that had helped to bring it into being, miscegenation [and the acceptance of the miscegenated by whites]" (50). Its end did not come about through racial wars (51). The termination of slavery in Latin America was not tied to major political convulsions (52). The *Sociedad de Castas* formally ended with the political wars of independence which were influenced by French revolutionary ideology.

In sum, contrary to the expectations posited by Table 2.1, it seems that a general climate of racial adaptation—the absence of racial wars and of major racist national social movements—does not require total homogeneity or an open society. There can be relative enduring systems of racial discrimination characterized by pockets of socioeconomically deprived racial minorities, that is, by persons found in cell 4. This alternative does not require the idealized equilibrium of a traditional society in which there are clearly defined and well-established interracial boundaries, for as we show for Cartagena, the infusion of miscegenated persons throughout the stratification system is conducive to neutralizing the racial awareness of socioeconomically deprived racial groups—the slaves in the past; the black slum dwellers currently.

Contrast Between the Infused and the United States Racial Systems

In contrast to the Iberian American experience with a large proportion of free blacks and the full acceptance of some coloreds in the white-dominant segment during the slavery and the postslavery periods, the United States experience illustrates the opposite case of continued segregation with its southern and northern variants: *de jure* and *de facto* segregation. Klein documents the resistance in the southern United States (Virginia) to enter into less-structured race relations than those represented by slavery, where the clear legal distinction of master and slave prevailed. For instance, in 1806 a law was enacted "which required newly emancipated persons to leave the state within twelve months" (53). After 1830, there were frequent petitions to the state legislature to "restrict every movement and action of the free Negro and attempt if possible the total extinction of this class through exportation" (54). These attitudes indicate that total segregation was the pre-emancipation ideal (cell 4). Those blacks who were not clearly segmented by slavery were treated as "foreigners" (55). The return-to-Africa movement of this period was diametrically opposite to the successful Haitian revolutionary movement, where the dominant white segment was violently returned to "Europe" (56). Nevertheless, ultimately both aimed toward increased homogenization (cell 2) through elimination or expulsion. Granted that in the face of northern antislavery pressures, the fear of uprisings was exacerbated, and as indicated by the Vesey and Turner rebellions of the early nineteenth century, free Negroes could be critical agents in revolts (57). Furthermore, it is possible that the economic structure "needed" the continuation of slavery (58). Whatever its causes, the fact that an ideology of racial segregation prevailed is unquestionable. In the South, where the bulk of blacks lived, emancipation was followed by *de jure* segregation. Because homogenization through the total expulsion of whites or blacks did not materialize, legal institutions were created to prevent racial homogenization (cell 2) and maintain a non-competitive, racially segmented society (cell 4). In the North, less formalized methods of segmentation than slavery and extensive *de jure* segregation were institutionalized, and segmentation has been largely maintained through the alternative mechanism of social avoidance and by occupational discrimination (59).

The United States variant of race relations has been characterized by a *"Herrenvolk* democracy," in which to most whites "people" has meant whites (60). That is, in a sense, blacks have been considered to be "aliens." In sharp contrast to the Latin American experience, acceptance of miscegenation has been quite low in the United States. According to Reuter, "the little intermarrying that took place in the early colonial days between Negroes and the white indentured servants ceased almost entirely as the status of the Negroes became fixed and understood" (61). Beginning in 1661 in Maryland, to 1923, when 29 states had laws against the intermarriage of blacks with other races, continuing to the present time, although anti-miscegenation laws have been ruled unconstitutional, racial intermarriage has been seen as an evil in the United States (62). As already noted, in Iberian America the situation was much different because there was a much earlier legalization of interracial sexual relationships.

The previous considerations indicate the historical closeness of race relations in the United States. Given this pattern, the tendency has been toward open conflict and violence, that is, movements from cell 4 to cell 3. Few persons with noticeable black ancestry move into cell 2 or are integrated into white society. In contrast to the Latin American infused racial system, the United States' system has been characterized by a continued bifurcation or segmentation of white and black societies, by a lack of acceptance of miscegenated persons in the white social system.

The Infused Racial System and the United States Ethnic System

We now turn to a brief comparison between the infused system of Latin America and ethnic relations in the United States, a topic of importance because in some critical aspects the black-white pattern of Iberian American race relations is similar to United States ethnic patterns. By contrasting Latin race relations and ethnic patterns in the United States, that is, relationships among caucasians with different national or religious origins, we are able to clarify the nature of racial discrimination in Latin America and establish ground to explain why there has been greater interclass, not racial conflict in this region.

United States history has been characterized by processes of ethnic homogenization of immigrant groups. As members of ethnic communities became "Americanized," they entered into processes of "miscegenation" with persons of other national backgrounds, which, in certain aspects, parallel the Latin American process of racial homogenization by *mestizaje.* In both cases, miscegenation has led to integration (cell 2). This process notwithstanding, some segregated ethnic ghettoes or communities have remained in existence in the United States (cell 4) (63). Again, in Latin America, there are ecologically segregated pockets with a highly Negroid population that have not experienced substantial miscegenation. In the United States, white Protestants have experienced less discrimination in the more intimate elite social cliques. Even today there are some elite clubs, residential areas, and businesses (64) in which Jews and Catholics are discriminated against. As suggested, there is some racial discrimination among Latin American elites, and this discrimination has parallels to elite ethnic discrimination in the United States in that racial and ethnic visibility is a barrier for integration into the apex of the national socioeconomic elite.

There are, however, fundamental differences between the two patterns. First, in the United States to some extent ethnic segregation has been the product of the desire of the minority (65). The presence of strong subcultural identities, of ethnocentric beliefs, and of a leadership encouraging endogamy has maintained group boundaries. In Iberian America, on the other hand, a strong case for voluntary segregation can be made mainly for segments of the Indian (66) but not the black population. Second, in the United States some minorities have been tied to highly productive economic niches that have created parallel or segmented elite structures (67). In Latin America, on the other hand, this process has not occurred with *negros* and *indios* (68). Furthermore, in the United States, ethnic ghettoes have benefited from the country's economic affluence, whereas the bulk of Iberian American blacks and Indians are in the lower class. Thus some groups found in cell 4 have been relatively affluent. In short, there appears to exist a greater political and economic underparticipation—less pluralism—in Iberian American race relations than in United States ethnic relations.

The above-mentioned differences notwithstanding, the process of individual assimilation in the dominant sectors is similar in both societies. If a United States Jew and a Latin American Negro graduated with honors from law school and sought acceptance into reputable elitist law firms (69) they would encounter powerful barriers. Clearly, the physical or highly visible handicap of the Latin American *negro* would preclude his acceptance (70). The road toward his success in penetrating this small exclusivist circle would have to be indirect. By marrying a lighter person, he would "improve his race," his "bleached" children thus having a greater probability of success than he has. Eventually, appropriate miscegenation will permit full elite membership. Although less visible than his Latin American counterpart, the United States Jew with ethnic parents—or not "miscegenated"—would also find it difficult to "pass." The processes of changing his cultural identity —changes in name, religion, and so on—can be painfully slow. Again, it would most probably take nonendogamous generational changes to "pass" (71).

Let us recapitulate. It is in the area of ethnic, not racial relations that the United States has experienced the process of "miscegenation" comparable to those of the Latin American republics. It is precisely in this area that discrimination and open conflict have been relatively lower, the presence of ethnic prejudice notwithstanding. Actually, as with Latin American race relations, the tendency in the United States has been to polarize the society in interclass, not interethnic, conflict. For example, white immigrant groups formed a labor movement that cut across ethnic boundaries. As suggested, in Latin America class conflict has also been more potent than racial conflict. We have also seen that total ethnic and racial homogenization has not occurred in the United States and Latin America, respectively, and that some discriminatory practices remain, particularly for those seeking to penetrate exclusivist socioeconomic elite sectors (72). Finally, racial discrimination in Latin America is accompanied by relatively more painful economic experiences than those of members of United States ethnic minorities.

What are the ideologies that reflect the United States and Latin American systems? The combination of economically powerful ethnocentric groups wishing to maintain segregated endogamy and of persons seeking assimilation has led to a pluralistic philosophy in the United States that can be synthesized by the slogan of "cultural pluralism and structural assimilation" (73). That is, the ideal has been that there should not be any economic discrimination, that persons seeking assimilation (cell 2) should not be discriminated against, but on the other hand, that those desiring to maintain their cultural identity (cell 4) should be able to do so (74). In Negroid Latin America, on the other hand, the infused system has been accompanied by a less-pluralistic outlook. First, the economic and educational poverty of the *negro* minority and the absence of a religious basis for endogamy has been accompanied by generalized beliefs about the inferiority of blacks (75). In Latin America there is little political representation for persons found in cell 4. These highly Negroid segments do not articulate racial pride or interests. Secondly, as a reflection of the pigmentocratic origin of the infused system, the majority of assimilated persons—those found in cell 2—underplay their Negroid ancestry. As we show, few miscegenated persons in Cartagena call themselves *mulato,* they prefer to employ terms that do not connote black ancestry (76). Furthermore, as noted, the apex of the social class pyramid is *blanco* (77). Finally, the significant penetration of miscegenated persons in these circles has often been accompanied by beliefs that race mixture has led to "degeneracy" and underdevelopment (78). Miscegenation, the bleaching process, has been viewed as an inevitable process, a fact of life among elite groups. It is in this light that we must interpret Wagley's statement that miscegenation has been the unplanned or "unstated race policy" (79) of the infused system. That is, racist sentiments have been accompanied by a tolerance of racial impurity.

We have described the ideology of the infused system in Negroid Latin America because this is the focus of our study. This does not mean that there are no other patterns. As noted, the size of the black population seems to affect racial mentalities. For instance, the infused ideology is not as clearly evident in areas like the Choco, where the population is virtually all black, nor in areas where there is virtually no black blood, such as Bogota. Similarly, the effect of minority size is also seen in some areas of Latin America with substantial Indian populations, in which the presence of unassimilated Indian majorities has been accompanied by the equation of Indianism (*Indigenismo*) with nationalism. To the extent that Latin American societies or countries are *mestizo,* not Negroid, racist tendencies have been minimized. Conversely, to the extent that they are European, feelings of racial "purity" have been reinforced. Nevertheless, throughout Latin America there has been ambivalence in racial matters reflected in ideological expressions of a preference for the European cultural-racial complex, such as Hispanism (*Hispanidad*). Yet most of these have been romantic in nature, not generally tied to racial violence, and have not been formally incorporated into official policies of segmented endogamy.

CONCLUDING REMARKS

In this chapter we have contrasted Latin American racial patterns with United States minority relations within the context of two ideal polar types of dominant-minority relationships: the open and the closed systems. The key characteristics of the open system are exogamy, racial or ethnic homogeneity, and an absence of racial group domination. The closed system is characterized by endogamy—segregated family groups—and by racial group segmentation and domination. The closed system requires deliberate segregation, that is, a myth of endogamy and the establishment of barriers against interracial marriages. Furthermore, given its hierarchical relationships, the closed system is prone to experience competition and conflict between racial groups. This is likely to occur in the long run even though the system is designed to prevent competition. In contrast, in the open system there is free or open individual (not group), competition among persons with different physical characteristics. Thus in this system there is no discrimination and conflict among racial groups.

Although the Latin American infused racial system originated with slavery and a pigmentocracy that formally established a legally segregated, noncompetitive, multiracial society, there developed during the early colonial period a system based on both substantial levels of miscegenation and the penetration of miscegenated persons into the uppermost levels of the society. This system has been characterized by racial upward mobility and by the transformation of racial characteristics into physical traits, particularly for some miscegenated types. In sharp contrast to the Iberian American phenomenon, the United States experience with miscegenation during the colonial period resulted in a legal and real bifurcation or segmentation of the population into two polar groups: blacks and whites. This system has not permitted the infusion or integration of nonwhites into white society. Actual rates of miscegenation notwithstanding, the myth of racial purity and the lack of acceptance of the miscegenated by whites still remains.

The analysis of the infused racial system is crucial to explain the absence of substantial racial conflict in Latin American societies. First, it is the most heterogeneous racial system found in the area, for it is characterized by significant proportions of whites, blacks, and miscegenated individuals with different combinations of genes. In Iberian America societal feelings of racial "purity" or predominance have been directly related to the presence of phenotypic Caucasians, and discrimination has been concentrated against the Negroid population. Racism has been minimized in *mestizo,* not Negroid societies. Although racist orientations have been maximized in the few fairly homogeneous European societies found in Latin America, the small size of their minorities has not posed a racial political threat in them. Conversely, minority racial awareness has been heightened in those scarce, fairly homogeneous black regions that are found in some Latin American republics. However, the fact that these regions are quite poor and isolated from their national societies diminishes the probability that they can generate anything but unsuccessful secessionist racial movements, unless they form coalitions with the relatively more integrated and less homogeneously Negroid regions. These areas have been characterized by the presence of the infused racial system. Indeed, the infused system finds itself in a critical position in the Iberian American scene, for it exhibits the eclecticism of the relative racist orientation of European, not *mestizo* Latin America and the presence of a substantial minority of the relatively discriminated Negroid, not *mestizo* population.

In terms of our model, the Iberian American infused system also exhibits an eclectic nature: it is neither open nor closed. This system contains both endogamy and hierarchical relationships among polar racial types (the discrimination principle) and exogamy and nonhierarchical relationships among whites and some miscegenated types (the integration principle). Thus, in terms of the four-cell model that was presented to typify both open and closed racial systems, the Iberian American racial system is not described by any one cell. Rather, some nonwhites are perfectly integrated into white society—the situation described by cell 2—and others —the bulk of the *negros*—are segregated from white society; that is, they are found in cell 4. This static perspective of the Latin American system has prevailed since the period of slavery and contrasts to the static characteristics of the

United States racial system in which nonwhites are found in cell 4—they are segregated from white groups.

Race relations in the United States can be dynamically described in terms of movements from segregated noncompetition (cell 4) to segregated racial group competition and conflict (cell 3). In Latin America, the dynamics of race relations fit a pattern by which individuals, not groups, move from racial segregation (cell 4) to miscegenated integration (cell 2). This movement, as well as the presence of nonwhite individuals in cells 2 and 4, finds its parallel in United States ethnic, but not race relations.

The Iberian American infused racial system and the United States ethnic system have experienced greater class conflict than racial or ethnic conflict, respectively. The reason for this is clear. Despite tensions, both systems have assimilated upwardly mobile minority individuals. In later chapters we document the sources of racial tension and the mechanisms by which they are overcome in Cartagena. But first, we must explore the factors that led to the infused system, to the infusion of persons of color throughout the Latin American social class pyramid.

NOTES

1. For a recent case, see *El Tiempo*, Bogota, January 30, 1970, p. 1 and February 1, 1970, p. 8.

2. For the weaknesses of these movements in Brazil, see Pierson, *op. cit.*, p. 206 and Fernandes, *op. cit.*, pp. 127 and 133.

3. For the need to place the study of race relations within the theory of social stratification, see Michael Banton, *Race Relations*, Basic Books, New York, 1967, pp. 259–292.

4. Of course, this does not mean that there cannot be other sources of intraracial group conflict, but we do not consider, for example, interfamily conflicts, such as the Hatfield-McCoy feud, as racial in nature, even though they do produce a bifurcation of superiority and inferiority between these subgroups.

5. Blalock has emphasized the role of avoidance in United States race relations. See Hubert M. Blalock, Jr., *Toward a Theory of Minority-Group Relations*, Wiley, New York, 1967, pp. 51, 111, and 121.

6. The definition is taken from van den Berghe, *op. cit.*, p. 10, our emphasis. Of course, Myrdal established that racial discrimination in the United States is highest in the family. See Gunnar Myrdal, *An American Dilemma*, McGraw-Hill, New York, 1944, pp. 60–62. More recent studies indicate a continued opposition to mixed marriages in the United States. See Herbert H. Hyman and Paul B. Sheatsley, "Attitudes toward Desegregation," in *Comparative Perspectives on Race Relations, op. cit.*, pp. 284–285.

7. Pierre L. van den Berghe, "South Africa: The Culture and Politics of Race," in *Comparative Perspectives on Race Relations, op. cit.*, p. 230.

8. For a recent systematic attempt, see Blalock, *op. cit.*

9. Pierson, *op. cit.*, pp. 185–186, our emphasis.

10. *Ibid.*, pp. 125, 147, 154, and 350.

11. Harris, "Race in Minas Velhas," *op. cit.*, p. 81.

12. The importance of religious reasons for the maintenance of segmented societies (in the long run) has been stressed by Hoetink, *op. cit.*, p. 104.

13. Actually, after the expulsion of the French white group, two temporarily separate states emerged, a Negro kingdom and a mulatto republic. Up to the present time, some sectors of the mulatto elite have been ambiguous as to their ethnic background, an ambiguity having a racial aspect, and have sought to identify themselves as colored "French men." See *Ibid.*, pp. 133–138.

14. See, for instance, Melvin M. Tumin, "Introduction," in *Comparative Perspectives on Race Relations, op. cit.*, p. 11. Many cases of increased interracial conflict have been related to real or perceived increases in economic competition. This situation has been considered as one of the major preconditions of urban race riots in the United States, beginning with Atlanta in 1906. See Ray Stannard Baker, *Following the Color Line: American Negro Citizenship in the Progressive Era*, Doubleday, New York, 1908, pp. 84–87; Elliot M. Rudwick, *Race Riot in East St. Louis* [1917], Southern Illinois Press, Carbondale, 1964, pp. 6–15; The Chicago Commission on Race Relations, *The Negro in Chicago: A Study of Race Relations and a Race Riot*, University of

Chicago Press, Chicago, 1922, pp. 596–602; Alfred McClung Lee, *Race Riot* [*Detroit, 1943*], Dryden Press, New York, 1943, pp. 10 and 90; Otto Kerner, *et al., Report of the National Advisory Commission on Civil Disorders,* Bantam Books, New York, 1968, p. 225. As Whitten can testify, migrations and economic competition can lead to increased discrimination, that is, the economic displacement of some blacks, in Latin America as well. See Whitten, *op. cit.*

15. See van den Berghe, "South Africa," *op. cit.*

16. According to Blalock, in the United States there is greater racial discrimination in craft-type unions than in less skilled occupations, Blalock, *op. cit.*, p. 85.

17. See Chapters 4 and 5.

18. See Joseph L. Love, "Commentary [on Henry H. Keith's 'The nonviolent tradition in Brazilian history: A myth in need of explosion?'']," in Henry H. Keith and S. F. Edwards, Eds., *Conflict and Continuity in Brazilian Society,* University of South Carolina Press, Columbia, 1969, pp. 241–247.

19. Jaime Jaramillo Uribe, "Esclavos y Señores en la Sociedad Colombiana del Siglo XVIII," *Anuario Colombiano de Historia y de la Cultura,"* 1, 1963, pp. 3–62.

20. For this usage in Brazil as well, see Pierson, *op. cit.*, p. 139.

21. That this competition has also included the working classes appears documented in Fernandes, *op. cit.*, pp. 135–136. Indeed, some optimistic interpreters of the Iberian American racial variant have traced the "mildness" of race relations found in the area to the greater "openness" of the Iberian system of slavery which was characterized by large proportions of free blacks. See, for instance, Klein, *op. cit.*

22. For instance, witness the cases of South Africa and the Southern part of the United States. We might note that this relationship is not linear. If the dominant group is extremely small, as was the case of the British West Indies, then political control tends to be based on metropolitan rule.

23. For data in support of this contention see Chapters 4 and 5.

24. As considered by Harris, the predominance of phenotypic whites in these circles leads to define these groups as white. This does not mean, of course, that persons cannot make racial distinctions, for in fact they do. See Harris, "Race in Minas Velhas," *op. cit.*, p. 72.

25. See Chapters 4 and 5.
26. Pierson, *op. cit.*, p. 153.
27. *Idem.*
28. Hoetink, *op. cit.*, p. 65, our emphasis. The infusion of black blood throughout the Spanish Caribbean elites is also reflected in the saying *"¿tu abuela donde está?"* The saying literally means "where is your grandmother?" and makes reference to the fact that socially pretentious persons have black ancestry.
29. Harris, "Race in Minas Velhas," *op. cit.*, pp. 72–73.
30. Ben Zimmerman, "Race Relations in the Arid Sertão" in *Race and Class in Rural Brazil, op. cit.*, p. 88.
31. *Ibid.*, p. 93.
32. Tumin with Feldman, *op. cit.*
33. Unfortunately, the absence of racial census data and of pertinent racial studies impedes a more precise analysis of this important topic.
34. For instance, in Quibdo, the capital of Choco, there is a monument to a prominent late political leader with the following inscription—*Padre del Departamento, Educador y Faro de la Raza.* This reference to the *raza*, that is, "the [black] race," is atypical in Colombia. We might note, however, that this leader married a white woman. At the time of this writing, one of his sons is the governor of the department. It appears that a low proportion of whites has also led to a relative openness of the elites in Portuguese Africa. See David M. Abshire and Norman A. Bailey, "Current Racial Character," in *Portuguese Africa, A Handbook, op. cit.*, p. 204. Of course, the impact of colonial rule highly limits the political role played by natives in these colonies.
35. We might note here that there is a definite regional connotation given to *negros* in Colombia to the point of being called according to the area of origin. For instance, some are called *chocoanos* and others *costeños.* There can also be salient cultural differences between some *negro* and *mestizo* groups, particularly in terms of family structure and attitudes toward work, differences that can lead to discrimination. See Guy T. Ashton, *The Differential Socio-Economic Adaptation of Two Slum Groups and The Working Class To A Housing Project in Cali, Colombia,* unpublished Ph.D. dissertation, Department of Anthropology, University of Illinois, Urbana, 1972. For the presence of

44   Framework for the Study of Racial Violence

cultural differences between some *negro* and *mestizo* groups in Brazil as well, see Hutchinson, *op. cit.*

36. Secondary sources have considered that miscegenation and the outmigration of blacks have produced this effect. See Lowenthall, *op. cit.,* and Fernandes, *op. cit.* The migration of blacks vis-a-vis the economic pressures of *mestizos* has been recently documented by Ashton for Cali, Colombia. See Ashton, *op. cit.* This source presents data suggesting that miscegenation is not currently frequent at the very bottom of the class-race pyramid.

37. Of course we are not implying that Haitian society is thoroughly homogenized. There still remains a value for lightness in segments of the society.

38. The discussion that follows draws heavily on Mörner, *op. cit.,* Chapter 5.

39. *Ibid.,* p. 54.

40. This system reflected church ideology. We might note here that the church maintained this outlook after the French and Russian revolutions. Consequently, it sponsored quasi-fascist corporatist experiments during the periods of escalated interclass conflict that preceded the World War II. Although the emphasis on corporatism is pluralistic, the church adopted nonpluralistic ideas in religious matters where repression was favored. See Leo XIII's encyclical letters *Libertas* and *Rerum Novarum,* and Pios IX's *Quadragessimo Anno.* For discussions of the corporatist philosophy, see R. Morse, "Toward a Theory of Spanish American Government," *Journal of the History of Ideas, 15,* 1954, pp. 71–93, and Juan Linz, "The Party System of Spain: Past and Future," in *Party Systems and Voter Alignments,* Seymour M. Lipset and Stein Rokkan, Eds., The Free Press, New York, 1967, pp. 198–282. As late as in the early 1950s, the church was promoting a corporatist structure in Colombia. See Félix Restrepo, S. J., *Colombia en la Encrucijada,* Biblioteca Popular de Cultura Colombiana, Bogota, 1951.

41. Mörner, *op. cit.,* p. 37.

42. Klein, *op. cit.,* p. 84. In 1805, a royal decree "declared that persons of 'pure blood' had to ask permission of the viceroy or the audiencia in order to marry 'elements of Negro and Mulatto origin.' " See Mörner, *op. cit.,* p. 39.

43. This has led several scholars to trace Latin America's greater interracial adaptation to the Spanish cultural-legal heritage. More is said on this point in the following chapter.

44. In this respect different attitudes toward the miscegenated have accompanied slave or van den Berghe's "paternalistic" system. See van den Berghe, *op. cit.*

45. Mörner, *op. cit.*, p. 68.

46. *Ibid.*, p. 69.

47. Quoted in *idem.*

48. As stated, the Indian-white variant kept patterns with a predominant ethnic, not racial segregation, racial discrimination being concentrated in Latin America against Negroid individuals.

49. Slavery ended late in Latin America, particularly in Brazil and Cuba in 1888 and 1886, respectively. It was not until the 1850s that slavery disappeared from all the remaining 17 Spanish American republics.

50. Mörner, *op. cit.*, p. 68.

51. Slave uprisings were usually isolated events, and the emancipation movements were characterized by a conspicuous absence of *negro* leadership. For Brazil, see Fernandes, *op. cit.*

52. This does not mean that in some instances it did not have some political consequences. The bloodless fall of the Brazilian Empire has been commonly tied to the abolition of slavery. We should note here that in the Northwest European variant the issue of abolition was not always tied to high levels of violence as in the United States. This was not the case in the British West Indies where the very small proportion of absentee whites led to an accommodation with British policies. See Genovese, *op. cit.*, pp. 27–34. As indicated by the recent developments in Rhodesia, the presence of a significantly large white group has been a necessary condition for a white-led secessionist movement in Anglo-Saxon societies. For a more detailed discussion of the relationship between population proportions and racial politics see Chapter 3.

53. Klein, *op. cit.*, p. 245.

54. *Idem.*

55. Similarly, in South Africa blacks are currently treated as a foreign group. See Hoetink, *op. cit.*, p. 110.

56. Many of the expelled white colonists settled in the Caribbean, particularly in Cuba, thus contributing to the development of the Cuban plantation system.

57. Klein relates the return-to-Africa movement to the Turner rebellion. Klein, *op. cit.*, p. 248. However, the implications that the presence of free Negroes is indeed an upsetting factor in slave

societies is developed in William W. Freeling's "Slavery and the Nullification Crisis," in *American Negro Slavery*, Allen Weinstein and Frank Otto Gatell, Eds., Oxford University Press, New York, 1968, p. 148, and in Charles Grier Sellers, Jr.'s article in the same volume entitled, "The Travail of Slavery," p. 186.

58.   According to Klein, "the Virginia whites fought all attempts to destroy slavery, even when it was shown to be uneconomic." Nevertheless, he indicates that the price of slaves rose up until the 1850s and that from 1790 until 1860, the slave force increased while the number of owners decreased. Klein, *op. cit.*, pp. 255, 176, and 186. These facts suggest the continued economic profitability of the system.

59.   Blalock, *op. cit.*, pp. 51, 111 and 121.

60.   See van den Berghe, *Race and Racism, op. cit.*, p. 77.

61.   Edward Byron Reuter, *Race Mixture: Studies in Intermarriage and Miscegenation*, Whittlesey House, McGraw-Hill, New York, 1931, p. 39. It seems that most societies experience an early stage of "fascination" between racial groups in which miscegenation is relatively accepted. For South Africa as well, see van den Berghe, *Race and Racism, op. cit.*, p. 98.

62.   Reuter, *op. cit.*, pp. 78–82.

63.   However, according to Blalock the residential segregation of Negroes is higher both in the North and South than for the ethnic minorities. Blalock, *op. cit.*, pp. 146–147.

64.   Reference is being made to top managerial positions of some enterprises. Commercial banking is a conspicuous case. For a good overview of the subtle but persistent discrimination and prejudice toward Jews in the United States, see Sidney Goldstein and Calvin Goldscheider, *Jewish Americans: Three Generations in a Jewish Community*, Prentice-Hall, Englewood Cliffs, N.J., 1968.

65.   Again on this point for Jews, see Goldstein and Goldscheider, *ibid.*, especially Chapter 8 on intermarriage and Chapter 11 on the retention of Jewish identity.

66.   Harris, *Patterns of Race, op. cit.*, p. 29.

67.   See Blalock, *op. cit.*, pp. 120, 140, and 154.

68.   Of course, the process has been repeated in some Latin American countries with some ethnic communities, Jews and Arabs in particular. Some Indian communities, as the Otovaleños of Ecuador, have also been relatively successful in business, but not to the extent of constituting a parallel national elite. The Otovaleño

case is being studied by Kathleen N. Klumpp in her dissertation in progress at the University of Illinois, Urbana.

69. Reference is being made to a traditionally established WASP firm and its counterpart in Latin America. It should be noted that in the United States ethnic barriers have started to crumble in these circles. As we document for Cartagena, a minority of highly Negroid persons graduate from the local university and attend prestigious private schools.

70. It should be noted again that in Indo-Latin America racial visibility is much lower, ethnic and class related difficulties being relatively more prevalent handicaps.

71. Obviously, in both contexts, persons seeking total assimilation, that is, to pass (cell 2), find themselves in conflictive situations because some segments remain segregated (cell 4). Of course, as previously noted, in contrast to the Latin American Negro the United States Jew will more readily find economically productive occupational alternatives by catering to his community of origin or practicing in firms with lesser ethnic orientations. On the other hand, the absence of racial economic parallelism in Latin America and the strength of prejudice against *negros* greatly handicaps the economic success of blacks in Latin America.

72. Obviously, the fact that some sectors find themselves in cell 4 leads to discrimination against those entering cell 2. See Blalock, *op. cit.*, p. 43.

73. See, for example, Milton M. Gordon, *Assimilation in American Life*, Oxford University Press, New York, 1964, especially pp. 231–265.

74. The tensions between these ideals is evidenced by the fact that discrimination still exists in the social system.

75. For instance, according to Harris in Minas Velhas, Brasil, this statement appeared in a school textbook: "Of all races the white race is the most intelligent, persevering, and the most enterprising. . . . The Negro race is much more retarded than the others. . . ." See Harris, "Race in Minas Velhas," *op. cit.*, p. 52.

76. See Chapters 5 and 6.

77. This does not mean, of course, that there are no miscegenated persons in this group, nor that the elite is not aware of its racial "impurity." Rather, given the facts that (1) the elite is predominately composed of phenotypic whites, (2) that there is racial

prejudice, and (3) that some miscegenated persons are fully accepted at this level, there is a tendency to suppress racial considerations by not openly giving a nonwhite definition to elite members.

78.   For Brazil, see Pierson, *op. cit.*, p. 211.
79.   Wagley, *op. cit.*, p. 151.

Chapter Three

. . . .

MISCEGENATION, THE CRUCIAL
INTERVENING VARIABLE

It should be apparent by now that we consider that both the acceptance of miscegenated persons by phenotypic whites and extensive miscegenation—two preconditions for the infusion of the miscegenated throughout the class pyramid—are critical determinants of the Latin American modality of racial adaptation. *Ceteris paribus,* tolerance toward the miscegenated, leads to miscegenation. The acceptance of extensive miscegenation, in turn, reinforces racial tolerance. In this chapter, we first present the logic behind these analytical statements that attempt to interpret the *adaptive* dynamics of the infused racial system of Cartagena. Then we discuss the main historical, sociocultural, and racial or physical interpretations that have been given for both the acceptance and the high levels of miscegenation found in most of Latin America. Although the possibility of testing these general or macroscopic interpretations with available data is very limited, they are nevertheless extremely important. As has been suggested, in some respects the patterns of race relations in Latin America have been stabilized since early independence and even colonial periods, and these grandiose interpretations have attempted to explain, at least implicitly, this phenomenon. Although the importance of dealing with them seems evident to us, we hope that by linking the interpretations to a "tolerance-miscegenation" syndrome we can contribute to the formalization of theory in the field, facilitate future research, and avoid the unilateral explanations found in much of the literature. It should be noted, however, that we do not purport to settle controversies which in several respects are insoluble. Our objective is to clarify the relationships of a set of variables in the structuring of Iberian American race relations as a basis for clearer thinking on the contrastive Latin American historical experience of low levels of racial strife amidst much higher levels of political and class conflict.

MISCEGENATION AND DISCRIMINATION

It is evident that tolerance toward miscegenated individuals describes a mild system of race relations. Although not as evident, this attitude is conducive to further miscegenation. It would be if miscegenation were the cultural ideal, for then interracial marriage would be the modal miscegenating tool and racial mixing would occur on a legitimate basis. However, given the frequent imperialist nature of extensive interracial contact, extramarital relationships have been a common instrument for miscegenation, particularly during colonial periods (1). This was the case in Latin America, where by the midsixteenth century "the words 'mestizo' and 'illegitimate' had become almost synonymous" (2). Thus miscegenation has had a connotation both of sexual exploitation by the dominant group and of illegitimacy to the point that van den Berghe has made it a common characteristic of all "paternalistic" systems of domination (3). Indeed, despite ideologies, substantial proportions of whites and blacks have actually produced a high density of miscegenated individuals in relatively closed societies such as the United States and South Africa.

Conversely, the low presence of whites in Iberian Negroid regions such as Choco, Colombia, have not produced substantial miscegenation (4). Thus the composition of the population appears to be a most critical variable in the determination of the volume of miscegenation. This is why the emergence of the infused Latin American system has required the presence of significant proportions of both whites and blacks.

Not only has miscegenation accompanied relatively closed racial systems; in Colombia, the frequency of legal marriages is directly related to class, and interclass relationships tend to be extramarital in nature (5). As in other Latin American countries legal marriages are infrequent among polar racial types, and extramarital *interclass* relationships are also characterized by the male having the dominant-lighter pattern. However, our data indicate that in Cartagena males tend to marry persons with equal or lighter racial characteristics (6). (The pattern established here is applicable in interracial and intraracial contexts throughout many areas of the world. The dominant pattern of extramarital interracial relations finds expression in dominant-race males and minority-race females. Conversely, interracial marriages predominate between minority males and majority females. Intraracial marriages also mirror the above in that there is a tendency for males to choose for a wife a female who is as close to the dominant physical type as he is, or more so. The causes for these manifestations are quite clear. Males initiate courtship, and the qualities desirable for a wife who will bear legitimate children are quite different from those of a lover whose rights are more limited.)

The previous considerations suggest the existence of complex interracial mechanisms. For our current purposes, it appears that the probability of sexual contact among the racial poles also is enhanced by the exploitative context of a class-race bifurcation in which the dominated race has frequent ecological-work contact with the dominant one. Nevertheless, judging from our experiences in pre-Castro Cuba and our field study in Cartagena, it seems that sexual contacts between the racial poles may not be as frequent as might be thought (7). Indeed, as already noted, the infused racial system is not open; lightness is preferred. Consequently, prejudice combined with the availability of lesser-Negroid women have impeded a fuller racial homogenization in Latin America (8). Racial homogenization has proved to be a painfully slow process in the infused system.

Despite the foregoing constraints to miscegenation and the emergence of an open racial system, it does appear that Iberian tolerance toward the miscegenated has also furthered miscegenation. This is particularly the case when a *cultural* definition is given to the term, as we do throughout this study —a most important consideration because to a large extent culture conditions biological miscegenation. For example, actual miscegenation notwithstanding, in the United States the tendency is to disregard miscegenation by defining individuals as black or white. We have already observed the Iberian American practice of defining *indios* as miscegenated or *mestizo* once they exhibit cultural assimilation, a most important factor for the lower racism of the Amerindian, as opposed to Negroid, complex. In addition, theoretically speaking, a cultural ethos accepting miscegenation leads to the emergence of a complex, and hence ambiguous, racial terminology that permits a sharp reduction in the number of persons found in the poles of the spectrum. As we show in later chapters, Iberian terminological ambiguity permits processes of "terminological miscegenation" by which highly Negroid individuals—even polar racial types—lose this identity by the employment of miscegenated terms that neutralize blackness. However, we must note again the eclectic nature or "imperfect" functioning of the infused system. The tendency toward miscegenating or reducing the number of persons found in the dark racial pole is accompanied by the counter tendency to increase the numbers in the light pole by giving a relative broad *blanco* social definition to light types. This practice, as opposed to assigning a miscegenated definition to the light extreme, contributes to the maintaining of racial prejudice against persons still found in highly Negroid aggregates. Rather than a cultural ideal of the infused racial system, miscegenation has been the accepted but unplanned "race policy."

We are now left with the proposition that the acceptance of extensive miscegenation is conducive to reducing the levels of racism in the society. The openness of a system of race relations is fundamentally related to the levels of miscegenation found in the society, because, as previously suggested, an analysis of extremes leads inevitably to this conclusion. Miscegenation erodes those conspicuous physical characteristics deemed to be undesirable in a racist society. Ultimately, it homogenizes the population, thus making discrimination an impossibility. Alternatively, total segregation requires a myth of racial purity and endogamy, that is, social distance in most intimate relationships. As the miscegenating process expands, the probability that persons of "some color" will be infused throughout the social structure increases. The Latin Caribbean saying *"¿tu abuela donde está?"* suggests the presence of this phenomenon (9). Indeed, as the process of miscegenation expanded in Latin America the frequency of legitimate mixed bloods increased substantially (10). Accepted miscegenation leads to ambiguous and fluid interracial boundaries. It transforms race into an achieved quality that diffuses and dilutes the power of racist thinking. Where miscegenation is possible ambitious persons can "improve" their race by approximating dominant group characteristics through their children, and as we show later, this has adaptive social psychological consequences in Cartagena. There is another important effect of miscegenation; it tends to change "prejudice of origin" into "prejudice of mark," (11) the former being characterized by an emphasis on genealogy, the latter on appearance. In effect, extensive miscegenation leads to situations, such as those common in Latin America, in which even full siblings can have marked physical differences (12). Given this situation, race becomes a relative matter, one of degrees, as opposed to fixed, castelike patterns. Under this condition, racial characteristics tend to become physical, descriptive qualities of individuals, a matter of esthetics—some children, the lighter ones, are more handsome than others—and there is a tendency to substitute racist designations for racial terms that convey affection, as is also the case in Latin America. Obviously, the acceptance of miscegenation leads to flexibility in racial matters.

To summarize the discussion in succinct form, we feel that the Iberian acceptance of miscegenated persons in the presence of sufficient proportions of whites and blacks has produced the tolerance-miscegenation syndrome that characterizes the infused racial system found in Cartagena. The syndrome can be represented schematically as follows:

$$\text{Racial tolerance} \xrightarrow{\hspace{2cm}} \text{Miscegenation}$$
$$\xleftarrow{\hspace{1.5cm}}$$

To conclude, we view the tolerance-miscegenation syndrome as the crucial intervening variable for our analysis because it relates the historical sociocultural and physical factors that produced the infused racial system to the racial adaptation that is its consequence.

IBERIAN AMERICAN CIVILIZATION AND THE TOLERANCE-MISCEGENATION SYNDROME

In this section we discuss the main interpretations that seek to explain the adaptive Latin American tolerance-miscegenation syndrome.

The Moorish Conquest

From a sociological point of view, historical interpretations are often considered to deal with unexplainable (i.e., taken as given) events that determine current behavior. In slightly different terms, they can be considered to register past events that condition the future, the assumption being that social processes are partly repetitious, traditional, or stable. More specifically, historical events can determine behavior through their impact on the development of cultural configurations.

Among the precolonial historical experiences that may have influenced Iberian cultural racial attitudes, the Moorish conquest deserves special consideration (13). According to this interpretation, having been conquered by darker and slightly Negroid populations, Iberians were less esthetically repulsed by dark peoples; more forcefully, Freyre considers that the Moorish conquest led to the sexual idealization of the dark woman—the *moura encantada*—that was transformed to apply to the people involved in the colonial situation. In effect, early Spanish chronicles praised the beauty of native women (14); several studies have suggested a preference for medium-brown over pale skin color (15); and our data indicate that among the lesser-Negroid groups of Cartagena there is still a widespread belief in the "sexual superiority" of the *mulata* (16). In more general terms, it has also been argued that the Moorish polygamous influence led to a greater laxity in familial matters, including an increased tolerance toward illegitimacy, a factor favoring a greater acceptance and volume of miscegenated persons (17). In any case, prior to the conquest of America, Iberians had experienced miscegenation with darker dominant peoples.

There is powerful logic behind the assumption that precolonial Iberian mingling with dark human groups, which had themselves miscegenated with Negroid populations, could have affected Iberian racial attitudes. The shifting and ill-defined boundaries that characterize Latin American race relations require perceptions of race as part of a continuum. Insofar as these attitudes reflected the physical realities of a dominant group, the contacts with the Moors should have fostered them.

Although there are no adequate data to evaluate fully the

impact of the Moorish conquest on colonial racial and race-connected attitudes such as illegitimacy, the analysis of racial terminology suggests that the conquest did indeed have an impact. First, both the term *morena,* which is derived from Moor, in the Iberian Peninsula and Iberian America, connotes an ideal of beauty to the extent that it is frequently employed in love songs. Second, this term connotes both white brunette types and miscegenated types who are "frequently lumped together in the romantic national idealization of *'morena' "* (18); that is, a term derived from the Moorish conquest lends itself to sexual idealization and racial ambiguity. Furthermore, both *morena* and *moreno* connote white physical types and are employed as euphemisms for *negros* in the area. In addition, the tendency to have a broad social definition of *blanco* is reflected in one of the definitions of *moreno,* which is "the darkest color that a person can have and still be considered to be white" (19).

Historically, racial terms derived from Moor were employed ambiguously during the early colonial period. In effect, the chronicler of the establishment of Cartagena referred euphemistically to Negroes as *morenos* (20). Mörner presents some interesting eighteenth-century racial terminology in New Spain that directly suggests that the process of racial upgrading and assimilation were tied to Moorish terminological derivations. For instance, during those times, descendants of Spaniards and mulatto women begat *morisco.* We might add, during the period a descendant of Spaniard and *requinterona de mulato* (a more miscegenated type) was considered to be white (21). The point is that derivations from the term Moor have been employed for sexual idealization and to designate darker groups and white persons, and that this terminological variation has served to soften and give relativism to racial patterns. In summary, it seems that this semantic ambiguity reflects a willingness to mingle with and a greater acceptance of nonwhites.

The Tradition of Slavery

There is another precolonial, historical argument that has been used to account for the relative acceptance of nonwhites by Iberians: a tradition of slavery that is traceable to antiquity. Prior to the sixteenth century, slavery was institutionalized in the Iberian peninsula with sub-Sahara Africans as one of the subjugated groups (22). This slavery was predominantly a "paternalistic" or "mild" type rather than a "plantation" or "harsh" type, with large proportions of the slaves being domestic servants, artisans, and semiskilled workers (23). In the thirteenth century, Roman-influenced Castilian legislation—*Las Siete Partidas del Rey Don Alfonso el Sabio* —reflected benevolent attitudes toward slaves. It considered slavery as an accidental condition, *contra razón de natura,* (i.e., against natural reason) and recognized a legal status for the slave, which included the right of manumission. This legal tradition was continued in Spanish America during the colonial period (24). Given the experience with a legal history of slavery, the argument goes that Iberian Americans had lenient attitudes toward slaves and were prone to manumit them, factors favoring acceptance, geographic mobility, and miscegenation. In more general terms, given their preplantation experience with slavery, Latin Americans did not experience a need for substantial legal innovations during the colonial period; they maintained their traditional, "benevolent" legal definitions. In contrast to this situation, as Anglo-Saxons institutionalized slavery in conjunction with the emergence of the plantation economy, they evolved harsher legal definitions for the subordinated groups, and, the argument follows, this led to highly discriminatory racial patterns. Indeed, it has been considered that slavery itself is a critical factor for increases in racial prejudice (25). Thus, if Iberians considered slavery as a condition "against natural reason," they were not as predisposed to have radical mentalities in which slaves, and more importantly, their descendants, were equated to "chattel." Several sources have considered that Latin American slavery was characterized by intimate, paternalistic, personal relations between masters and slaves (26). Miscegenation and manumissions typify Iberian American slavery. The syndrome that is presented is one in which miscegenation contributes to manumissions (27), and the manumitted miscegenated persons contribute to further miscegenation. This system can be contrasted to the ideal type of the plantation system where the economic profitability of slavery is maximized and the ratio of masters to slaves is low with corresponding regimentation and impersonality, processes that reduce the possibility of miscegenation within the master-slave context.

Various scholars have traced the mild nature of Latin American slavery to the legal system. For example, Humboldt makes the case for the role of Spanish legislation, "directly the reverse of French and English," in the high levels of manumissions in Cuba (28). Noticeably, the French were predominantly Catholic but did not have the Iberian tradition with slavery, nor had they experienced the Moorish conquest; they did not develop the "bland" Iberian racial patterns. However, it is necessary to be cautious with legal evidence depicting slave systems, for there is not necessarily a strong correlation between formal norms and actual behavior. Indeed, in another context, Humboldt considered that "nothing is more illusory than the extolled effects of those laws which prescribe the model [to treat slaves]" (29).

Although most sources have concluded that Iberian American slavery was relatively mild, there is documentation that plantation slavery was repressive in both the Iberian and non-Iberian American contexts and that manumissions in both types of societies were related to economic or market conditions (30). These findings have led some sources to reject the role of a tradition with slavery—and of Iberian cultural factors—in affecting racial attitudes, that is, the acceptance of miscegenation and manumissions. In Mörner's words, "if slavery in a Latin American environment appeared to be 'mild' the explanation usually will be found in the existing socio-economic structure" (31). In some instances, restrictive Marxist interpretations have been upheld even when there are no sufficient data to determine the relative harshness of Iberian and non-Iberian plantation systems, nor to compare the relative net impact of economic variations on manumissions within these two cultural complexes. For example, although plantation slavery predominated in Brazil (32), some historians have considered that manumissions were "customary" (33), in this country. However, Hoetink argues that although "the United States never witnessed a situation like that in Brazil in 1888, the year in which slavery was abolished, when there were already three times as many free people as there were slaves," he considers that "a little further back in Brazilian history [when the plantation economy was profitable]" the figures were comparable to those of the Deep South (34). Unfortunately, Hoetink does not support this statement with hard data. Indeed, as noted by Genovese, the treatment of slaves in specific countries varied historically according to economic conditions (35). In addition, there are several indicators to establish the harshness of a slave system (e.g., manumissions and living conditions), and the results obtained from one indicator need not necessarily correspond to those obtained from another. Although harshness has been tied to commercialization, this relationship does not logically hold for all the indicators. For example, manumissions, an indicator of paternalism, logically is inversely related to the economic profitability of slavery. In contrast, the cost factor is directly related to providing better living conditions for the slaves.

The difficulties of evaluating the impact of the tradition with slavery on Iberian American patterns of race relations should be apparent by now. Yet there is a powerful argument that weakens the relationships between slave systems and national patterns of race relations as posited by strict economic determinists. It is a fact that the extent of plantation slavery varied geographically and temporally through Latin America, and that this does not seem to have significantly altered the emergence of similar patterns of race relations in these societies. In some countries, like Colombia, the impact of the plantation economy was minor (36). In others, such as Cuba, urban slavery was always of importance (37). In still others, like Brazil, the plantation system dominated slavery (38). If we add to this list non-Iberian societies such as South Africa and Curaçao, where plantation slavery was not a crucial institution (39) but where the "soft" patterns of the Iberian American infused system did not develop, the tenuous relationship between slave systems and the evolution of patterns of race relations becomes obvious.

In the light of this evidence, those who favor the role of historical slavery in the determination of the relatively "softer" Iberian American racial patterns could attempt to salvage their interpretation by emphasizing its cultural role in the determination of milder racial ideologies or mentalities, as contrasted with the actual treatment of slaves. It could be argued that although the commercial revolution of the sixteenth century led to the establishment of harsh plantation slave systems, in Latin America this produced the breakdown of traditional practices mainly within the plantation context. More importantly, it could be considered that although Iberian American plantations were particularly cruel, the Iberian historical experience with "bland" slavery led to a *cultural* predisposition that reduced the need to generate new, radical mentalities in which the slaves, and their descendents, were equated to "chattel" and given a caste status in the society (40). In more general terms, allowance would be given to "the necessity to recognize that ideas, once called into being and rooted in important social groups, have a life of their own . . . , [and that] the economic and ecological processes enable us to account [only] for the room given [to the legal, moral, religious and institutional inheritance and its survivals] to breathe" (41). Traditional slavery can be seen as having led to general cultural orientations, reflected in the legislation, by which people felt relatively more comfortable toward slave-related individuals. Iberian Americans, then, found less of a necessity to establish fixed and segregated boundaries with these groups. They did not see the need to create myths about physical compartmentalization in race relations, including the descendants of slaves, a necessary condition for a relatively closed, not infused, system. This paradox of tolerance amidst feelings of inequality has been a frequent theme in the literature. Its logic does not require the manipulation of extreme interpretations. That is, a tolerance toward the miscegenated need not be linked to a highly benevolent slave system nor to a highly ascriptive system in which whites accept the miscegenated because they are entirely secure about their status. Rather, a comfortable attitude toward slavery or "exploitation" can be logically linked to racial leniency. Without entirely contradicting some economic deterministic interpretations, then, given this historical experience in the face of manumissions—which were at least partly determined by economic conditions— Iberian Americans were more capable of coping with and absorbing the descendants of slave populations. The application of the precolonial slave experience to include general, relaxed attitudes toward slave-related groups would, therefore, transcend the particular nature of the slave systems at hand, the point being that in the determination of national patterns of race relations, it is not as important how kindly particular subjugated or underprivileged groups are treated, but what occurs to their descendants. As is illustrated with our Cartagena data, where the bulk of the blacks have infamously low socioeconomic conditions, if the miscegenated are integrated with the middle and upper levels of "white" society, there are powerful forces favoring interracial adaptation. We have already noted that during the nineteenth century, slave uprisings were frequent in Brazil. Yet these events were confined to particular areas and did not escalate into major racial movements. If we consider that according to Hoetink the racial situation in Brazil—the bleaching process, by which biological and "terminological" miscegenation permitted persons to forget black ancestry—150 years ago was similar to the current one (42), it is possible to understand the dual phenomenon of assimilation and harshness.

Let us recapitulate. Some sources have linked Iberian American "soft" or infused racial relations to a tradition of "bland" slavery, which led to paternalistic patterns, the mingling of the races, manumissions, and the acceptance of the miscegenated. There has been a strong polemical debate over the harshness of slave systems in the New World in which economic interpretations have sought to disprove historical and cultural ones. Although it is possible to trace intracultural differences in slave systems to economic considerations (i.e., it appears that plantation systems were relatively harsher) similarities in the acceptance of the miscegenated and in other corollary patterns of race relations have accompanied differences in the type of slave economy. Furthermore, harsh racial systems have emerged in societies where slavery was virtually absent. Consequently, until better data are gathered, the overall relationship between slave systems and racial patterns appears to be tenuous. It is in the area of general cultural orientations toward the slave-related population that a history of bland slavery can be seen as possibly having exerted some mitigating influences by generating less radical mentalities toward the descendants of the slaves, and avoiding extensive psychosocial distance with this population, particularly with miscegenated persons. Nevertheless, there are no data to test this proposition adequately. Given this situation, it is preferable to avoid unilateral opinions. We feel that Iberian American racial patterns have been determined within the broad context of its colonial civilization. This leads us to the consideration of the racial implications of the patterns of the colonization of Latin America.

The Latin American Pattern of Colonization

Latin America was colonized by a medieval civilization that was resistant and impervious to the modernizing currents of the Renaissance and Protestantism. As established in the previous chapter, underpinned by church doctrine, the Iberian form of colonization consisted of the transplantation into the New World of the medieval corporative society. Although nonpluralistic in religious matters, this medieval orientation was ecumenical in that it gave a place to all groups in the social "organism." As indicated by colonial legislation and administrative decisions, blacks and Indians were considered as an integral part of the social system. We have already stated that colonial Anglo-Saxons were more prone to define racial groups as "alien," and, consequently, to segregate them (43).

There has been a vivid polemic on the contrastive nature of the ethos of both types of colonization. In the Hispanic world, frequent reference is made to the *Leyenda Negra* (44), which is seen as having denaturalized the Spanish colonization by depicting it as a brutal and greedy enterprise. Those praising the Hispanic colonization, on the other hand, have emphasized such aspects as the early establishment of cultural institutions (including universities), extensive religious proselytization, and the acceptance of racial mingling itself as evidence that Spaniards were led by noble ideals. This experience has been contrasted to the Anglo-Saxon system in which the colonial enterprise was relatively autonomous from the crown, did not emphasize religious proselytization, and was tied to the "expulsion" of native populations (45). Typically, Anglo-Saxon settlements are seen as "materialistic," that is, led by mercantile companies, void of religious ecumenism, and desiring to establish exclusivist settlements—what, as previously noted, van den Berghe calls *"Herrenvolk* democracies." Of course, anti-Hispanic counterarguments are also heard—the brutality of the conquest, as witnessed by the virtual elimination of some native populations, the greed for gold of the *con-*

quistadores, and so on. No enterprise of the proportions of the colonization of Latin America can be characterized by simplistic emotional criteria. Indeed, Beals has noted the complexity of colonial policies. According to him there were three distinct policies toward Indians: extermination, pluralism, and assimilation (46). In this section, we outline some of the basic characteristics of the colonization and relate them to the tolerance-miscegenation syndrome.

The colonization of Latin America was characterized by the very active role played in it by the crown and the church (47). Influenced by the religious outlook, the Spanish government placed a premium on territorial expansion and the control of populations who were evangelized. This orientation led to the establishment of tutelary relationships between the metropolitan government and its new subjects; consequently, it was accompanied by relatively high levels of administrative centralization. Indians and Negroes had souls to be saved; therefore, they deserved legal protection by the crown. Given these practices, the metropolitan government has been depicted as having blocked the crystallization of strong local power structures inimical to the interests of the colored (48), and as the champion of the latter. Although this legal tutelary situation is undeniable, there is a polemic as to its actual consequences, that is, the effects on race relations of the crown's mediation role. First of all, as already noted, racial groups received legal discriminatory treatment by the metropolitan government, and, of course, the colonization itself was brutal in many respects (49). But of greater importance, the extent of the actual applicability of the formal-legal structure established by the metropolis in the colonies can be questioned. Although Klein considers that there was a "correlation between law and practice (50)," there is evidence supporting the interpretation that this relationship was weak, at least in some areas. According to Mörner for example, although within the *Sociedad de Castas* the legal status of the Indians was only second to that of the Spaniards, in reality their social status in many communities was at the bottom of the pyramid, below the position of the black slaves (51). Actually, in addition to the dearth of empirical data, the analysis of legal institutions is complicated by two other factors. First, there were frequent contradictions in the legislation, and it permitted multiple exceptions (52). Second, colonial legal institutions can be logically related to opposing consequences. For instance, in terms of one of our variables—miscegenation—because only Indians were subjected to the tribute of the *mita*, it can be argued that this favored increases in miscegenation to elude it. However, because only married Indians were entitled to lands in the "reservations"—*resguardos*—this institution should have promoted endogamy (53).

As with the previous discussion of the role of a tradition with bland slavery, interpretations must be tentative again. However, it seems to us that the legislative record of the Spanish crown reflects a desire for inclusion of racial groups in the social fabric of the society. Furthermore, although the metropolis sponsored only directly intermarriage with daughters of *caciques* and indirectly in the case of the *encomenderos* (54), the widely acknowledged fact is that the colony consisted of an unparalleled enterprise in planned cultural homogenization and acculturation (55). In our opinion, these practices contributed to the reduction of interracial psychological barriers and distance. In this medieval Catholic world, there was no place for individualistic, autonomous groups with different religious visions (56). As shown by the similarity of racial patterns in Portuguese and Spanish America—the former having experienced relatively more decentralized patterns of colonization—more than the actual mediation role of the metropolitan structures of government the ecumenical cultural orientation that presided over both colonizations would have reduced feelings of racial separateness. This leads us into a discussion of the role of Catholicism in Iberian American racial patterns, but first, a few additional words on corollary points that have been made on the function of the Hispanic colonizing political structure.

The Hispanic colonization of the New World has often been contrasted to its Anglo-Saxon counterpart in terms of their respective immigrant male-female ratios. The high male-to-female ratio of the Spanish (and Portuguese) colonization has been singled out as a most important factor that led to high levels of miscegenation in the area (57), and it has been partly linked to political aspects of the colonization. According to Klein, the already-mentioned Spanish premium on territorial expansion was paralleled by metropolitan policies that did not encourage white family migration and favored male migration. In his words,

> In the history of Spanish migration to the Indies [in the first two centuries of colonization] the system of white indenture was never carried into effect. . . . Those who could meet the qualifications [to migrate] were required to pay for their own passage. Although large numbers were transported free under particular expeditions supported either by the crown or by private funds, they were primarily soldiers rather than peasants or laborers. . . . Even if a large number of Spanish peasants and workers had wished to emigrate, the Spanish vessels of the sixteenth century were incapable of carrying such a volume of free white passengers profitably, especially under the [centralized] fleet system (58).

Thus it is assumed that political centralization contributed to the migration of men directly by fostering military migrations and indirectly by increasing migration costs.

In addition to these political factors, it has often been argued that the Hispanic male-female ratio was influenced by the widespread desire of Spaniards to make quick profits and return to Europe, as opposed to settle in the colonies (59). Obviously, these transient attitudes would have reduced the number of female migrants and fostered illegitimacy and miscegenation in the New World.

The relationship between miscegenation and a high male-female ratio is evident. Hoetink considers that both variables have been positively related in Latin America and in non-Latin Caribbean societies, such as Jamaica, Surinam, and Curaçao (60). Nevertheless, there are no sufficient data to determine the ratio for colonial Latin America. Although Mörner has made it his main interpretation for miscegenation in Iberian America, he considers that "almost everything remains to be done" in the investigation of the point (61).

In addition to the sex ratio, it has been argued that the proportion of white settlers over the black population is an important determinant of racial tolerance and miscegenation. We have already accepted the importance of this ratio in the determination of the volume of miscegenation and in the materialization of the infused racial system. Quite simply, extensive miscegenation is facilitated by a high male-female ratio and requires substantial proportions of populations of both groups. However, there is evidence that such mechanistic interpretations cannot explain the Iberian American pattern of racial *tolerance*. Indeed, high and low proportions of blacks have been accompanied by caste relationships in the non-Iberian American context. It seems that although significant proportions of whites and blacks are necessary for substantial biological miscegenation, this ratio is not a sufficient condition for the materialization of a racially tolerant system. As already noted, it is not miscegenation *per se* but the cultural definition given to it that accounts for the infused system.

To summarize, it has been argued that the centralized, tutelary role of the Spanish colonial corporate system, which placed a premium on territorial expansion by a predominantly male colonization and provided the legal inclusion of all racial groups in the society, contributed to the emergence of the tolerance-miscegenation syndrome. If we contrast the relatively more centralized Spanish pattern to the Portuguese American one and make allowance for the incongruency between law and practice that characterized both colonizations, it appears that the actual mediation of the central government structure was probably not an important factor in determining the syndrome. In our opinion, the ecumenical cultural orientation of the colonization with its combined emphasis on expansion and inclusion contributed more than mechanistic factors, such as the male-female ratio, to the emergence of the infused racial system. After all, decisions as to the size of the sex ratio are largely determined in the long run by cultural orientations, and the infused system is characterized by a predominantly *blanco* elite. Since these orientations are so deeply rooted in the Catholic system, we now turn our attention to a discussion of the role played by the church in the tolerance-miscegenation syndrome.

The Role of the Church

In the colonization of Iberian America, the Catholic church played a role second to no other organization. We have already noted that Catholic doctrine underpinned the medieval corporatist political outlook which defined nonwhites as an integral part of the colonial social system. Furthermore, we have considered that religious ecumenical acculturation also served the cultural function of reducing psychoracial barriers in Latin America, factors that are conducive to the acceptance of nonwhites. However, some sources believe that the church had a direct structural impact on race relations through its direct tutelary role. Such figures as Las Casas and Pedro Claver are examples of religious intervention against local power structures to favor the Indians and Negroes, respectively (62). According to this interpretation, then, the church contributed to the development of soft patterns of race relations not only by its ideological contribution—defining nonwhites as human beings and manumissions as good deeds (63). A more direct intervention is traced to such factors as the facts that in Spanish America manumissions could be made by a simple declaration in a church and that the Catholic church was legally the prime guarantor of the conduct of the manumitted, practices that contrast sharply with the United States counterpart of requiring masters to post a bond when manumitting slaves (64). The tutelary role of the church was also extended by the incorporation of religious ordinances into civil legislation (65).

The previous arguments notwithstanding, the role of Catholicism in the determination of the mild patterns of Iberian American race relations has been attacked on several grounds. First, it has been noted that the French did not evolve these patterns (66). This indicates that although Catholicism may be a necessary condition for the Iberian American patterns, it is not a sufficient one. More specifically, it is the combination of Catholicism, a tradition of slavery, and the Moorish conquest that determined the Iberian patterns. Because the French had only the first factor, they can consequently be placed in a middle position in the soft-harsh continuum (67). Second, as previously noted, the relative softness of Iberian over Northwest European slavery has been questioned, particularly within the plantation context. Although there are no sufficient data to evaluate this latter interpretation, if correct, it would undercut the thesis about the direct mediating influence of the church (68). Third, it has been argued that the church played an insignificant role in the Latin American abolitionist movements of the nineteenth century and that more humanitarian slave systems materialized in Latin America from the late eighteenth century on, when the ideological and political power of the church declined (69). In this sense the intellectual currents of the Enlightenment appear as a more powerful force in mitigating race relations in the area. Finally, to the extent that miscegenation was and is the product of extramarital relations, the effectiveness of the direct involvement of the clergy in the daily lives of a nominally Catholic population can be questioned. Indeed, no other than Klein himself considers that not even a high density of priests led to high rates of marriage in eighteenth-century Cuba (70). However, we should note that relatively lax sexual mores have been associated with Catholicism, as opposed to puritanism. Of course, rather than actual miscegenation *per se*, it is its greater openness or tolerance that characterizes the infused system.

Unfortunately, again, any conclusion on the role of Catholicism must be tentative. In our opinion it is probable that the impact of the church in racial patterns, even more so than that of the metropolitan government, was more through its contribution to sponsor cultural orientations that reduced psychoracial distance than by the direct mediation of the clergy against racial exploitation. Let us clarify this important point. The lack of congruence between ideology and practice can lead one to question the impact of the former in human relations. For example, because slaves are treated harshly in a Catholic society, the role of the church in race relations can and is questioned. In parallel terms, given the death of substantial numbers of workers in Stalinist Russia, one could erroneously deny the impact of Marxist ideology in the status of the working classes in Soviet society. Although there is never a perfect correlation between ideology and reality, this does not deny entirely the independent role of the former in shaping events. Obviously, the role of nonwhites in the Catholic ideology of the times cannot be compared with the central position of the working class in Marxist philosophy, but we feel that the evangelical enthusiasm of Catholicism in colonial Latin America contributed to the reduction of the psychological distance among racial groups and that this distance is a necessary condition for a highly segmented society.

The Latin American Cultural Ethos

There is another important Iberian American cultural orientation that can be linked to racial tolerance and miscegenation: the traditional Latin American ethos of *personalismo* and *machismo* (71). In the personalistic culture, persons are valued in terms of their uniqueness. "Although . . . the Rights of Man [are held] in high verbal esteem, the underlying emphasis is upon the inherent uniqueness of each person. The individual is valued precisely because he is not exactly 'like' anyone else" (72). This leads to the "personification" of relationships. That is, one must demonstrate warmth in human interaction and avoid impersonal social distance. *Personalismo* is accompanied by a high presence of *familismo* and *amiguismo*. The two traits—literally, familism and friendism—characterize patterns of interracial interaction in the area. According to Hoetink,

> The everyday contact between members of heterogeneous groups in Iberian society is undoubtedly marked by social suppleness, by an apparently spontaneous (albeit often artificial and superficial) warmth, which finds its physical expression in the *abrazo* and other physical expressions of social contact. All this can be said to flow from a sophisticated and well-developed technique for creating the requisite atmosphere for such contacts in a socially, economically, and racially divided society, where objectively speaking many points of friction exist between various groups. The latent conflict is not reduced, but is so completely submerged by this deluge of uninhibited mutual friendliness that it is apparently checked, at least during the temporary contact, and the reflex show of friendliness is hardly recognized as artificial (73).

These cultural traits find symbolic expression in the *abrazo* given to a Negro, even by a prejudiced person, a practice recognized in the literature (74), and is manifested verbally in statements such as *"negro, pero bueno gente";* that is, he is black, but he is so nice. In the personalistic culture, given the tendency for individuals to relate to others on a personal basis rather than as members of a categorical group, racial characteristics are apt to be transformed into physical characteristics of individuals. Furthermore, there is an interaction between the complex and ambiguous Iberian American racial terminology and the personalistic orientation. For example, as already noted, the terms *negrito* and *negrita* (little male and female Negro, respectively) are used to depict affective ties among persons that do not consider themselves to be black, and personal sentiments lead to the manipulation of racial terminology to favor the lightening of individuals (75). In short, an affective dimension is given to race relations.

There are still other racial ramifications of *personalismo*. A personalistic orientation has been considered to lead to paternalism in situations of dominance: the paternalistic *patrón-peón* relationship. Klein makes reference to the *compadrazgo* (76), a corollary of this relationship, in Cuban slave society, in which runaway slaves "resorted to the curious *padrino* (godfather) system where [they] could use third parties to intercede in their behalf before the master" (77). Of course, students of Brazil have also noted the personalistic-paternalistic aspects of master-slave relationships in this area and have linked them to a mild system of race relations by projecting their historical survival (78).

Machismo, the he-man syndrome, can also be linked to the tolerance-miscegenation syndrome. As a crude aspect of *personalismo* that stresses sexual prowess, one of *machismo*'s underlying themes is that the male will try to "get away with murder," while demanding chastity from "his" women. The cunning, picaresque, or "sinful" dimension that accompanies *machismo* (79) is conducive to sexual exploration, mingling, and illegitimacy. Given the availability of racially subordinated women, it leads to miscegenation of the population and relaxed attitudes toward mixed bloods.

Several explanations have been forwarded for the *personalismo-machismo* cultural ethos. Vasconcelos has considered that tropical climates are propitious to the warm interpersonal interaction we have related to *personalismo* (80). However, the literature has extended the traditional Iberian ethos to include various climates. It appears that climate has only a modifying effect on *personalismo*. Apparently, interpersonal relations are generally less formal, more carnavalistic, and less distant in tropical Latin America. Incidentally, these areas are also characterized by a concentration of the black population (81). Second, Catholicism has been singled out as an important determinant or reinforcer of *personalismo* (82). The cult of saints and Catholic ritualism fit well in cultures with a high propensity to personify. However, despite the laxity associated with Catholicism, not puritanism, *machismo* sexual patterns are antinomial to church dogma and doctrine. Finally, the personalistic-familistic aspects of the traditional cultural ethos can be also linked to the socioeconomic structure. Underdeveloped economies are generally low in impersonality; they are characterized by a dearth of secondary organizations. This leads us to a consideration of the plausible role that the predominantly *Gemeinschaft* colonial society had in the formation of Latin American racial patterns. But first let us clarify our position.

The Latin American traditional cultural ethos, with its tendency to personify relationships, is conducive to the lessening of social distance between individuals with different racial characteristics. Furthermore, the *machismo* element, with its strong emphasis on sexual prowess, can be seen as conducive to legitimize sexual exploration and miscegenation. These cultural orientations interact with the Moorish-influenced racial terminology to produce ambiguously defined racial boundaries, particularly between similar racial types. Nevertheless, the analysis reveals once again a situation of tension, particularly in terms of the role of Catholicism, which on the one hand reinforces personalistic tolerance and on the other opposes in principle the miscegenating tendencies of *machismo*. Although *personalismo* in the context of a colonial economic structure of dominance is conducive to the development of paternalistic ties and miscegenation, caution is necessary with this interpretation. Indeed, the Iberian pattern of race relations is not one of racial mingling, because racial boundaries are well established. The peculiarity of the infused racial system is precisely the opposite: the competitive acceptance and infusion of persons of color throughout the social structure.

Thus, as revealed by our data (83), the infused system does not reflect a racially ascribed, highly stratified multiracial society.

The Colonial Economy

Latin American societies have generally been characterized by the low penetration of capitalism (84). Sources linking this precapitalist economic system to low levels of racial conflict have considered that the economy had in this respect a favorable impact on the cultural system and the social structure. As previously noted, the prevalence of personalistic, affective, cultural orientations that can be linked to racial cordiality has been partly explained in terms of a precapitalistic, underdeveloped economic system. Furthermore, the colonial economic structure has been depicted as essentially static and ascriptive, a society in which racial competition is minimal and subordination is widely accepted. In this type of society, subordination and racial boundaries are internalized. Consequently, there is sufficient psychological security for racial "mingling" (85). Within this system, then, whites are not threatened, and nonwhites do not experience any substantial mobilization. In contrast to this benevolent and nonconflictive equilibrium, the argument goes, the universalistic and competitive cultural and structural aspects of the more modern economies lead to greater racial conflict because groups do not uphold ascriptive standards and there are high levels of competition and mobilization. In these societies, then, there are insurmountable cultural and structural pressures toward racial equality. Paradoxically, it is the presence of these pressures that, it is felt, exacerbate racial prejudice because of the threatening thrust of equalitarianism. This, in turn, is believed to lead to greater degrees of segmentation and conflict—to *Herrenvolk* democracies. Of course, these arguments have led scholars to consider that racial conflict will escalate in Latin America as the process of economic modernization proceeds (86). Historical evidence, such as the relatively greater discrimination in universities as opposed to the guilds in colonial Latin America (87), can be complemented with current findings relating increases in prejudice to competition (88) in support of this interpretation. In addition to the previous arguments, the wide bifurcation in social status that characterizes colonial economies is considered to weaken family organization and foster both sporadic interclass sexual interaction and concubinage —particularly under ecological working conditions in which the dominated race interacts with the dominant one— processes increasing the levels of miscegenation in the society (89). There is evidence that interclass concubinage still has high prestige among some segments of the Colombian lower classes and that the former practices continue to be carried out (90).

The previous considerations notwithstanding, arguments in opposition are found in the literature; that is, high levels of racial discrimination and, we might add, of political and interclass conflict can be linked to economic underdevelopment (91). Blalock himself, who, as previously noted, relates discrimination to competition, presents propositions that predict greater discrimination in underdeveloped economies (92). In effect, the scarcity of resources and new jobs and the high levels of unemployment of these societies suggest relatively greater competitive pressures in underdeveloped economies. This structural aspect of the problem is ignored by some sources because they erroneously consider the economy as being basically static and ascriptive (93). However, that there was significant racial upward mobility during preindependence periods and that, as we show, there is current mobility into relatively aristocratic elites suggest that these assumptions are subject to question. In fact, an eclectic interpretation has been made that in Latin America the static colonial society was well institutionalized during a prolonged period, and that this led to adequate levels of racial homogenization through miscegenation, so that when more competitive economic systems materialized they did not produce substantial levels of racial, as opposed to class, conflict (94).

To evaluate the validity of an economic interpretation of race relations, it is necessary to differentiate the impact of this system on general cultural orientations from the impact of one of its structural characteristics, that is, the actual levels of intergroup competition. It seems to us that a case can be made that precapitalist, *Gemeinschaft* societies are prone to experience cultural orientations that are conducive to mitigate certain types of conflict. As already noted, personalistic, affective, and even paternalistic orientations, which foster miscegenation and dependency and mitigate the cruder aspects of racial prejudice, can be linked to the economy (95). However, there is no simple relationship between the economic system, these cultural orientations, and the patterns of race relations. Quite simply, there are noneconomic factors that also affect racial patterns in important ways. It has already been observed that the relationships between slave systems defined in terms of broad concepts, such as the plantation and nonplantation dichotomy, are not very useful to explain the contrasts between Iberian and non-Iberian American patterns of race relations. Similarly, there are precapitalist and preindustrial societies with high and low levels of segmentation. For instance, in contrast to Iberian America, Guyana is characterized by low levels of miscegenation and high segmentation and conflict between its black and East Indian populations. This suggests that there are other autonomous cultural factors that also mold racial patterns.

In addition to the described cultural effects of the economy, racial patterns are also influenced by a specific structural characteristic of the economic subsystem, that is, its degree of competitiveness, often operationalized in terms of population proportions. To repeat again, given the high levels of competitiveness of industrial capitalist societies, it has been argued that this system maximizes racial prejudice and physical segregation. Conversely, precapitalist societies are assumed to experience minimum competition, mobility, and physical segregation. The empirical links between segregation and competition are not as strong as one might hope, a condition suggesting that the competitive structural interpretation is somewhat "upside down." First of all, actual economic competition is inversely related to segregation. For instance, in the United States white immigrant groups have been subjected to lesser segregation but have actually competed more with other white groups than with blacks. Expressed in other terms, the blacks, who have experienced the most discrimination in the United States, are the group who, empirically speaking, has competed the least with white groups. Second, precapitalist societies are not static. In effect, it has been documented that in Latin America nonwhites have experienced mobility and have penetrated exclusivist socioeconomic and political elites. Furthermore, the fact that Latin American societies have experienced substantial levels of political and interclass conflict suggests the dynamic aspects of these societies. There has been mobilization, at least among elite and middle sectors, the latter being mostly miscegenated or nonwhite in the infused system, and this has not led to high levels of overt racial strife. The confusion in this respect found in some of the literature can be attributed to an inadequate analysis of the elites and to the error of interpreting the "dynamics" of the society mainly in terms of an "elite-mass gap" that is thought to be unbridgeable (96). The degree of competitive penetration of nonwhites in the Cartagena elite and middle sectors and other corollary points is presented in the following chapter. The point we wish to make here is that although the elite-mass gap hypothesis is correct in that, indeed, non- or low-miscegenated blacks —the lower classes—virtually do not compete with "pure" whites—the upper classes—in the area, in Cartagena there has been substantial competition for positions between *blancos, mulatos,* and *mestizos.* In Colombia this competition also includes blacks and *mestizos* (97), and it has not produced high levels of racial violence. Actually, job competitiveness is also present in all the racially nonhomogeneous towns of the Cartagena area, and it is possible to assume that economic underdevelopment—the scarcity of positions—should exacerbate it.

Let us recapitulate. There are cultural aspects associated with a precapitalist economic system that favor the tolerance-miscegenation syndrome. Personalistic and affective cultural orientations, and the paternalism linked with a seigneurial system, can be seen to favor racial tolerance. In contrast, an equalitarian rather than a seigneurial cultural ethos appears to reinforce racial prejudice and social distance. That is, some *cultural* orientations historically associated with a capitalist system, such as competitive equalitarianism, individualism, and puritanism, or Protestant as opposed to Catholic humanitarianism, can be logically linked to discrimination. However, as previously exemplified with Guyana, a precapitalist, preindustrial economy is not a sufficient condition for the emergence of the cultural characteristics of the infused racial system. Quite simply, the links between the economy and culture are weak enough to permit culturally determined differences in a given economic system. The actual competitiveness of the economic system—a *structural* characteristic—has also been considered as a fundamental determinant of racial patterns. According to this interpretation, prejudice and discrimination are directly related to competition often operationalized by demographic proportions. In the light of our evidence, we consider that there is a sacred cultural aspect to prejudice that transcends economic structural characteristics. For example, caste relationships materialized in the Anglo-Saxon world with different white-black ratios. In effect, in many ways there is a cultural atavistic dimension to racial prejudice; that is, it can be seen as a case of cultural lag vis-à-vis economic modernity. In our opinion the competitive structural variable cannot account for the final causation of prejudice and segmentation; rather, competition is a factor that triggers conflict and gives particular forms to discriminatory structures within the parameters established by the culture. Here is where its predictive value lies. Expressed in different terms, intergroup competitiveness cannot entirely account for prejudice; it simply exacerbates discrimination and leads, both in Latin America and elsewhere, to "slight" increases in it. Competitiveness can explain short-run variations in prejudice within particular cultures, but not "substantial" differences in prejudice. In a continuum of segregation for example, between Mexico and Brazil and the United States and South Africa, a better mechanistic predictor of racial acceptance and adaptation is the degree of penetration of the miscegenated found in the society, which in turn must be explained by other variables.

The Somatic Distance

There is an important additional variable to explain the differences between Iberian and non-Iberian American racial patterns: the somatic, physical, or racial distance between groups (98). According to this interpretation, social groups develop a "somatic norm image," that is, a

complex of physical (somatic) characteristics which are accepted by a group as its norm and ideal. . . . The somatic norm image is the yardstick of aesthetic evaluation and ideal of the somatic characteristics of the members of the group. The socio-psychological reality of this norm image is demonstrated by the fact that without it, it would not be possible for an individual to be physically vain, or to be hurt in his physical vanity (99).

This esthetic preference normally corresponds with the physical characteristic of the dominant group. This leads, then, to maximize racial discrimination against those groups who deviate the most from the norm. The acceptance of these esthetic standards produces those practices common in Latin America and the United States by which individuals seek to "whiten" themselves (100).

According to this interpretation, the mild Latin racial patterns correspond to the relative somatic closeness or similarity between Iberians and nonwhites, a condition that was partly affected by precolonial miscegenation with the Moors. The physical resemblance of Iberians with nonwhites, particularly with *mestizos,* but not Negroids, and the problems that this presented to maintain a legally segmented society were acknowledged during the colonial period. According to Mörner, "expressions such as 'taken for Spaniard' or 'reputed to be Spanish' " (101) were frequent during the period and reflected the difficulties of assigning a position to somatically similar individuals in the Hispanic colonial discriminatory caste system. Actually, some sources went as far as to consider that "there were many mestizos who '. . . from the advantage of a fresh complexion, appear to be Spaniards more than those who are so in reality' " (102). Furthermore, the physical similarities between Indians and *mestizos* contributed to an early distinction between both groups in ethnic (e.g., patterns of dress) as opposed to racial terms a practice that continues to exist in Latin America. In effect, in the 1770s, Concolorcorvo considered that

the Indian is not distinct from the Spaniard in the shape of the face. When one of them enters the service of one of us (i. e., the whites) who treats him with charity, then his first measure is to teach the Indian cleanliness, to wash his face, to comb his hair, to cut his nails. When this is done and he is clad in a clean shirt, the Indian, though otherwise maintaining his own dress, passes as Cholo; that is, as somebody who has some Mestizo admixture. If his service is of use to the Spaniard, he gets a (Spanish) dress and shoes are put on his feet. Within a couple of months he is a mestizo by name (103).

Although the color and hair of Negroids (104) rendered them relatively more distant than the *mestizos* from the Iberians, during the colonial period the somatic closeness of mulattoes and whites was also considered to be a factor that made their racial designation a difficult task (105). More recently, the similarity between the Iberian brunette type and the light mulatto type has been considered to be the key factor for the fluidity of racial patterns in the area. For instance, Hoetink states that

> the [Iberian–non-Iberian] difference in incidence of intimate social relations between a section of the coloured group and the whites does not imply a "cultural" or "moral" difference in the attitude of the whites. The explanation is wholly amoral: the Latin whites simply accept "coloureds" in their midst because by their physical criteria, they are not "coloured". . . . It is exclusively the lesser somatic distance which has caused the higher incidence of "coloureds" in the white group (106).

Although according to our data the predominantly white elite of Cartagena are aware of nonwhite physical characteristics, even when these are present among other elite members (107), this finding need not imply the total rejection of the somatic interpretation. There is evidence that the somatic distance can explain some of the variations in racial patterns. But we must note here that, obviously, the hypothesis implies that a somatic closeness sponsors the acceptance of miscegenated persons and miscegenation, and that as this latter process proceeds, the somatic norm tends to darken, thus permitting increases in racial upward mobility or "passing."

There are two facts that support a physical or somatic interpretation of race relations. First, a critical difference between Iberian and United States race relations is the "privileged" position of the *mulatos,* not the blacks, that is, the group that is somatically closer to the whites (108). Although it could be argued that Iberian Americans are more paternalistic toward Negroes—the colonial-economy hypothesis—the fact is that in the Cartagena area, discrimination is high against "pure" blacks. In terms of intermarriage between whites and blacks, there is little difference between the Latin and non-Latin patterns. Second, if the hypothesis is correct, *mestizos*—persons without Negroid characteristics—should experience less discrimination than *mulatos,* and this is the general case in Latin America.

There has been some confusion in the literature regarding this point. Some studies have suggested that both in the colonial period and currently, Negroes have had a higher status than Indians (109). This has obscured the already-mentioned fact that in Latin America, Indians basically have an ethnic, not racial, definition and that *negros,* not *indios,* are relatively more integrated into national society. For example, even in the economically underdeveloped and relatively isolated Colombian region of the Choco, Negroes speak Spanish and prefer the national style of dress, whereas the Indians maintain their tribal language and dress in their native costumes. A frequent pattern of social interaction between *negros* and *indios* in this area is one in which the former ridicule the latter for their ethnocentric, nonassimilated patterns. An additional source of confusion about the relative position of *mestizos* and *mulatos* in Iberian American society can be traced to regional-ethnic differences between both types that can lead to cultural preferences for the latter in some areas (110). However, as we later show, the miscegenated middle classes of Cartagena prefer the self-designation of *mestizo,* not *mulato* (111). It is interesting to note that the middle-class club of this city, whose membership is miscegenated and pervasively Negroid, has for its symbol an Indian, not black, rebellious *cacique* of the colonial period. Actually, the less discriminatory patterns of *mestizo,* not Negroid Latin America can be interpreted in terms of the relatively fewer racial differences between *mestizos* and whites (112). In the 1920s, the Mexican philosopher Vasconcelos adopted this interpretation and extended it to the United States. In his words,

North Americans are very firm in maintaining their resolution of racial purity; but that is because they are faced with the Negro, that is the opposite pole, the opposite of the elements that can mix. In the Iberian American world, the problem does not present itself with such crude dimensions; we have very few Negroes and most of them have already been transformed into a mulatto population. The Indian is a good bridge for miscegenation (113).

The previous considerations notwithstanding, a noncultural, physical deterministic interpretation of racial patterns is unwarranted. Although *ceteris paribus,* as the somatic distance is reduced interracial psychological distance is also diminished, there are cases indicating that cultural factors have an independent effect on race relations. For example, although East Indians are somatically closer to blacks than the Iberians, the former have maintained highly segmented relationships with the blacks in Guyana, where group conflict has recently become a fundamental societal problem. It seems that the somatic distance can best account for intracultural variations in societies characterized by the acceptance of the miscegenated. That is, it can explain differences in discrimination between *mestizo* and *mulato* Latin American societies. Nevertheless, the somatic distance cannot explain racial differences between highly segmented societies with a low acceptance of miscegenation, such as South Africa and the United States. In this case, competitive factors such as relative size of the racial groups seems to be a more adequate mechanistic predictor. Finally, somatic distance cannot account for differences in racial patterns between societies that accept miscegenation and those that do not, such as between the infused racial system and the case of Guyana.

CONCLUDING REMARKS

Up to this point we have addressed ourselves to the analysis of issues posed by a particular type of system of racial domination: the infused racial system. We have described some of its critical characteristics in the context of two ideal-type polar racial systems: the open and the closed. Briefly, the former is characterized by racial homogeneity and competition between individuals with different physical characteristics. The latter evidences patterns of racial heterogeneity and dominance, the myth of racial purity and endogamy, and a propensity for racial group conflict.

Within the framework of these two polar systems we find the properties of the infused system to be eclectic. First, although miscegenation has been extensive there are still individuals who define themselves in terms of the two racial poles: whites and blacks. Second, there is a pattern of endogamy and dominance of *blancos* over *negros*. In conjunction with these characteristics of the closed system, there also exist elements of the open system that center on the role played by the miscegenated in the society. The unique aspect of the infused system is not that mixed bloods have a mediating role between whites and blacks but rather that a significant proportion of them are accepted and intermarry freely with persons who define themselves as white. Consequently, in this system the power of the myth of racial purity is extremely weak; the miscegenated are infused throughout all strata of the society's single stratification pyramid. In addition, competition within this pyramid is carried on by individuals with different racial characteristics, not by racial groups. Nevertheless, there is little competition between the polar racial types. Finally, despite discrimination, the tensions and conflicts produced by this system are focused upon class rather than racial differences.

The infused racial system is not a contemporary development, for it materialized in Latin America during the colonial period when the tolerance-miscegenation syndrome was already evident. That is, *ceteris paribus,* acceptance of the miscegenated leads to further miscegenation which in turn reinforces racial tolerance. In the presence of sufficient demographic conditions and racial dominance, substantial miscegenation occurs. Although this is a fairly universal phenomenon, acceptance of the miscegenated is not a historical constant. What characterizes the Iberian variant is precisely this acceptance, which is reflected in the cultural-terminological patterns. This cultural orientation of acceptance furthers miscegenation. It is the cultural definition of miscegenation, as opposed to biological miscegenation, that conspicuously differentiates the Iberian variant. In the Latin American infused context, acceptance has furthered miscegenation by reducing the number of persons found in the discriminated-against pole. The bleaching process reduces the number of Negroid individuals found in the society. It erodes Negroid identity throughout the racial continuum. Finally, the acceptance of extensive miscegenation reinforces racial tolerance, for it leads to a situation in which a large proportion of phenotypic whites have *legitimate* relatives with visible racial mixture. Thus the tolerance-miscegenation syndrome produces a recursive system that builds upon itself.

The infused system materialized in areas where there were sufficient proportions of whites and blacks. It did not find expression in areas, such as Argentina, where blacks were too few and extensive European migration absorbed the black population, nor did it materialize in those few regions that have been sufficiently isolated to maintain a virtually all-black population, such as the Choco region of Colombia. Furthermore, the infused system did not develop in areas, such as Mexico, where there were very small proportions of whites and blacks as compared with an overwhelming Indian population. In terms of racial homogenization Negroids have been the most difficult to absorb, a factor emphasizing the concentration of prejudice against them and the utility of the somatic interpretation for societies characterized by the acceptance of miscegenation. Where the predominant gene pool has been European with a residual of Indian, as in Argentina, the miscegenating process has led to societies that define themselves as basically European. In contrast, where the predominant gene pool has been Indian, as in Mexico, the tendency has been toward the development of a highly homogenized, "miscegenated" racial system.

The common factor that runs through the Iberian variant is the tolerance-miscegenation syndrome which is conditioned by the racial nature of the various proportions. To the extent that the proportions of whites have increased, the societies have become predominantly *blanco*. Paralleling this pattern has been the case where the dominance of Indian proportions has led to basically *mestizo* or miscegenated societies. These patterns set in high relief the potential for conflict where there are sufficient proportions of whites and the most negatively perceived racial group—the *negros*. Yet conflict has not occurred because of the development of the infused system under these conditions. Although it appears that racial minority awareness has been heightened in those uncommon regions found in Latin America with a virtually all-black population that have been described in the anthropological literature, their scarcity, poverty, and isolation have impeded the crystallization of effective racial movements in them. The economic development required for effective political action has materialized in Negroid Latin America with the development of the patterns of dominance characteristic of the infused racial system.

Although racial proportions have had an impact in Latin America, the patterns of miscegenation that naturally occur have been accepted to produce relatively homogeneous racial societies. Homogenization is apparent even in the infused system where *racial* heterogeneity finds its greatest expression. Despite the racist tendencies of whites toward blacks, a mechanistic competitive interpretation of race relations in Iberian America based upon population proportions leaves much to be desired. The mild Iberian American pattern of race relations cannot be accounted for in terms of a static system in which there has been little competition between persons of different racial makeup for scarce resources.

In the Iberian pattern racial proportions have influenced the racial self-identity of the dominant group without producing the rigid boundaries of a caste system between whites and nonwhites, regardless of proportions; in contrast, the Anglo-Saxon modality has been one of white domination and clear racial boundaries. In these societies, particularly under condi-

tions of a preindustrial paternalistic system, substantial miscegenation occurred. However, this has not been accompanied
by the legitimation and acceptance of the miscegenated. Indeed, increasing proportions of nonwhites have tended to produce *de jure* segregation, as in the southern United States and
South Africa. Nevertheless, this propensity has not been linear. As in the former British West Indies, when the number of
whites has been quite small white domination has been based
on metropolitan colonial control. This leads us into the question of political breakdown. In the Anglo-Saxon world where
there has been a substantial proportion of blacks and whites
the racial issue has tended to be tied to abrupt secession, as in
the United States and Rhodesia. However, the small proportion of whites in the British West Indies led to the peaceful abolition of slavery because of the noted dependence of whites on
the metropolis. In contrast, in Iberian America the wars of independence had only a residual racial aspect. The infused
system that accompanied significant proportions of *blancos*
and *negros* produced a pattern of white and miscegenated
leadership. In Portuguese Africa, however, despite an observed relative acceptance of the miscegenated, a very small
colonial Iberian population has not sufficiently penetrated the
societies to produce an infused system with the consequent
strengthening of black nationalism.

In this chapter we have analyzed the historical, sociocultural, and physical factors that have been advanced to explain
the presence of the infused racial system. This was necessary
because the system was established during an earlier historical
period. What were the causes of the infused racial system? As
we have seen, it is possible to relate logically a series of causal
factors operating under the condition of sufficient proportions
of whites and blacks to this racial system. At the highest level
of analysis (the macrosocietal) two ahistorical interpretative
models of racial domination are found in the sociological literature: the paternalistic—*Gemeinschaft*—type and the
competitive—*Gesellschaft*—type. In the perspective of the

open and closed system dichotomy both sociological models refer to closed racial systems. Under the paternalistic system, there is a prevalent ideology of ascription and elitist rule. Racial groups accept their position in the stratification system and do not compete for power. Interracial contacts take on a nonthreatening, tutelary aspect. These contacts are frequent and "intimate." The competitive system, on the other hand, is characterized by an ideology of achievement and equalitarianism. Racial groups attempt to compete in the stratification system for power. Interracial contacts are of a threatening nature. Therefore, these contacts are avoided, and when they occur, are highly tension producing.

Both systems, as formulated in the sociological literature, contain the seeds for their own destruction. In effect, the intimate nature of the paternalistic system leads to high levels of miscegenation. Faced with a substantial proportion of mixed bloods, the dominant group can either accept or reject them. In the former case, the system becomes infused. In the latter, faced with the threat posed by the miscegenated, the system must establish impersonality and social distance or legal segregation between racial groups. This leads, of course, to the compartmentalization of the competitive model. The long-run weakness of the competitive system, on the other hand, is found in the contradiction between its ideology and its practice, which makes it prone to racial conflict and violence.

With the conspicuous exceptions of the Moorish conquest with its impact on the *acceptance* of dark populations and the somatic or physical determinist interpretation, most of the factors that have been considered to produce the tolerance-miscegenation syndrome, and its resultant infused racial system, can be seen to exemplify "paternalistic" *themes*. Indeed, the tradition with slavery; a relatively unproductive colonial economy characterized by miscegenation and manumissions; a colonial structure heavily influenced by the hierarchical, ecumenical, and benevolent orientations of the Catholic church; and the *personalismo* of a *Gemeinschaft* society, all can be linked to paternalistic orientations. However, the question still remains on the accuracy of interpreting the Iberian American infused system as the product of the outlined *Gemeinschaft* sociological *model*.

Without denying the stress posed by a capitalistic-competitive system on miscegenation and racial subordination and its underlying tendency to the racial radicalism manifested in *Herrenvolk* democracies, nor the impact that paternalistic factors may have had in Iberian American race relations (114), it appears that the paternalistic-*Gemeinschaft* sociological interpretation of the Iberian infused system is inadequate for the following reasons. First, as already noted, there is evidence that the colonial society was not a highly stratified, multiracial system, for there is support for the position that racial boundaries were not well established, and that processes of racial acceptance and mobility were conspicuous during the colonial period. That is, the acceptance of the miscegenated cannot be explained in terms of the presence of marked racial boundaries. Second, it appears that racial tolerance accompanied colonization, thus preceding the emergence of the infused system. That nonwhites did not threaten the *conquistadores* did not determine the infused racial system. As revealed by the crucial, early employment of Moorish-derived terms to give ambiguity to and soften racial definitions, the Moorish conquest, a historical element that transcends the *Gemeinschaft-Gesellschaft* sociological dichotomy, favored the development of the infused system. In addition, there is evidence that the somatic likeness was important in facilitating racial assimilation and "passing" during the colonial period.

The previous considerations do not imply that some of the elements we have linked to a *historical*, paternalistic interpretation did not have an impact in the Iberian American racial modality. Most notable among these elements was the impact of the Catholic church with its corporate, humanitarian philosophy, as opposed to the puritanical, individualistic equalitarianism associated with *Herrenvolk* democracies. However, as we have noted, Catholicism did not produce the infused system within a French context. Similarly, both slave and non-slave societies have produced mild and harsh racial systems.

In the Western Hemisphere the only elements unique to the Iberian pattern are the Moorish conquest, the tradition with slavery, and the *personalismo-machismo* of the ruling group. As noted, the colonial preindustrial economy was accompanied by low levels of acceptance of miscegenation within a non-Iberian context, Catholicism was present both in harsh and mild racial systems, and segmentation and low levels of miscegenation accompanied relationships between blacks and East Indians, somatic likeness notwithstanding. Unfortunately, within this hemisphere we do not find sufficient combinations of the forementioned elements such that by a process of elimination we could assign priorities to the analyzed factors in the determination of the tolerance-miscegenation syndrome and its infused racial system. Consequently, it is preferable not to adopt unilateral interpretations. Rather, we view the tolerance-miscegenation syndrome as the product of the constellation of historical, sociocultural, and physical factors discussed in this chapter. To conclude, if we had to adopt a mechanistic predictor for a mild, Iberian-style discriminatory racial system, it would be the volume of accepted miscegenation present in the society. A good predictor of the openness of mild racial systems, such as those of Iberian America, is the somatic likeness. Indeed, as exemplified within Colombia, *mestizo* societies are better integrated than *mulato* ones.

Now that we have discussed the major interpretations for the emergence of the infused system, in the next four chapters we focus our analysis on the structural characteristics and social-psychological processes that pinpoint the sources of conflict and adaptation of this system. By analyzing in detail the functioning of the race-class system of Cartagena we are able to provide empirical evidence that explains why discrimination has not generated significant levels of overt racial conflict in Latin America.

NOTES

1. These periods seem to have been generally characterized by high rates of miscegenation.

2. Mörner, *op. cit.*, p. 43.

3. See van den Berghe, *Race and Racism, op. cit.* This is not to say that, in the context of slavery, extramarital relations did not imply a tolerance of sorts. It is well known that lovers and mulattoes were often freed. For Latin America, see, for instance, Mörner, *op. cit.*, p. 117. For the United States, see Maurice R. Davie, *Negroes in American Society*, McGraw-Hill, New York, 1949, p. 35. Of course, a similar case can be made for domestic servants, who were often concubines and have constituted an "elite" group. It is probable that these benevolent aspects of "paternalistic" systems have led some sources to suggest their preference over those systems of discrimination that maximize avoidance and minimize sexual contact. See van den Berghe, *Race and Racism, op. cit.*, p. 18. It has been argued that in the United States the racism of the slaveholders and slave areas was relatively mild; see Genovese, *op. cit.*, pp. 107 and 111.

4. For Portuguese Africa see Abshire, *op. cit.*

5. Although these generalizations are valid for Colombia as a whole, according to Gutiérrez de Pineda there are important regional or ethnoracial differences. The Negroid complex of which Cartagena forms a part is characterized by a low frequency of legal marriages. This contrasts sharply with the Andean *mestizo* complex in which slavery had a lesser impact, areas which have experienced a greater church influence. See Virginia Gutiérrez de Pineda, *Familia y Cultura en Colombia*, Coediciones de Tercer Mundo y Departamento de Sociología, Universidad Nacional de Colombia, Bogota, 1968, especially pp. 15–18, 51, 66, 70, 210, and 217–218.

6. See Chapter 4 and Daniel Lemaitre, *Flor de Corralitos de Piedra*, Ediciones Corralito de Piedra, Cartagena, 1961, p. 117. For pertinent non-Colombian interpretations, see, for instance, Mörner, *op. cit.*, pp. 51, 67, and 72; and Hoetink, *op. cit.*, pp. 38, 41, and 152.

7. Of course, in Latin America miscegenation transcended the master-slave and other exploitative interclass sexual relationships. Poor European immigrants and *criollos* and the predominantly male African groups also participated in the three-way process

—whites, Indians, and blacks—which led Vasconcelos to speak of a Latin American "cosmic race." See Mörner, *op. cit.,* pp. 40, 67, and 76–77 and Vasconcelos, *op. cit.* Although generally disregarded in the literature, the presence of the somatically closer Amerindian types in the infused racial system contributed to racial assimilation.

8. This may be a reason for the alleged historical reduction of miscegenation in Negroid Latin America. See van den Berghe, *op. cit.,* p. 70.

9. The saying literally means "where is your grandmother?" and makes reference to the fact that socially pretentious persons have black ancestry.

10. Mörner, *op. cit.,* pp. 44 and 66.

11. The terms are quoted in Hoetink, *op. cit.,* p. 53.

12. See Pierson, *op. cit.,* p. 134.

13. This interpretation has been emphasized by Gilberto Freyre. See his *The Masters and the Slaves,* Knopf, New York, 1946 and his *Brazil: An Interpretation,* Knopf, New York, 1945.

14. For Cartagena, see the sixteenth-century chronicle of Juan de Castellanos, *Historia de Cartagena,* Biblioteca Popular de Cultura Colombiana, Bogota, 1942, p. 7. However, Mörner considers that these statements which were frequent in the chronicles were largely the product of "the literary taste of the times." See Mörner, *op. cit.,* p. 22.

15. See van den Berghe, *Race and Racism, op. cit.,* pp. 66 and 71, and Hoetink, *op. cit.,* p. 170.

16. See Chapter 5.

17. Pierson, *op. cit.,* p. 327.

18. Hutchinson, *op. cit.,* p. 33.

19. See the official Castilian dictionary of the *Real Academia Española.*

20. See Castellanos, *op. cit.,* pp. 186, 199, and 204.

21. Mörner, *op. cit.,* p. 58.

22. However, according to Pierson it was not until 1433 that the first African slaves were imported into Portugal. See Pierson, *op. cit.,* p. 31.

23. See Mörner, *op. cit.,* p. 111. The "privileged" position of non-fieldhand slaves is widely accepted in the literature. Although the

employment of the term capitalistic presents some problems because of the "irrational" implications of slavery for the optimal
materialistic allocation of resources, for our purposes Gray's definition of the slave plantation system as "a capitalistic type of
agricultural organization in which a considerable number of un-
free laborers were employed under unified direction and control
in the production of a staple crop" is adequate. The definition is
quoted in Klein, *op. cit.*, p. 128. For the classic critique of the
economic rationality of slavery, see Max Weber, *The Theory of
Social and Economic Organization*, Oxford University Press,
New York, 1947, pp. 276ff. However, although acknowledging
differences, Genovese has argued for the paternalistic aspects of
all slave systems. Genovese, *op. cit.*

24. See Klein, *op. cit.*, pp. 57–85. The Siete Partidas were influenced by the Roman Justinian Code. Of course, the Catholic
Church has been singled out as a fundamental determinant of
this "soft" slave system. See *ibid., passim.*, and the earlier classi-
cal work by Frank Tannenbaum, *Slave and Citizen: The Negro
in the Americas*, Knopf, New York, 1947. A parallel case has
been made for Moorish influence on Iberian slavery. See Pierson,
op. cit., p. 79. More is said later on the role of the church in Iberian race relations.

25. For instance, Adams has related the "mild" Hawaiian racial patterns to the absence of slavery. See Romanzo Adams, "The
Unorthodox Race Doctrine of Hawaii," in *Comparative Perspectives on Race Relations, op. cit.*, pp. 81–90. However, for the
view that slavery is more clearly understood as a class rather
than a racial phenomenon see Genovese, *op. cit.*

26. See, for instance, Freyre, *op. cit.*, Pierson, *op. cit.*, and Klein,
op. cit.

27. Pierson notes the direct relationship between miscegenation and
manumission. According to him, in 1822 in Brazil over 75 percent of the mixed bloods were emancipated, as contrasted with
less than 20 percent of the Negroes. Pierson, *op. cit.*, p. 161.

28. Quoted in Klein, *op. cit.*, p. 201.

29. See Mörner, *op. cit.*, p. 115.

30. See Hoetink's review of the literature in Hoetink, *op. cit.*, pp.
23–31. Klein has documented the privileged position of Cuban
urban, as opposed to plantation, slaves. For Colombia, King considers that blacks received better treatment in the city of Carta-

94   *Miscegenation, the Crucial Intervening Variable*

gena than in the mines of Choco. See James Ferguson King, "Negro Slavery in New Granada," in *Greater America, Essays in Honor of Herbert Eugene Bolton*, Books for Libraries Press, Freeport, New York, 1945, pp. 311–312.

31. Mörner, *op. cit.*, p. 125.

32. According to Poppino, as late as in the 1870s, five of every six were plantation slaves. See Rollie E. Poppino, *Brazil, The Land and People*, Oxford University Press, New York, 1968, pp. 173–174.

33. Mörner, *op. cit.*, p. 117.

34. Hoetink, *op. cit.*, p. 29.

35. Genovese, *op. cit.*, p. 65.

36. See Robert C. West, *Colonial Placer Mining in Colombia*, University of Louisiana Press, Baton Rouge, 1952, p. 84.

37. In this sense see Klein, *op. cit., passim.*

38. Poppino, *op. cit.*, pp. 174–184.

39. See van den Berghe, *op. cit.*, p. 97 and Hoetink, *op. cit.*, p. 112.

40. Harris has argued in demographic mechanistic terms that the lower proportion of whites in Brazil than in the United States was conducive to improve the status of the miscegenated because of the need to staff intermediate class positions. Harris, *Patterns of Race, op. cit.*, pp. 86–89. However, as noted by Genovese, small proportions of whites did not lead to the noncaste relations with the miscegenated that characterize the infused system in the British West Indies. Genovese, *op. cit.*, pp. 106–108. More is said on the important role of demographic variables in the following section.

41. *Ibid.*, pp. vii and 12.

42. Hoetink, *op. cit.*, p. 36.

43. According to Banton, "the cause for the coloured man's complaint may well lie in the British [not Latin] tradition of maintaining a greater social distance, and the appreciation of cultural distinctiveness." See Michael Banton, "White and Coloured in Britain," in *Comparative Perspectives on Race Relations, op. cit.*, p. 70.

44. Its literal translation is the black legend. Most of the arguments that follow find parallels in Portuguese America.

45. Klein vividly reproduces the anti-*Leyenda Negra* position. See Klein, *op. cit.*, particularly part 1.

46. Beals, *op. cit.*, p. 239. He considers that these policies were determined by "differences in the Indian societies and in the experience and purposes of the Spanish at given times and places." See also page 241.

47. The crown played a more direct role in the Spanish brand of colonization, which politically was more centralized than the Portuguese one.

48. Of course, the virtual collapse of political organizations after the independence from Spain suggests the presence of weak local political organization.

49. For the role of economic motives in both capitalistic and noncapitalistic colonization see Genovese, *op. cit.*, p. 17.

50. Klein, *op. cit.*, pp. 95–96.

51. See Mörner, *op. cit.*, p. 60. Pierson has also acknowledged the disparity between law and practice in colonial Brazil. Pierson, *op. cit.*, p. 52.

52. Mörner, *op. cit.*, p. 36.

53. See the discussion of these institutions as applied to Colombia in Gutiérrez de Pineda, *op. cit.*, pp. 36–38.

54. See Mörner, *op. cit.*, pp. 37–38. According to him, the former were relatively frequent. For one such case in the colonization of the Cartagena area, see Castellanos, *op. cit.*, p. 96. We have already noted that in 1514, the liberty to marry Indians was definitely decreed. However, it was as late as 1806 when total freedom for whites to marry persons of Negro origin was decreed.

55. If we control for factors such as size of native populations and economic development, there is no question of the success of these policies. Of course, the process of acculturation ran both ways between dominant and subordinate groups. For example, in Brazil today some whites participate in the *candomblé*, an African influenced ritual. See Pierson, *op. cit.*, pp. 102 and 238.

56. This cultural unity of Catholicism has led Pierson to consider it an important factor in Brazilian race relations. See Pierson, *op. cit.*, p. 194.

57. Several sources have considered the ratio as a crucial determinant of both racial tolerance and miscegenation. For Hawaii, see Adams, *op. cit.*, pp. 85–86. Mörner has made it his main interpretation for Latin America. See Mörner, *op. cit.*, p. 134. Pierson emphasizes this point for Brazil; Pierson, *op. cit.*, pp. 111–112. He also notes the importance of the high male-female

ratio in early colonial South Africa in the production of high levels of miscegenation, which was reduced by the subsequent arrival of Dutch females; see pp. 113–114.

58. Klein, *op. cit.*, pp. 142–143.

59. Klein considers that the different patterns of settlement were affected by the belief that the British Isles were overpopulated. *Ibid.*, p. 167. However, according to Mörner, "it seems as if [in the sixteenth century] there was a demographic pressure on available resources" in Spain. Mörner, *op. cit.*, p. 15.

60. Hoetink, *op. cit.*, p. 172.

61. Mörner, *op. cit.*, p. 15. However, he considers that, especially at the beginning of the colonization, male immigration prevailed and that about 40 percent of the 12 million European immigrants who arrived in Latin America in the 1850 to 1930 period returned to Europe. *Ibid.*, p. 133.

62. Klein considers that the church was the most important influence in race relations over the long run, and he contrasts it with what he considers to have been a clergy controlled by local economic interests in the United States. See Klein, *op. cit.*, pp. 106 and 196. Several sources have singled out the Quakers as being a special case in the United States characterized by more evangelical attitudes. See, for instance, Blalock, *op. cit.*, p. 78. Incidentally, Saint Pedro Claver (1580 to 1654) operated in Cartagena. See Angel Valtierra S. J., *San Pedro Claver, El Santo Que Liberó Una Raza*, Santuario de San Pedro Claver, Cartagena, 1964.

63. For pertinent comments see Genovese, *op. cit.*, pp. 99–100.

64. Klein, *op. cit.*, pp. 98–99 and van den Berghe, *op. cit.*, p. 82.

65. Klein, *op. cit.*, p. 92.

66. However, it has been considered that the French church had less power than its Iberian counterparts. See Genovese, *op. cit.*, p. 43.

67. Tannenbaum, *op. cit.*, p. 65.

68. We might note here that during the colonial period there were instances in which there were racially separated church organizations. See Pierson, *op. cit.*, p. 164.

69. Mörner, *op. cit.*, pp. 113–114. According to Pierson, "the clergy as a group did not support abolition [in Brazil]." Pierson, *op. cit.*, p. 54. Also see Harris, *Patterns of Race, op. cit.*, p. 16. Genovese has noted that abolition began in the Anglo-Saxon world. Genovese, *op. cit.* pp. 13–14.

70. Klein, *op. cit.*, pp. 96–97.
71. For a description of this cultural ethos, see Gillin, *op. cit.*
72. *Ibid.*, p. 29.
73. Hoetink, *op. cit.*, p. 22.
74. See, for instance, *ibid.*, p. 36.
75. See Hutchinson, *op. cit.*, p. 30.
76. *Compadrazgo* is the institution by which godparents are included in an extended family.
77. Klein, *op. cit.*, p. 155. The term *padrino* includes general paternalistic-familistic relationships, which do not require the actual existence of the religious bond.
78. See, for instance, Pierson, *op. cit.*, pp. 45–50; Hutchinson, *op. cit.*, p. 16; and Freyre, *op. cit.*, *passim.*
79. Terms have been coined to describe this cultural aspect, such as *malicia indígena* and *picardía criolla.*
80. See José Vasconcelos, "La Raza Cósmica, Misión de la Raza Latinoamericana," *Conciencia Intelectual de América, Antología del Ensayo Hispanoamericano (1836–1959)*, in Carlos Ripoll, Ed., Las Americas Publishing Company, New York, 1966, pp. 321–337.
81. It is perhaps this coincidence that underlies Needler's consideration that Negroid Latin American nations are relatively less stratified than Indian ones. See Martin C. Needler, *Political Development in Latin America: Instability, Violence, and Evolutionary Change*, Random House, New York, 1968, Chapter 6.
82. See Hoetink, *op. cit.*, p. 49.
83. For pertinent data see Chapter 4.
84. Of course, Catholicism and economic imperialism have been considered to have blocked the economic modernization of the area. For the traditional medieval anticapitalist Catholic orientation see Leo XIII's encyclical *Rerum Novarum.*
85. For a summary of most of the arguments relating increases in racial conflict to a capitalist economy and its links to Parsons' pattern variables, see van den Berghe, *op. cit.*, pp. 31–33.
86. See, for instance, Harris, "Race in Minas Velhas," *op. cit.*
87. See Mörner, *op. cit.*, p. 63, and Klein, *op. cit.*, p. 144. Greater discrimination at the university level was compounded by a "precapitalist" disdain for manual work. This placed a high premium on professional education. For relevant Colombian–United

States comparisons indicating that holding economic development constant, the former society places a greater premium in
these activities, see Payne, *op. cit.* It can be argued that this attitude led not only to the openness of guilds to the colored, but
also to a "coupon-clipper" or *rentista* mentality that fostered the
hiring-out of slaves, a practice that led to higher levels of manumissions.

88. In this respect, see Whitten, *op. cit.* Incidentally, our data indicate that increases in segregation in the Cartagena area are tied
to increases in the economic complexity of a virtually preindustrial society. That is, discrimination increases from the village
to larger economically more developed towns. In addition, perceptions of discrimination are related to upward mobility. See
Chapters 5 and 8.

89. See van den Berghe, *op. cit.,* p. 32.

90. See Gutiérrez de Pineda, *op. cit.,* pp. 53, 66, and 70.

91. For Latin America, see, for instance, Merle Kling, "Toward a
Theory of Power and Political Instability in Latin America,"
Western Political Quarterly, 9, 1956, pp. 21–25, and Needler,
op. cit. Personalismo, an orientation that is reinforced by economic underdevelopment, has also been linked to escalated political and class conflict in the area. See Mauricio Solaún, *Sociología de los Golpes de Estado Latinoamericanos,* Universidad de
los Andes, Bogota, 1969, pp. 114–118. It is possible that *personalismo* produces opposite effects in race relations because of its
noted impact on miscegenation.

92. See Blalock, *op. cit.,* pp. 49, 67, 71, 168, and 204.

93. See van den Berghe, *op. cit.,* pp. 31–33.

94. This argument fits van den Berghe's interpretation for Mexico.
See *ibid.,* Chapter 2.

95. The seigneuralism of slavery has been linked to paternalism and
relatively lower levels of prejudice in the United States. See
Genovese, *op. cit.,* p. 107. Similarly, "as capitalist industrialization and urbanization advance in Brazil, more evidence of racial discrimination appears." *Ibid.,* p. 109.

96. These ideologically based analytical deficiencies have been extended to non-Latin American areas as well. See Charles C.
Moskos, Jr. and Wendell Bell, "Emerging Nations and Ideologies
of American Social Scientists," *The American Sociologists, 2,*
1965, pp. 67–72.

97. Ashton, *op. cit.*

98. This theory has been developed by Hoetink, *op. cit.*

99. *Ibid.*, pp. 120–121.

100. It should be noted that our interviews in Cartagena indicated that even some lower-class miscegenated persons showed a disdain for marked Negroid characteristics, mainly because of the difficulties that they pose to adopt dominant stylistic patterns of beauty and demeanor.

101. Mörner, *op. cit.*, p. 69.

102. Quoted in *ibid.*, p. 68.

103. Quoted in Mörner, *op. cit.*, pp. 68–69.

104. Some of the literature has considered that in Latin America the hair is a more important characteristic than color in racial designations. See Hoetink, *op. cit.*, p. 168. However, our data indicate that extreme color is a sufficient condition to classify a person as *negro*. See Chapter 6.

105. Mörner, *op. cit.*, p. 69.

106. Hoetink, *op. cit.*, p. 168.

107. See Chapters 4 and 6. Actually, it is not uncommon for persons with recognizable nonwhite characteristics to be considered particularly handsome in the area.

108. Hoetink, *op. cit.*, p. 164.

109. See, respectively, Mörner, *op. cit.*, pp. 30–31 and Charles Wagley, *Amazon Town, A Study of Man in the Tropics*, Macmillan, New York, 1967, p. 141. However, it should be recalled that Indians received better legal treatment, which included the early right to marry whites, during the colonial period.

110. Perhaps this is the case of the *caboclos* in some areas of Brazil. See Hutchison, *op. cit.*, p. 30.

111. Mörner extends this practice to other Spanish speaking countries as well. See Mörner, *op. cit.*, p. 2.

112. According to van den Berghe, *op. cit.*, Mexico has lower levels of racial discrimination than Brazil. Similarly, there is greater racial homogenization and integration in *mestizo* Andean Colombia than in the Negroid Coastal regions.

113. Vasconcelos, "La Raza Cósmica," p. 331. Our translation.

114. Even today, particularly among polar racial types, there are

some paternalistic manifestations. For example, the Colombian national press annually publishes pictures of the predominantly white contestants for the Miss Colombia title; often she is dancing and being carried by lower class Negroes of the Cartagena area. Of course, these situations represent "affection," not equality, among polar racial types.

Chapter Four

. . . .

THE CLASS-RACE STRUCTURE
AND THE POTENTIAL FOR
RACIAL CONFLICT IN CARTAGENA

In Chapter 2 we introduced the racial configuration of the class structure of Cartagena under the term of the infused racial system. We now turn to a more precise description of this system as it is found in Cartagena. Our analysis focuses on both its static and dynamic aspects. After the discussion of the system we establish hypotheses concerning its potential for conflict, hypotheses that are tested in the following chapters.

Although difficult to measure (1), there is no better standard of measurement of discrimination than the deliberate exclusion of persons from positions in the class structure on racial grounds. Consequently, by applying a racial scale from white to black to the different layers of the class structure, we are able to explore the degree of discrimination that exists in the society. To obtain a better picture of the racial situation in Cartagena, we also investigate the degree of openness of the Cartagena elite. This seems to be an important step in understanding discriminatory relationships in the society for the following reasons. It has been argued that elite positions are highly ascriptive in developing societies. Were this to be the case in Cartagena, we could expect that elite membership is restricted to a few select families who established their prominence at some time in the past. We could then expect to find that not only blacks—descendants of slaves who were not members of elite families—but other groups as well have been excluded from elite membership. That is, given these conditions, a case could be made that class prejudice based on tradition, as opposed to racial factors, is of paramount importance in the upper levels of the stratification system of Cartagena, and that this situation is more conducive to the promotion of class conflict rather than race conflict. Finally, to explore the dynamic aspects of race in the local class structure, we also analyze interracial marriage patterns. Our aim is to explore trends in miscegenation that can be linked to processes of upward mobility. If Cartagena experiences processes by which ambitious individuals can approximate dominant racial characteristics through their descendants, then the potentiality for racial conflict in the area is reduced.

HISTORICAL PERSPECTIVE

At this point a brief historical statement is needed to place this study of Cartagena in context with the development of the city. During the colonial period, the crown exercised a fundamental role in the growth and welfare of Cartagena. The seventeenth century saw a mercantilist colonial policy on the part of Spain in which Cartagena served as a mandatory port city for one of the two prescribed routes between the metropolis and South America (2). Early in that century, Cartagena was established as one of the major slave markets in the New World; thus it was an historic port of entry for blacks into Colombia (3). Today, only one other large port city—Barranquilla—has a comparable proportion of phenotypic Negroes.

Although the deterioration in the volume of trading between Spain and her colonies, which occurred during the first half of the eighteenth century, was not conducive to its further development, the general liberalization of colonial trade under Carlos III and the consolidation of Cartagena during his reign as a major port for the Spanish Armada contributed to the importance of the city until Colombia's independence from Spain in the early nineteenth century (4). Cartagena's role as a military port—*plaza fuerte*—enabled it to receive the *situado,* a subsidy from other colonial territories, that contributed to its economic welfare. During the eighteenth century, Cartagena was a commercial center whose direct influence spread as far south as Quito (5).

With independence, Cartagena no longer served as an important port. Within a period of a few decades, its population abruptly declined. Although there is a disagreement among sources as to its size about 1810—estimates are between 50,000 and 20,000 (6)—there is consensus that in the 1880s its population was less than 10,000 inhabitants (7). Although the loss of its colonially determined importance was a prime factor in the decline of the city (8), the literature speaks of additional factors that contributed to this deterioration. In 1815 the Spaniards, in their attempt to reestablish their control over Colombia, successfully seized the city. After 108 days, Cartagena surrendered. The Spanish interim governor estimated the civilian dead at 3,000 (9). The combination of the termination of its military role and the violence concomitant with Colombia's independence from Spain took a heavy toll from Cartagena's elite. Bossa has traced the migration and death of prominent Cartagenians to these events (10). This initial depletion of its elite has been interpreted as an important cause for the relative economic stagnation of the city during the nineteenth century (11).

In 1880 a native *cartagenero,* Rafael Núñez, was elected president of Colombia. As a result, the political power of the Cartagenian elite was enhanced, and the city itself benefited by attention from the central government in the form of public works and industrial subsidies (12). However, as indicated by Table 4.1, not until the first decade of this century did its population size achieve preindependence levels. For all practical purposes, during the nineteenth century Cartagena was a

TABLE 4.1   Population of Cartagena during the
Twentieth Century (Census Years)

Year	Population
1905	9,681
1912	36,632
1918	51,382
1928	92,494
1938	84,937
1943	97,680
1951	128,877
1964	242,085
1969	297,173

Sources: *Anuario Estadístico de Colombia, 1943*, p. 30; *Anuario Estadístico de Colombia, 1953*, p. 18; *XIII Censo Nacional de Población, 1964, Resumen General*, p. 30; and *Boletín Estadístico de Bolívar, Enero y Febrero 1969*, p. 1.

ghost town. In effect, a prominent Cartagenian industrialist and writer reports that in the 1880s there was such a shortage of people that real estate owners would search for occupants who would merely maintain their buildings (13). Notwithstanding the efforts made under Núñez, the strategically located Barranquilla on the Magdalena River supplanted Cartagena as the most important Atlantic port city of Colombia. Throughout this century, Barranquilla has kept this position.

There is no written history of the recent social changes of Cartagena. However, official statistics indicate that it is among the most rapidly urbanizing cities of Colombia (14). Its industrial growth is also visible. Furthermore, there is a chronicle of political and economic events (15), which permits us to explore the important topic of elite mobility in the city. The point that must be stressed here is that Cartagena is a city of *abolengo* (i.e., of lineage or strong tradition) that has experienced periods of socioeconomic decline, followed by processes of rapid urbanization. This socioeconomic deterioration notwithstanding, the importance of aristocratic orientations in Colombian culture (16) has contributed to the high social reputation of the Cartagena elite in the national society (17). Thus Cartagena provides us with a setting that is quite propitious to the analysis of the relationships between social change and racial conflict.

THE STRUCTURE OF CLASS
AND RACE IN CARTAGENA

Let us turn our attention now to the contemporary structure of class and race in Cartagena. The following diagram gives what for our purposes is an accurate picture of this relationship (see Figure 4.1). From its analysis, two clear conclusions emerge concerning the relationship of race and class in Carta-

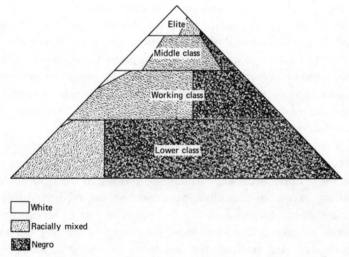

Figure 4.1   Class and race in Cartagena.

gena. First, and most important, is the fact that persons of some color—the miscegenated—are found at every class level. Second, only the polar extremes of the class structure are racially segmented; that is, there are virtually no Negroes at the elite level, and there are practically no whites at the lower-class level. Thus the system is eclectic for it has characteristics of both the open and closed racial models.

Because our interpretation of race relations in Cartagena rests largely on the accuracy of the race-class pyramid described by Figure 4.1, before we discuss its implications for racial conflict we must present a detailed description of the methods employed to construct it.

The Class Structure

There are no adequate census data to construct a class diagram of the city of Cartagena. The most recent estimate available utilizes a three-category classification and places 7.5 percent in the high socioeconomic stratum, 27.7 percent in the middle stratum, and 64.8 percent in the lowest stratum (18). However, no criteria are given for these determinations. Yet, like other developing countries, the class structure of Cartagena is composed of a very large and poor lower class and a relatively small middle class. It is precisely the preponderance of the lower class and the low ratio of middle-class persons that distinguish the class structure of Cartagena from a comparably sized city in the United States.

It is beyond the scope of our investigation to determine precisely the class structure of the city. Because our goal was to obtain a fairly accurate estimate of the racial distribution of distinct layers of the class pyramid, we established distinct groups of people who clearly belonged to the different class levels. To this end we followed a strategy of seeking out the ecological and institutional locations of the distinct social strata.

To investigate the elite we obtained lists of the most exclusive social club of the city, of the local Chamber of Commerce and the Association of Manufacturers (19), and of senators and governors. Thus we could determine the social elite from the club membership, the economic elite from the economic associations, and, of course, the political elite. These sectors were combined to obtain a cross-classification of the total elite stratum.

To determine the middle class the strategy followed was to make an analysis of educational institutions. Secondary sources have established that the majority of university students in Latin America and in Colombia have a middle-class background (20). Consequently, we investigated graduating classes from the University of Cartagena. After further exploration, we learned that the private secondary schools in the area had predominantly middle-class student (21). Therefore, we analyzed yearbooks and class pictures from these schools. Finally, we made several visits to a local middle-class club to familiarize ourselves with its membership.

Whereas the distinction between the upper and the middle class along the lines employed in this study are relatively clear, the difference between the lower levels of the middle class and the upper levels of the working class are much more diffused. However, it is clear that the bulk of persons in service occupations, particularly those involving manual work, can be considered to be members of the working class. This does not mean that there are segments of this sector, such as sales clerks in major department stores and bank tellers, who should not be considered as members of the lower middle class. For this reason, to determine the working class we observed service workers and manual workers, paying particular attention to status differences within the work groups. Finally, our analysis of the lower class was based on observations made in the slum areas of the city. Given the conditions of extreme poverty in these areas, the location of their residents at the very bottom of the social pyramid is evident.

Racial Characteristics of the Class Groups

Research on race relations was complicated because in addition to the impossibility of constructing a class pyramid for Cartagena from census data, after 1918 Colombian censuses have avoided any racial or color classification. Consequently, we utilized our assessments of the racial composition of individuals in the four class groups (22).

Compared with the population of any large United States city in either the north or south, the overall population of Cartagena is darker in pigmentation, and clear racial contrasts such as those found in the United States are, lacking. Miscegenation between whites, blacks, and Indians has been so extensive that racial classifications are difficult to make (23). One rarely sees very white skin, blond or light brown hair, and green or blue eyes on the streets of the city. With the exception of a small proportion of clearly phenotypic Caucasians and a few Orientals, there are many cases where it would be very difficult to argue whether a person with light brown or white skin color was either pure Caucasian or of some mixed ancestry.

In addition to extensive miscegenation, there are two other factors that complicate racial classifications, one somatic and the other geographic. Most Cartagenians with Caucasian ancestry can trace their background to Iberian stock. This means that the somatic norm is straight or wavy black hair, brown eyes, and in many cases a swarthy complexion. Then, even in families where the pigmentation is very white, the Caribbean sun can add many shades to their complexion. This results in a somatic likeness to a *mestizo*—a person with both Indian and Caucasoid genes. However, the great bulk of the population, at least two out of every three people, probably more, do have some distinguishing physical characteristics that are Negroid, indicating the overwhelming presence of Negro blood throughout the entire population.

Now that we have a working picture of the class structure and of the racial mixture of the population, we must put the two together. To do this we applied the following methods to the previously described segments of the class structure. Basically, two approaches were used to determine racial group characteristics: the direct and indirect. The direct method entailed the authors acting as participant observers and systematically counting and categorizing groups in the city by race. The indirect method entailed our racial classification of pictures of *cartageneros*. The use of these photographs provided an efficient method of inquiry, yet it had certain drawbacks. In some cases, the quality of the photos led to interpretation difficulties, particularly with older pictures. Another phase of our indirect approach was a special elite investigation. In this case, we asked several members of the socioeconomic elite to give a racial designation to our sample of elite members. This approach was necessary because of the relative inaccessibility of the elite to extensive systematic observations by the researchers.

Racial classifications in an area that has experienced such high levels of miscegenation as Cartagena are very difficult to make, a factor that, of course, adds ambiguity to race relations. It should be noted that in addition to Negroid ancestry, the population under investigation has experienced a significant degree of racial mixture with Indian elements. Given the particular somatic similarity of *mestizo*, but not *mulato*, types with Iberians, the task was complicated further. We constructed three categories therefore to classify persons: white, racially mixed, and Negro. Persons were classified as racially mixed if their pigmentation, their hair type, or their physical facial characteristics denoted conspicuous noncaucasian ancestry. Within this group we placed both persons with clear *mulato* and *mestizo* characteristics. Persons were classified as Nergo only if they revealed no visible sign of racial mixture. This method underrepresents Negroes, because our criteria were more restrictive than those prevailing both in the United States and Cartagena (24).

Let us begin at the top of the social ladder with the elite. Our primary source of data for the racial characteristics of the elite comes from the information provided by seven persons belonging to the socioeconomic elite on a random sample of 109 social, economic, and political elites. Table 4.2 summarizes the results. The reader may question the validity of an analysis based on information from seven persons. The selection of a small number was based on two factors. First, as defined by us—club and economic association memberships—

TABLE 4.2   The Racial Classification of the Elite *

| Classification | $N1$† | Racially | | | $N2$‡ | Total % |
		White	Mixed	Negro		
Social only	(13)	63.1%	35.4	1.5	(65)	100.0
Economic only	(15)	41.0%	53.4	5.6	(39)	100.0
Political only	(14)	43.9%	33.3	22.8	(66)	100.0
Social and economic	(36)	66.9%	32.5	0.6	(178)	100.0
Social and political	(24)	66.9%	31.7	1.4	(145)	100.0
Social, economic, and political	(7)	76.1%	21.7	2.2	(46)	100.0
Total N	(109)				(539)	

* There are seven possible combinations of the different elite types, and only one did not exist empirically: a combination of economic and political only. The lack of existence of this type of elite might be explained as follows. Given a high economic and political status, individuals also achieve a high social position; that is, they have been admitted to the exclusive social club.

† $N1$ is the number of subjects in each category.

‡ $N2$ is the total number of racial classifications for the category. There is not perfect agreement between the number of rankers and number of subjects because, first, we did not ask persons to make comments on members of their own family and second, each ranker did not know every subject well enough to wish to comment on every one of them.

the Cartagena socioeconomic elite is quite small. Many of its members are interrelated by ties of consanguinity or affinity. As a consequence, we selected few respondents to maintain the right of privacy. Second, we also interviewed a larger sample of elite members (see Chapter 5) and asked them for their racial self-designation. This complementary information allows us greater confidence in the results.

Table 4.2 indicates that the Cartagena elite considers itself as not being purely white. As previously noted, Latins are aware of subtle racial differences. The penetration of the elite includes persons who received classifications of the term *negro*. That is, some persons were sufficiently Negroid that our respondents employed this polar racial term. However, this does not mean that these subjects were pure Negroes. Our observations indicate that with the exception of rare persons among the political elite, there are no somatic Negroes at the elite level, particularly in its social realm. Periodic visits to the exclusivist social club—to be a member of this club is to assert that you have made it socially—indicated the presence of racially mixed persons but not Negroes. Furthermore, our analysis of pictures of the club membership in the late nineteenth century showed a 4 to 1 ratio of whites to racially mixed persons; there were no Negroes. Also, we viewed 25 pictures of past presidents of the club, and they were all white.

Our data suggest that of all elite sectors, the social realm is the most difficult for nonwhites to penetrate as evidenced by the higher proportion of whites in all the social-elite categories. The political elite seems relatively more open to nonwhites in that the largest percentage of *negros* appears under the political-only category (25). However, as indicated by the economic-only group, there are a number of heavily miscegenated persons who arè economically successful persons (26). Further, the apex of the class pyramid, that is, the social-economic-political category, overrepresents whites. These structural features suggest evidence of deliberate racial discrimination, particularly at the social-elite level. But before we make any assertions concerning discrimination in these circles, we must place our analysis within a context of social mobility, which is presented in the section that follows.

Let us now analyze some of the implications of the responses that were obtained. As noted, the socioeconomic elite is aware of its racial impurity. In this respect, "money does not whiten" in Cartagena. Although we cannot quantify the extent to which racial designations follow "origin," as opposed to "mark" or physical appearance, and it appears that both criteria operate, we feel that the latter is more pervasive. In effect, individuals belonging to the same family were often given different racial definitions according to their physical characteristics. Although ancestry is a factor in racial designations, it appears that this criterion is mitigated by the factor of time; as one respondent related to us in an informal interview, "I know that I have some black blood, but, sincerely, I cannot tell you exactly which ancestor had Negroid blood." Of course, the substantial levels of miscegenation that existed during the colonial period have been conducive to the erosion of the extremely racist prejudice of origin because of the frequency by which Negro blood is acquired from miscegenated, not black persons. Further confusion over racial origin is probably introduced by the factor of migration. That is, it appears that conspicuous mixed marriages are often followed by migrations to erode the social memory (27).

Throughout the text we have argued that racial discrimination in Cartagena is centered against the polar racial type and that among racially similar individuals, particularly when they are of the same social class, there is a tendency to suppress racial categorizations and consider racial traits as individual physical characteristics. However, as noted, in a few instances persons at the elite level were given the polar racial designation of *negro* by some respondents. Does this imply that the system is more open than we thought? The answer is no. First of all, their number is extemely small. Secondly, we feel that the *negro* designation responds more to attempts on the part of our respondents to be "scientific" coupled with their subjective tendency to use the term *negro* with laxity (28). Of course, as previously observed, personal sentiments affect racial designations, and, we might add, in Cartagena female respondents tend to employ harsher racial definitions. Indeed, our findings do not contradict the tendency to avoid the racial categorization of persons belonging to the same class, for our informal interviews revealed that on different occasions a respondent would give different racial designations to the same person. That is, there is a tendency to suppress racial categorizations in normal social intercourse among persons belonging to the same class. It is in this respect that we must accept the proposition that "money whitens" because nonwhites can receive a "white" *social* definition; that is, they can be treated as *blancos* and accepted into intimate circles that discriminate racially against outsiders.

Let us turn our attention now to the middle class. To assess the racial composition of this class we looked at the educational institutions in the city and at a middle-class social club. We first analyzed the yearbooks from three secondary schools in the area: two boys' schools and one for girls. For the first boys' school we analyzed the graduating classes for the years 1940 to 1959. During this time period slightly over 300 students earned degrees from the school. Slightly less than two-thirds of the graduates appeared to be white and over one-third racially mixed. Most were light skinned. There were no phenotypical Negroes (29). For the second boys' school we were able to classify racially the graduating classes from 1919 to 1945. During this 26-year period, the school graduated 229 students (30). Only 3 out of every 10 students were not white.

We also obtained three yearbooks from a prestigious girls' school, covering the years 1958 to 1960 for all grade levels, from kindergarten through the final year of high school. Over 300 students were pictured in these books. The girls' school seems to practice greater racial selectivity, as only 2 out of

10 of the girls were clearly miscegenated and there were no Negroes. Furthermore, the hair type of the girls pictured showed an important difference when compared with that of the boys. Whereas some of the *mulatos* at the boys' school had kinky hair, none of the miscegenated girls had kinky hair (31).

Our analysis of students at the University of Cartagena was based on the graduating class pictures of its law school from 1943 to 1964. Table 4.3 contains our racial classification of these lawyers by year. Again, these students are predominantly white (two-thirds) with a fair proportion of racially mixed persons and very few somatic Negroes—less than 5 percent. These racial proportions follow naturally from the evidence presented for the racial composition of the private *colegios,* for if a person must have a secondary school diploma to enter the university and if the high schools are predominantly white, it follows that the university will be predominantly white also (32).

In contrast to the elite social club of Cartagena, the

TABLE 4.3   Classes of the Law School by Race and Year

Year	Negro	Racially Mixed	White	Total
1943	2	6	21	29
1944	2	10	13	26
1946	3	3	15	20
1947	1	4	21	26
1951	1	4	28	33
1952	5	7	28	40
1959	3	15	11	29
1960	0	13	22	35
1961	0	8	17	25
1962	0	5	17	22
1963	0	12	23	35
1964	0	17	20	37
Total	17	104	236	357
Percent	4.8	29.1	66.1	100.0

middle-class club is much less elegant. It has no swimming pool, nor air conditioning, though it does have a large, pleasant pavillion. The club has about 200 members. Some are clearly Negro, but the majority of the membership are light brown and brown; some could easily pass for white. The cost of membership is much less than at the elite social club. The relatively low cost, coupled with the many light and white persons seen there, leads us to conclude that it is a club for a particular income level person and not a club developed for those excluded from other clubs on racial grounds. It is noteworthy that this club clearly contains many persons who are not *blancos* (33).

The emergent picture of the racial composition of the middle class based on our observations is the following. The dominant proportion of middle class *cartageneros* is white, a substantial minority is miscegenated, and a small percentage is Negro. This generalized picture is subject to modification for the following reasons. First, by looking mainly at private high schools and the law school of the University of Cartagena, we are concentrating on the solid middle class. Second, because of the previously mentioned difficulties in utilizing our picture materials, we are fairly certain that we have underrepresented *mestizo* types. Also, to a lesser extent, the somatic likeness of light *mulato* types with Iberian Caucasians leads us to feel that we have underrepresented *mulatos*. Thus we have modified our data interpretations concerning the proportions of white and the miscegenated to say that the latter group predominates at the middle-class level. This does not imply that a substantial number of phenotypic whites are not found in the middle class of Cartagena (34).

We now turn to an analysis of the working class. In the course of a two-month period, we observed over 500 persons in over 60 business establishments and work groups. Our observations indicated noticeable differences of racial composition among businesses and type of occupation. Employees of the larger and more prestigious businesses, such as national chain stores as opposed to a small local store, showed a much lighter racial composition. In the former type of establishment there was a virtual absence of somatic Negroes. A similar marked difference in racial composition was also found along occupational lines, where the closer the job was to middle-class status, the greater was the probability that a Negro would not be found in that position. For example, although in a given hotel somatic Negroes were employed as waiters, the croupiers in its casino were all light. Similarly, with the exception of the janitorial personnel, bank tellers tended to be darker than policy-level bank employees. The most striking evidence on this point lies in the realm of the purely manual labor type of employment. Within the working class it was among construction workers, bus drivers, and furniture movers that the largest proportion of heavily Negroid persons was found. This apparent discriminatory evidence notwithstanding, the case can be made that there is a virtual absence of occupational racial discrimination among particular levels of the working class. Although as we approach the occupational levels that approximate middle-class status somatic Negroes are less likely to be found, it is highly probable that within each hierarchical level there will be a random racial distribution. For example, in a restaurant the waiters can range from Negro to white (or virtually so), and the cashier can be clearly a *mulato,* so that a more Negroid person is in a hierarchical superordinate position to a light person. Our observations indicate that this randomness of race, which produces work situations where light and dark persons work as equals and where darker persons are superior to lighter ones, is a very common pattern in Cartagena.

Additional evidence for this point can be drawn from an analysis of a segment of the marine infantry, a unit of the military that draws heavily from the working class. We observed three platoons of trainees (120 men) training on the beach. Of the trainees, none was phenotypically white or Negro. They ranged from light to dark brown. There were nine regular cadre training the men, and two of them were highly Negroid. One of these was a member of the high-status paratroopers. As a whole, the infantry school is almost totally devoid of whites and contains few Negroes (35). In sum, the racial composition of the working class overall is dominated by miscegenated persons with a substantial proportion of highly Negroid persons, particularly at the lower levels, and a virtually insignificant proportion of whites.

At the bottom of the class pyramid lies what we have termed the lower class. For our purposes, we have defined this group as being formed by the inhabitants of the slums. The abysmal living conditions of this group, which reflect their lack of education and unstable employment, clearly places them on the lowest rung of the social ladder. Most of these people live in what is locally termed *barrios de invasión* or *tugurios,* that is, in areas where the people neither own or rent the land on which they construct their dwellings. Rather, they simply invade unused land, build shacks out of wood and waste materials, and inhabit them. Among the cities of Colombia, Cartagena is noted for the geographical preponderance of its slums. This has led to the establishment of a major program of slum rehabilitation by the government. After inspecting several of these *barrios* and noting little difference among them in their racial composition, we randomly selected one for detailed racial analysis.

This *barrio* is located on the northern edge of the city, and like most of the *tugurios* of the city, it is extremely poor in appearance. The houses, one-room affairs made out of wood and salvage materials, provide little more than shade from the sun and minimal protection from the rain. There is no running water; thus the inhabitants must buy water from a wagon that passes through the streets during the day. Animals abound in the area—dogs, cats, chickens, and pigs. One can count the ribs on any of them.

In the *barrio*, we observed 106 persons in approximately 40 households. The most striking racial characteristic was the darkness of the people. None was white and only 10 could be considered light brown. Approximately 60 were dark brown and 5 out of every 6 had very kinky hair. Thirty-seven, or slightly over one-third, appeared to be somatically Negro.

Although we observed that only approximately one-third of the people in this *barrio* were somatically Negro, we feel that actually there were many more. First, as already noted, because of the predominance of very dark skin color and of kinky hair, local Cartagenians would term most of these people *negro*. Second, many of these persons may have been genotypically Negro but appear to have some racial mixture. We say this because health deficiencies, especially malnutrition, prevails in these *barrios,* and this has a tendency to remove pigmentation from the hair, to lighten it, and to pale or sallow the complexion, so that a genotypic Negro suffering from malnutrition can appear to be phenotypically racially mixed. These factors lead us to conclude that the bulk of the lower class is heavily Negroid with a relatively smaller proportion of clearly miscegenated types.

Our conclusion concerning the racial composition of the class structure of Cartagena is the following, then, as represented in Figure 4.1. Whites dominate at the elite level, particularly the exclusivist social elite sector. However, within the elite, a significant proportion of persons are visibly of racially mixed ancestry, and persons termed *negros* by our respondents have penetrated the political-elite sector especially but also are found in the economic-elite sector. Nevertheless, somatic Negroes have not penetrated the social-elite realm. The middle class as a whole is dominated by miscegenated persons, with a substantial proportion of whites. Negroes are also found in the middle class in small but significant numbers, which makes this class the most racially heterogeneous stratum of the class structure. Racially mixed persons also dominate in the working class, but their hegemony within this class is less than in the middle class because there is a substantial proportion of Negroes at this level. White persons are not frequent in this class. Finally, the lower class is dominated by Negroes and virtually devoid of whites.

DYNAMIC ASPECTS OF CLASS-RACE RELATIONS IN CARTAGENA

Our analysis up to this point simply describes the racial composition of the class structure of Cartagena from a static perspective. As indicated by Figure 4.1, race is not randomly distributed throughout the class pyramid; rather, there is an inverse relationship between blackness and social status. The probability of finding a white person in the lower class is virtually nil, and, conversely, the probability of finding a Negro at the elite level is also virtually nil. This pattern suggests the presence of racial discrimination in the society. However, to obtain a more sophisticated understanding of the consequences of race in Cartagena, we must separate patterns of historical dominance from those of deliberate racial exclusion. In other words, we must find out the extent to which class position is ascriptive, as opposed to achieved, in the society. If, for example, class position is based solely on family inheritance, then one could say that tradition, not racial factors, accounts for this nonrandom racial distribution.

The first method we employed to investigate the openness-closedness of the social elite of Cartagena was to compare lists of politically or economically prominent persons during the nineteenth century and from the period 1900 to 1930 with the present membership list of the exclusivist social club. Table 4.4 presents this comparison. The persistence of tradition in determining social elite status is indicated by the fact that over half the politically or economically prominent men's names of the nineteenth century are represented today in the club. The proportion drops slightly for women's names because female last names disappear in the third generation. However, this is not a totally static group because even some of the prominent

names of the early twentieth century are not registered in the club.
Although this method yielded interesting results, it was clearly not sufficient to obtain a clear picture of the openness-closedness of the elite. To obtain a better picture we engaged in a focused study of the current socioeconomic elite of Cartagena utilizing the following method. First, we enumerated every person in this group from lists of the local Chamber of Commerce, Association of Manufacturers, and social club. This produced 74 persons. Second, we selected five of these

TABLE 4.4   Historically Prominent Names in Social Club *

			Percentage of Names Currently in the Club	
Period	Father's Name	Mother's Name	Father's	Mother's
Nineteenth century	49	10	55.1	40.0
1900–1930	27	11	66.7	45.5

Source: Bossa Herazo, op. cit. and Membership List of Club, 1969.
* Our ability to employ both father's and mother's names stems from the Colombian custom of using both names to identify oneself.

people to provide information on a random sample of 27 individuals. Again, we chose this small number on purpose. To maintain a sense of anonymity and personal privacy, it was important to investigate a small number of persons. Third, we obtained the following information for our subjects: (1) their age, (2) the length of their family background in Cartagena, (3) their financial situation, including their economic mobility, (4) the history of the wealth of their family, and (5) for those that had suffered economic loss, we explored the reasons.

The results of our investigation indicate that the socioeconomic elite is composed mainly of traditional, aristocratic families with a small but significant proportion of recent achievers of social and economic success. We say this on the basis of the following evidence, (see Table 4.5). It is clear that old families dominate this group, that is, families that have had high status for four generations or more. The traditional aspect of the group is further underlined by the fact that less than one-third of our subjects were under the age of 40, and as can be observed in the table, only 15 percent of our subjects are self-made men. It should also be noted that mobility through the mechanism of marriage is quite common, a condition underlining the ascriptive aspects of the system.

TABLE 4.5   Migration and Family Status

	Frequency	Percentage
Old family	12	44.4
Grandfather married old family	2	7.4
Grandfather came	5	18.5
Father married old family	1	3.7
Father came	1	3.7
Subject married old family	2	7.4
Subject came	4	14.9
Total	27	100.0

Now that we have a picture of the background of the socio-economic elite, we turn to the analysis of their financial situation. Contrary to the popular conception that underdeveloped nations are generally characterized by a few extremely rich people and a small middle class, the former does not seem to be the case of Cartagena. In the industrial and commercial sectors under scrutiny, businesses are relatively small. Even in the agricultural sector, where the *latifundio* pattern prevails, the capitalization and productivity of the land is low. These factors reduce the net worth of individuals. Table 4.6 presents the financial situation of our elite sample. While it can be seen that great wealth is not required to penetrate this elite level— a factor that would tend to make the system more open—it would be unwarranted to make any inference without taking into consideration the fact that the accumulation of wealth to become "comfortable" in this society is an uncommon feat.

Thus far we have seen that the socioeconomic elite group is heavily represented by traditional families and is not exceptionally wealthy. An indication of the source of this wealth is

TABLE 4.6   Financial Situation *

Situation	Frequency	Percentage
Millionaire	4	14.8
Rich	9	33.3
Comfortable	12	44.5
Must work to support himself	2	7.4
Total	27	100.0

* The definition of these categories is as follows: millionaires are persons who have the equivalent of one million dollars (U.S.) or more. The other categories do not have a dollar equivalent but are subjective definitions by our respondents.

presented in Table 4.7. In contrast to the data in Table 4.5, which showed the preponderance of old-family influence, here we see that the source of wealth for almost half of our sample was due to the economically successful efforts of either the subject or his father. This seems to indicate that there is a high proportion (48.3 percent) of self-made men. However, the juxtaposition of Tables 4.7 and 4.5 reveals the important role that traditional factors play in influencing a person's ability to achieve social and financial success. We can see this in two ways. First, although old families persist, old money does not persist as a major source of wealth. This implies that wealth tends to deteriorate throughout the generations. Second, there is a greater tendency to make money rather than to marry into it. Given the fact that the bulk of the socioeconomic elite is tied into old families, we must conclude that persons attached to these families have a high potential to be financially successful. In other words, the traditional group is quite resilient.

An indication of the deterioration of wealth through the generations is found in the fact that eight of our subjects— 29.6 percent—experienced financial losses in terms of their situation as compared with their parents. The list of reported

TABLE 4.7   Sources of Family Wealth *

Source	Frequency	Percentage
Old money (four generations)	1	3.4
Grandfather married money	0	0.0
Grandfather made money	7	24.1
Father married money	2	6.9
Father made money	9	31.0
Subject married money	5	17.3
Subject made money	5	17.3
Total	29	100.0

* Two subjects had two sources of wealth.

factors that produce this economic deterioration is headed by high fertility, followed by a discontinuation of the family's main business and by familial quarrels. Also important but to a lesser degree were such factors as bad administration, vices, and just plain economic risks. Thus, for example, a family fortune is divided among many children, or a son prefers to engage in a less-profitable but more-prestigious business than the father's, or divisiveness among the children leads to inefficiency and decline of the family business.

Let us summarize. The structural static analysis of the racial composition of Cartagena suggests the presence of racial discrimination. The dynamic analysis of mobility patterns among the social and economic elite indicates that there also is racial discrimination. In effect, although this group experiences some mobility, heavily Negroid persons are not found here. If we contrast the economic-only elite with the social and economic elite—see Table 4.2—we discover that the former group is relatively more Negroid. This suggests that economically successful persons who are Negroid are excluded from the social elite. Indeed, our respondents who belonged to the socioeconomic elite perceived economically successful persons that are outside of their inner circle as relatively more Negroid. This is not difficult to understand because, as already noted, there is a tendency to give a racial categorization to racial physical traits when dealing with persons that belong to a different class-status group. It is precisely against persons wishing to enter this exclusivist social circle that racial prejudice is heightened. The frustrating aspects of this process that runs counter to the "money whitens" syndrome should not be underestimated. All the gatekeepers are not always the most noble or prominent members of the social elite. Fortuitous factors, such as interpersonal rivalries with a key club member or the absence from the admissions committee of a particularly racist individual on a given day, can determine the rejection or acceptance in club membership.

Racial discrimination against Negroid persons notwithstanding, to understand the potentiality for overt racial conflict in the society it is necessary to explore the nature of racial boundaries in a physical sense. Of particular importance is to determine whether or not there is a lightening or bleaching process operating in Cartagena by which Negroid characteristics are attenuated intergenerationally (36). This racially dynamic element consists of a process by which "ambitious" Negroid individuals marry lighter persons. The offspring of these marriages are of a lighter racial type than their darker parent and, consequently, are less subjected to racial barriers (37). For reasons that we detail in the following section, the presence or absence of this process for the middle class is particularly crucial for the generation of racial conflict.

There is evidence that this dynamic pattern exists in Cartagena among the middle class. To explore the existence of this phenomenon we analyzed the racial composition of marriage patterns from photographs that were available in four photographers' studios. To confirm the middle-class position of these people we made a background check of their homes. Table 4.8 summarizes the results. It is clear from these data that lightness is valued in marriage. A substantial proportion of men marry women who are lighter than themselves. Few men marry darker persons. In the two cases where this occurred

TABLE 4.8   The Racial Characteristics of Marriage
Partners from Four Photo Studios

Studio	Both Partners White	White Male, Negroid Female	Both Partners Negroid		Total
			Male Darker than Female	Same Shade	
No. 1	3	—	2	5	10
No. 2	—	—	—	3	3
No. 3	—	—	4	—	4
No. 4	—	2	19	22	43
Total	3	2	25	30	60
Percentage	5.0	3.3	41.7	50.0	100

the females were very light skinned and extremely beautiful mulattoes. We do not have comparable data for elite marital patterns, but from the comments of our respondents in our elite study, it is clear that politically or economically successful men tend to follow this pattern of miscegenation through marriage.

Although there is a low possibility to engage in the bleaching process by the lower class, we have suggestive evidence that slum dwellers in Cartagena tend to follow this pattern within their heavily Negroid context. Of the 28 married couples (normally consensual) that we investigated, in 19 cases the men were of the same color as the wife, and in 8 cases the male was darker than the female, indicating the value of lightness. Despite the bleaching tendency there are cultural and structural factors that have impeded a fuller racial homogenization. First is the value placed on lightness. This orientation reduces the frequency of even extramarital sexual relationships between the poles. It appears that historically once a sufficiently large proportion of miscegenated individuals were produced sexual contact between the poles was reduced. In Cartagena today there are virtually no *negras* in the brothels attended by *blancos*. Thus the bulk of the miscegenation process occurs between racially close individuals. Second, there is the structural problem that the majority of the *negros* are found in the lower class. As Ashton has noted (38) and which our observations substantiate, although these black aggregates show a preference for sexual unions with lighter physical types, their possibility for a successful engagement in the bleaching process is minor. Quite simply, these aggregates lack the mediums of exchange—money or physical attraction— necessary for successful miscegenation. In short, the relatively economically *successful* Negroids are the ones that participate through marriage in the bleaching process.

IMPLICATIONS FOR CONFLICT OF THE CLASS-RACE STRUCTURE OF CARTAGENA

At the outset of this study, we established a dual pattern for Colombia of substantial levels of class-related political conflict amidst a minimum of overt racial conflict. We have also considered the eclectic nature of the Cartagena racial system. That is, two principles operate simultaneously in the area. On the one hand there are substantial levels of racial integration (the integration principle) because the miscegenated are infused throughout the class structure. On the other, there is racial discrimination (the discrimination principle) centered on the polar racial type and manifested in the inverse relationship between blackness and social-class position. At this juncture of our analysis we are prepared to give a preliminary structural explanation for the absence of overt racial conflict in Cartagena.

In Cartagena major racial discrimination is practiced mainly at the social-elite level. It is a fact that somatic Negroes are barred from entry into this realm by gatekeepers. However, as indicated by Figure 4.1, a significant number of miscegenated persons have entered into these exclusivistic, familistic circles. Nevertheless, these individuals constitute an exception to the principle of denying entry to nonwhites. Indeed, we have seen that economically and politically successful individuals belonging to relatively Negroid groups are generally excluded from the elite-social realm. (See the political-only and economic-only groups in Table 4.2). Given this indication of racial exclusion, what are the factors that operate against the generation of overt racial hostility among this economic and political group?

First, although racial discrimination exists, it is of an ambiguous nature because, as we have seen, some miscegenated persons have been accepted into the social elite. Further, if we recall the traditional influence, as indicated by the hegemony that old families have in the social-elite sector, that also denies membership to white persons into these circles, it is clear that racism is not the only decisive factor for exclusion. This latter case of denial is most conspicuous among economically successful Cartagenians of Arab ancestry, who have often been denied access to this group. It is not that racial characteristics are not important at this level of the class pyramid, for they certainly are. Rather, because race is only one of the factors for exclusion, racial discrimination is ambiguous. There are many whites who are also excluded from these circles.

Second, as previously noted, the argument that status-seeking, upwardly mobile nonwhites tend to marry lighter persons to "improve" their race is plausible. The race-class pyramid of Cartagena, with its substantial numbers of non-Negroid *mestizos* at all but the lowest class level, facilitates this process because lightening needs not be accomplished through liaisons with status conscious *blancos*. In this respect, the racial heterogeneity of the Latin American infused system facilitates successful miscegenation. Of course, this pattern reduces racial hostility and also reduces the number of *negros* found at this level of the class pyramid, for they tend to lighten their descendants. Thus it is unlikely that Negroes will be able to supplant the lighter racial types at the top of Cartagena's class structure.

Third, the lack of economic segmentation between whites and nonwhites at this top level of the social system—the weakness of racial pluralistic structures (39), coupled with the need for economic success in order to knock at the door of the social elite—means that these economically successful nonwhites have both colleagues and clientele who are white. Under these conditions any overt racial protest could prove to be highly costly. Further, the number of economically successful Negroes who could attempt penetration into the social elite is small. This factor, coupled with their personal success measured against the baseline of all of the Negroes of Cartagena, makes it propitious for them to accept their situation with relative complacency. In sum, it appears that at the top level of Cartagena's class structure the principle of integration outweighs the principle of segregation to produce racial adaptation.

At the middle-class level, as indicated by Figure 4.1, racial heterogeneity finds its greatest expression. It is at this level that the greatest potential for the generation of a racial movement is found because persons here are sufficiently educated to articulate protests over racial inequality and because substantial numbers of persons with different racial characteristics compete for scarce resources at this class level (40). However, middle-class grievances have taken on class, not racial, overtones. What are the factors that underlie this phenomenon? First, whites who find themselves at this class position, rather than in the elite, logically cannot resort to racists arguments to explain their class position. Second, there are other reasons why the miscegenated—the predominant group of this class —have a low propensity to voice racial protest. Most importantly there are substantial numbers of whites at this class level, and all are aware that there are significant numbers of miscegenated persons at the elite level (41). Thus, again, the principle of integration leads to racial adaptation at this class level. This principle is also supported because many of the miscegenated are not highly Negroid individuals. Many are *mestizos* who acknowledge their racial impurity and, given their somatic closeness to *blancos,* do not experience substantial racial discrimination, a factor that reduces the number of persons available to be mobilized for racial conflict. The racial heterogeneity and mingling found at the middle-class level contribute greatly to the ideology of equalitarianism that pervades this sector.

As indicated by our data, at this level of the stratification system the more Negroid the person is, the more racial discrimination he is likely to experience. However, there are factors that subdue the expression of racial tensions among this group. The more Negroid a person is, the greater the probability that he will, *ceteris paribus,* manifest feelings of racial oppression. Yet, given existing educational and economic constraints, extremely Negroid persons are small in number at this level and can consider themselves relatively successful. By following the marital pattern of the city, that is, marrying a lighter person, they can facilitate the mobility opportunities for their children.

As we descend the stratification pyramid, the principle of discrimination becomes more evident because persons become more Negroid (and should perceive the lightness at the top of the structure). However, the integration principle also operates at this level. Indeed, as noted, at the working-class level there is virtually no occupational discrimination because the juxtaposition of occupational hierarchies on race is quite random (42). Consequently, the principle of integration should neutralize the principle of discrimination at this level of the class structure and produce an absence of consensus about the presence of discrimination.

It is at the lowest class level that the concentration of blacks and their socioeconomic deprivation should lead to the prevalence of the principle of discrimination. Some of these slum dwellers are recent migrants from highly homogeneous, heavily Negroid villages and settlements along the Caribbean coast. Although prior to migration these people are probably aware of racial differences and "white" domination in the national society, they experience a more direct contact with the larger society for the first time in Cartagena. This phenomenon may be interpreted as conducive to an increase in the racial awareness of this group. It may do so. However, to generate a broad national social movement mainly based on racial lines, as is currently the case in the United States, it is necessary to develop leaders among the middle or upper classes who can articulate grievances and mobilize support among high proportions of the black masses. For the reasons already stated, this potential racial leadership has not been recruited from these classes.

CONCLUDING REMARKS

In this chapter we have attempted to explain some of the static and dynamic structural factors that produce a climate of racial adaptation amidst discrimination in Cartagena. This climate has coexisted in a country with a history of substantial levels of class-related political violence without producing substantial levels of overt racial conflict. Some sources have interpreted the absence of racial strife in Latin America as being the product of a static, traditional equilibrium in which noncompetitive, quasi-feudal relationships of dominance between the races are clearly established and accepted. This interpretation cannot explain the absence of racial strife in contemporary Cartagena for the following reasons. First, although a superficial and static contrastive comparison of the "white" elite and the "black" lower classes might lead to the foregoing interpretation, the fact is that racial boundaries are quite fluid in Cartagena. The dynamics of race in the area consists of an infusion of persons of some color (the miscegenated) throughout the social structure. Although imperfect, as indicated by Figure 4.1, there is a considerable degree of racial integration in Cartagena. Second, Cartagena is not in a political and class sense a static society. Actually, it has experienced substantial social changes. From an important port city during the colonial period through a severe decline in the nineteenth century to the current period of urban and industrial growth, Cartagena has exhibited changes unequaled by many cities. For these reasons, the social mobilization concomitant with the current urban and industrial growth of the city has led to the strengthening of class, not racial conflicts.

The Cartagena dual racial system of racial dominance and integration appears to have materialized during an early historical period. Indeed, we have found a "traditional" elite with segments who can trace their background to the early independence period and at the same time acknowledge their miscegenated ancestry. It also appears that the class-race pyramid of Cartagena—the infused racial system—has existed in this city for centuries. Indeed, except for the expansion of the middle-class sector, this structural configuration of race relations has been maintained with only minor changes throughout much of the history of the city. In this sense we believe that our structural interpretation for current racial adaptation can be extrapolated to explain the historical absence of substantial racial conflict in the area. Thus it seems that the nature of traditional race relations in Cartagena has produced a strong basis for obtaining a durable interracial peace, even in the presence of rapid social change. At this point, we would venture to predict that further modernization will be accompanied by major interclass crises, not racial ones. But before we extrapolate into the future, it is necessary to obtain a more complete picture of racial patterns in the area. To do this we now turn to the analysis of the social-psychological mechanisms of race that characterize the prevalence of the principle of integration in the Cartagena area.

NOTES

1. For the major difficulties found to measure discrimination, see Blalock, *op. cit.*
2. Segovia, *op. cit.*, p. 21.
3. Aquiles Escalante, *El Negro en Colombia*, Facultad de Sociología, Universidad Nacional de Colombia, Bogota, 1964.
4. Segovia, *op. cit.*, pp. 23 and 24. The major fortifications which still beautify the city date from the reign of Carlos III.
5. Jorge Juan y Antonio de Ulloa, *Noticias Secretas de América*, Ediciones Mar Océano, Buenos Aires, 1953, pp. 158–178. It is interesting to note that according to this source, although Cartagena was a military port, a large share of its trade consisted of contraband. Even today visitors can see some local *contrabandistas* in operation.
6. See respectively, *Almanach de Gotha pour l'anné, 1810*, p. 9 and Donaldo Bossa Herazo, *Cartagena Independiente: Tradición y Desarrollo*, Tercer Mundo, Bogota, 1967, p. 88.
7. See *Almanach de Gotha pour l'anné, 1889*, p. 643 and Segovia, *op. cit.*, p. 29.
8. According to a source, during the years immediately prior to independence, Cartagena depended more on its military than commercial, that is, export-import, services. See Martín Alonzo Pinzón, "Zaguán," in Donaldo Bossa Herazo, *op. cit.*, p. 14. In this sense, its welfare was highly dependent on its continuation as a colony.
9. See Eduardo Lemaitre, *Antecedentes y Consecuencias del Once de 1811. Testimomios y documentos relacionados con la gloriosa gesta de la independencia absoluta de Cartagena de Indias*, Cartagena, 1961, pp. 141–150.
10. See Bossa Herazo, *op. cit.*, pp. 47 and 48. According to him, three sons of the still socially prominent Pombo family died of hunger during the siege.

11. Segovia, *op. cit.*
12. Pinzón, *op. cit.*, pp. 16 and 17.
13. Daniel Lemaitre, *op. cit.*
14. Departamento Administrativo Nacional de Estadística (*1964*), *op. cit.*, p. 30.
15. Bossa Herazo, *op. cit.*
16. For the prevalence of these orientations, even when contrasted to other Latin American countries, see the important study of José Gutiérrez, *De La Pseudo-Aristocracia a la Autenticidad,* Tercer Mundo, Bogota, 1961.
17. See Dix, *op. cit.*, p. 46.
18. Instituto De Crédito Territorial, *Desarrollo Urbano en Cartagena: Filosofía y Criterios,* Oficina de Rehabilitación de Tugurios, Cartagena, 1969, p. 2.
19. Unfortunately, we were unable to obtain lists of persons belonging exclusively to the agricultural elite. However, given the traditional nature of this elite, many of these persons are included in the social club.
20. For Colombia, see Robert C. Williamson, *El Estudiante Colombiano y Sus Actitudes,* Facultad de Sociología, Universidad Nacional de Colombia, Bogota, 1962.
21. We learned this from interviews with six directors of local schools.
22. This description is based on the observations of the authors. One is a native North American with considerable familiarity with the interracial picture in both the northern and southern United States, and the other a native Latin American, who has traveled and worked extensively in Latin America. Therefore, the observations are tempered by a cross-cultural perspective.
23. The extent of this problem has been noted also for Brazil and Puerto Rico. See Wagley, *op. cit.*, p. 7, and Tumin with Feldman, *op. cit.*, p. 197.
24. This consideration is based on a test of racial designations administered in Cartagena, in which we found that *cartageneros* termed persons *negro* whom we considered racially mixed. See Chapter 6.
25. It is interesting to note that politics has been the most accessible sector of the elite for minority groups in the United States.
26. It should be recalled that this category corresponds with the relatively modern industrial and commercial sectors.

27. For Brazil, see Zimmerman, *op. cit.*, p. 109.

28. See Chapter 6.

29. It should be noted here that the quality of the photographs, especially the older ones, in many cases was not very good. Thus our classification of racially mixed persons tended to be restricted mainly to persons with *mulato* characteristics. It is very possible that persons who were actually *mestizos* were classified as white. Therefore, our analysis quite probably overrepresents whites, not the miscegenated. As previously noted, our definition of Negro excluded persons that were not somatically Negro, who would probably be termed *negro* by locals.

30. The reason for the relatively small number of subjects is that during the early years a typical graduating class contained only six or seven students. This figure gradually increased to over 20 in 1945.

31. In our field observations, we did see some men with their heads greased and tightly wrapped. This used to be a very common practice among Negro men in the United States to make their hair wavy or straight instead of kinky. They usually slept and worked with their hair greased and wrapped in a stocking (it was called a "mammy's leg") so it would stay straight when they engaged in evening social activities. It seems that the use of hair straightener among women in Cartagena is much more widespread. The term *morena alisada* is used to describe such females. One American who lives in the city but sends his children to school in the United States reported to us that when word gets around that he is going to the United States to visit his children, he is besieged with requests from local women to bring back hair-straightening kits.

32. It should be noted that although virtually free and compulsory, public education in Colombia and in Cartagena is highly inefficient. In 1969, of the 72,985 children between the ages of 5 and 14 years, 36,802, or only about half, were registered in the city's schools. See Departamento de Bolívar, *Boletín Estadístico de Bolívar, Enero y Febrero, 1969*, p. 7.

33. In this respect, we did not find parallel racial clubs in Cartagena for the middle class. This parallelism is suggested by Harris for Minas Velhas, Brazil. See Harris, *op. cit.*, pp. 78 and 79.

34. The racial self-designations of the middle class obtained from our survey data reinforces this conclusion. See Chapter 5.

35. This branch of the military contrasts strikingly with the cadets of

the Naval Academy in terms of race. The cadets are mainly drawn from the predominantly white-*mestizo* middle-class elements from the interior of Colombia. Few of them have Negroid characteristics. It is interesting to note the differing social patterns of these two units. Although the Marine Infantry base is located in Bocagrande, the peninsula of the city where the upper and upper-middle classes reside, when the troopers have free time, they are bussed to the center of the city. The Naval Academy is located across the Bay from the elite residential area. When they are off duty, they are under strict order to spend their time *only* in the elite area (Bocagrande) and are subject to negative sanctions should they be caught in other sections of the city.

36. Of course, in Chapter 2, we argued that this process was necessary to move persons from a state of racial segregation (cell 4) to miscegenated integration (cell 2).

37. Of course, Pierson has considered that this is the case in Bahia, Brazil. See Pierson *op. cit.*, p. 154.

38. Ashton, *op. cit.*

39. See the discussion in Chapter 2.

40. Harris, "Race in Minas Velhas," *op. cit.*, p. 78.

41. For data in support of the mechanisms of adaptation introduced in this section, see the following chapter.

42. In Puerto Rico, Tumin and Feldman found that the lower the class position the greater the proportion of persons that felt that skin color was irrelevant. See Tumin with Feldman, *op. cit.*, p. 205.

Chapter Five

· ·

SOCIAL CLASS
AND RACIAL ATTITUDES

In the previous chapter we argued that to generate a major racial social movement, there is a need for the feeling on the part of the minority that they are discriminated against and oppressed and for elements of the middle or upper classes to feel sufficiently disturbed by the situation to provide leadership for the minority masses. Our structural analysis has led us to consider that the infused racial system of Cartagena was adaptive because the factors of integration seemed to outweigh factors of discrimination. To test our hypotheses we have surveyed the racial attitudes of various class groups in the city, focusing on those attitudinal configurations that are adaptive and those that describe sources of racial tension. In this chapter we provide documentation for some of the propositions that we postulated in earlier chapters. The questionnaire that was employed to survey the racial attitudes appears in Appendix A.

CLASS GROUPS SURVEYED

Following the four-tiered class pyramid outlined in the previous chapter, we surveyed the racial attitudes of the elite, middle, working, and lower classes. We were particularly interested in exploring whether differences in status among class subgroups have an effect on racial attitudes for, as noted, there are two themes that pervade the literature. The first considers that upward social mobility heightens racial awareness and produces strain (1). The second theme posits that miscegenation is the adaptive tool of upwardly mobile minority individuals (2). Ideally, we would have analyzed upwardly mobile persons at each of the class levels. However, given the sampling difficulties involved in determining these groups, we limited our exploration to the investigation of upwardly mobile subgroups at the middle- and working-class levels.

The first group surveyed, the elite, was defined as individuals who belong to the exclusivist social club. A random sample of 24 persons was selected from the club directory and interviewed. We divided the middle class into two groups: the solid middle class and aspirants to middle-class status. The solid middle class was composed of bureaucrats and nonelite professionals, and businessmen. Interviews with 24 members of this class were completed from a larger list of persons provided us by key locals. Middle-class aspirants were located efficiently because, fortunately, in Cartagena there is a governmental institution whose purpose is to provide the acquisition of white-collar technical-educational skills for upwardly mobile persons. Courses in bookkeeping, accounting, typing, and shorthand are available for students mostly of working-class origins. From a list of persons undertaking courses in secretarial skills we selected a sample of 50 individuals who were then interviewed. We also divided the working class into three distinctive subgroups: labor leaders, stably employed semiskilled workers, and servants. We were particularly interested in surveying labor leaders because they exemplify successful, intraclass, upward mobility. Furthermore, given the traditional politicization of labor unions in Latin America, including Colombia, this group could have a greater racial awareness and provide grass-roots leadership for a racial social movement. At the time of our field research, local union leaders were taking an extension course in the University of Cartagena, and we distributed our questionnaire to all 29 of them. The stably employed semiskilled workers provided us with the element of the solid working class. As with the aspirants to middle-class occupation, we were able to obtain lists of workers enrolled in night school classes. In this case, a management-governmental educational institution developed to increase the skill level of employed workers provided instruction that ranged from language classes to skilled crafts such as welding and sheet metal work. From the enrollment lists we took a sample of 48 individuals who were interviewed. We also included domestic servants to get a fuller picture of Cartagena's working class. We went to an area of the city where practically every household employed servants, randomly selected one house on each street, and interviewed the servant or servants who were employed there. This produced a sample of 30. Our final task was to interview members of the lowest stratum of the social order: the slum dwellers. To do this we randomly selected a slum settlement in the outskirts of the city and interviewed one person from every fourth household. The sample size for this group was 41.

SOCIODEMOGRAPHIC CHARACTERISTICS
OF THE CLASS GROUPS

The first and most important feature of the class groups is their racial composition. Through direct and indirect methods of observation we had determined the class-race pyramid of Cartagena (3) and had concluded that although class and race are directly related (the discrimination principle) there also exists the infusion of miscegenated persons throughout all levels of the Cartagena class structure (the integration principle). Our direct observation of the persons interviewed corroborated the previous conclusion. However, we also wanted to determine whether our racial designations of class groups corresponded to the designations that they gave to themselves. To do this we asked our subjects to define themselves racially. Table 5.1 presents the results.

TABLE 5.1   Racial Self Designations of the Class Groups in Percentages

Designation	Upper Class	Middle Class		Working Class			Lower Class
	Elite	Solid Middle Class	Middle-Class Aspirants	Labor Leaders	Solid Working Class	Servants	Slum Dwellers
Blanco	71	29	10	10	10	—	—
Trigueño	8	8	14	—	10	7	2
Moreno	4	4	16	3	54	60	22
Mestizo	12	38	38	38	12	13	12
Mulato	—	4	—	21	4	7	2
Negro	—	4	16	10	6	13	51
No information	4	13	6	17	4	0	10
Total	100	100	100	100	100	100	100

As expected, a substantial majority of the elite defined themselves as white—*blanco*. Further, in support of our previous data, a significant proportion of the elite recognized its miscegenated background; more than one in four respondents employed a non-*blanco* term for themselves. Interestingly, no one employed terms indicating black blood, such as *mulato* and *negro*. As previously noted, this terminological manipulation by which miscegenation is acknowledged while suppressing a Negroid identification is what permits discrimination to coexist with "passing" at this level of the class pyramid. As indicated by middle-class responses, our conceptualization of this class as the most racially heterogeneous group is recognized by middle-class *cartageneros* themselves. In effect, particularly at the solid-middle-class level, there is an acknowledgment of the presence of all racial types. Furthermore, as previously observed, the bulk of this class group is miscegenated with a significant proportion of whites. The inverse relationship between blackness and high class position is suggested by the greater frequency of persons calling themselves *negro* among the middle-class aspirants. Indeed, our observations indicated the relatively Negroid characteristics of this subgroup. As we approach the lower levels of the class pyramid, the frequency of the term *blanco* declines, thus supporting our characterization of the Cartagena class-race structure. As a corollary, there is an increase in the usage of terms connoting black blood that achieves its maximum at the lowest class level—the slum dwellers. In sum, the responses of our subjects support our characterization of the infusion of miscegenated persons throughout the Cartagena class structure. That is, *cartageneros* themselves describe a situation in which persons with different racial designations compete freely within each class group, thus supporting the contention that feudalistic or racially rigid boundaries do not exist in the area. Nevertheless, there is a predominance of polar racial types at the extremes of the class pyramid. Finally, the relationship between racial designations and class position is imperfect because of the manipulation of the ambiguous racial terminology that we have considered to characterize the Iberian American infused racial system. The analysis of this complex nomenclature and its implications for racial conflict-adaptation are presented in Chapter 6.

The overall median age for the class categories is about 30 years, with a fairly even distribution; the middle-class aspirants, the solid working class, and the servants tend to be younger by approximately 5 years.

The sex ratio for our sample as a whole is almost evenly split between males and females. There is, nevertheless, variation by class groups. In the samples roughly three-quarters of the elite and solid middle class are males, and 9 out of 10 of the labor leaders and the solid working class are also males.

The middle-class aspirants and the servants are all females because of the nature of their occupations. The middle-class aspirants were being trained in secretarial skills and, in Cartagena, male servants are also very rare. Our sample of slum dwellers overrepresents females (75 percent) because the interviews had to be conducted during the day when many men were absent.

Our subjects were a relatively urban group in that about half of the persons in each group were born in Cartagena, and anywhere from a half to three quarters of them have lived in the city for at least 10 years. The two major exceptions to this pattern are the elite, who are almost totally urban in that 9 out of 10 of them were born and raised in Cartagena, and the servants who are the least urban group because most of them were born in small towns.

RACIAL ATTITUDES OF THE CLASS GROUPS

In the previous chapter we argued that racial discrimination in Cartagena is unevenly distributed throughout the class structure and that it is practiced most heavily against highly Negroid persons. The principle of discrimination should consequently find maximum expression against the lower classes. Conversely, the principle of integration should find its greatest expression among those groups that contain few Negroes, that is, the middle and upper classes. These considerations logically lead to the conclusion that perceptions of racial discrimination should be inversely related to position in the class structure. However, we have discussed some structural peculiarities of the class groups that appear to modify this proposition. First, as we have noted, the exclusivist elite members maintain institutions of deliberate racial discrimination against newcomers. Thus perceptions of discrimination should be high at the elite level. Second, we have observed that within the working class itself there is virtually no occupational racial discrimination, a factor that should mitigate perceptions of discrimination. It is, then, at the middle- and lower-class levels that the integration and discrimination principles, respectively, should hold. Indeed, the predominantly miscegenated middle class should be little concerned with the racial factor. On the other hand, the extremely poor and heavily Negroid lower class should be most aware that the lighter types are at the top of the class structure, a condition that promotes feelings of racial discrimination. This configuration can be complemented with a hypothesis about perceptions of discrimination on the part of middle-class aspirants. In this group the combination of darkness with their working-class background should lead to relatively high feelings of discrimination, for as we have suggested, upwardly mobile persons tend to experience a combination of class and race prejudice. That is, whereas persons who have penetrated a class position are able, *ceteris paribus*, to transform their racial characteristics into personal physical, not "racial" attributes, those who are attempting penetration are viewed in more categorical racial terms.

To test these ideas and refine our conceptualization we asked our social class sample a series of questions designed to measure their perceptions of racial discrimination in Cartagena. The first questions are contained in Table 5.2. Questions 1 and 4 asked if discrimination exists in Cartagena in broad general terms. Questions 13, 18, and 19 were more specific in that they focus on personal life experiences and ecological locations of discrimination.

The analysis of the first two questions indicates that, indeed, the discriminating elites are most aware of racial discrimination. The middle-class aspirants, who are upwardly mobile oriented and more Negroid than the solid middle class, also showed relatively high sensitivity in racial matters; they too are more aware of the existence of discrimination, for in addition to the described mechanisms of discrimination that operate against this group, these aspirants are all females, and as we have seen in Chapter 4, the miscegenation-bleaching process operates to the disadvantage of darker women. We also found, as expected, that the majority of the solid middle class believes that a climate of racial tolerance predominates in Cartagena and that the slum dwellers perceive of their existence as one of racial discrimination. Within the working-class groups, the solid working class is just about evenly split on the question of whether discrimination exists in Cartagena or not. It appears that at this class level the discrimination principle by which the lighter types are on top of the class pyramid is balanced by the integration principle that operates *within* this class position and leads to the absence of racial discrimination within this level. It is interesting to note that the highly politicized and relatively Negroid labor leaders, although aware of discrimination (see question 4) are relatively complacent in racial matters (see question 1). In this respect it appears that successful upward mobility within a class group is conducive to diminishing the importance of the racial factor in Cartagena. Finally, the servants, as a group of rural female migrants who have found "homes" in Cartagena, have little awareness of racial discrimination. Their low aspirations and expectations combined with their inarticulateness appear to lead to this response.

Turning to the question of discrimination at a more specific level, we see that in terms of life experiences (question 13), the basic pattern remains with the exceptions of the solid middle class and the slum dwellers. Why should a majority of the middle class consider that in their life cycle friendships are lost for racial reasons? In our opinion the answer to this question lies in the particular racial heterogeneity of this group, which contains the polar racial types. As we have seen, racial discrimination in intimate relations is most pronounced between the racial poles. Further, at this class level there is a certain amount of selectivity necessary for the functioning of the bleaching process. As for the slum dwellers, who expressed that in their life cycle friendships were not lost for ra-

TABLE 5.2   Percent Distributions of Perceptions of Discrimination by Social Class

	Upper Class	Middle Class		Working Class			Lower Class
	Elite	Solid Middle Class	Middle-Class Aspirants	Labor Leaders	Solid Working Class	Servants	Slum Dwellers

Is there racial discrimination in Cartagena? (Q. 1):

	Elite	Solid Middle Class	Middle-Class Aspirants	Labor Leaders	Solid Working Class	Servants	Slum Dwellers
Yes	67	21	62	31	48	20	66
No	33	79	34	69	46	73	34
No information			4		6	7	
Total	100	100	100	100	100	100	100

Are persons treated differently because of racial characteristics? (Q. 4):

	Elite	Solid Middle Class	Middle-Class Aspirants	Labor Leaders	Solid Working Class	Servants	Slum Dwellers
Yes	67	38	60	55	48	20	61
No	25	62	30	34	35	73	34
No information	8		10	10	17	7	5
Total	100	100	100	100	100	100	100

In the life cycle of a person, as he grows older, are friendships lost for racial reasons? (Q. 13):

	Elite	Solid Middle Class	Middle-Class Aspirants	Labor Leaders	Solid Working Class	Servants	Slum Dwellers
Yes	83	58	74	48	40	33	39
No	17	42	24	52	56	67	58
No information			2		4		2
Total	100	100	100	100	100	100	100

Is there a sector in the city where only colored people live, where it is dangerous for a white person to visit? (Q. 18):

	Elite	Solid Middle Class	Middle-Class Aspirants	Labor Leaders	Solid Working Class	Servants	Slum Dwellers
Yes	62	46	50	38	44	47	*
No	38	50	46	59	50	33	
No information		4	4	3	6	20	
Total	100	100	100	100	100	100	

144

	Upper Class	Middle Class		Working Class			Lower Class
	Elite	Solid Middle Class	Middle-Class Aspirants	Labor Leaders	Solid Working Class	Servants	Slum Dwellers
Are there places here where Negroes are not admitted? (Q. 19):							
Yes	58	50	54	59	58	40	68
No	42	50	38	38	33	47	32
No information			8	3	8	13	
Total	100	100	100	100	100	100	100
Is it better to have white or dark skin in Cartagena? (Q. 3):							
White	75	46	36	34	23	20	32
Dark	4	8	28	34	40	33	49
No difference	17	46	30	31	31	47	17
No information	4		6		6		2
Total	100	100	100	100	100	100	100
Are there many important people here that have nonwhite ancestors? (Q. 5):							
Yes	96	83	48	62	35	20	5
No		4	2	10	6		
Don't know	4	12	50	28	58	80	95
Total	100	100	100	100	100	100	100
What is most important in life, money, education, or racial characteristics? (Q. 7):							
Money	12	4	4	10	8	7	
Education	58	83	90	69	79	80	85
Racial characteristics			2	3		13	10
Don't know/other	29	12	4	17	12		5
Total	100	100	100	100	100	100	100

145

TABLE 5.2   Percent Distributions of Perceptions
of Discrimination by Social Class (*Continued*)

	Upper Class	Middle Class			Working Class			Lower Class
	Elite	Solid Middle Class	Middle-Class Aspirants	Labor Leaders	Solid Working Class	Servants	Slum Dwellers

If a person with dark racial characteristics
dresses well and is educated, is he
treated the same as a light
person? (Q. 8):

Yes	67	83	78	76	75	93	80
No	33	12	22	24	23	7	20
No information		4			2		
Total	100	100	100	100	100	100	100

* This question was not asked to slum dwellers because of its possible
sensitive nature to them.

cial reasons, this is understandable given the relatively high
racial homogeneity of this group.

To explore the existence of racial tensions we asked if there
is a sector in Cartagena where only "colored" persons or *personas de color* live, where it is dangerous for a white person to
visit? (question 18). Practically all class groups acknowledged
the presence of Negroid slum areas and characterized them in
terms of their criminality. The group most sensitive to this
was the predominantly white elite. These responses indicate
that Cartagena cannot be characterized as a "happy" racial
feudalistic system. Question 19—are there places here where
Negroes are not admitted?—received a majority affirmative
response by virtually all the class groups. If we contrast this
response pattern with that of questions 1 and 4, which revealed less consensus about discrimination across the class
groups, it appears that there is a general awareness of discrim-

ination against *negros,* the polar racial type. In other words, when the term *negro* is included in a question there is an increase in awareness of discrimination because in Cartagena, as we have seen, miscegenated persons are not highly stigmatized. Indeed, most *cartageneros* consider themselves mixed bloods. Finally, if we superimpose questions 18 and 19 we find that the poles of the class-race pyramid are highly aware that discrimination exists.

The previous discussion indicates that, in a static sense, the poles of the race-class pyramid are characterized by the discriminators and the discriminated against. From a dynamic point of view we find that in Cartagena interclass upward mobility produces a heightened awareness of the racial factor. However, intraclass mobility appears to increase racial complacency. Were we to conclude the analysis at this point and attempt to make inferences about the potential for racial mobilization in the area, we *might* posit that there is a possibility for a coalition between the emergent segments of the middle class and the oppressed lower classes to form a racial-social movement. Nevertheless, our data indicate'the presence of adaptive mechanisms that coexist with those that produce tension. Indeed, even among racially "dissatisfied" groups there is a significant minority that does not perceive the presence of racial discrimination in Cartagena.

Let us explore some of the adaptive mechanisms. First, when asked if it is better to have white or dark skin in Cartagena (question 3) only the discriminators gave a preference for white skin (4). The lack of a clear preference for a particular skin color by most class groups is indicative of the operation of the tolerance-miscegenation syndrome. Indeed, as evidence for the tolerance aspect of this syndrome is the fact that very high majorities of every class group felt that if a person with dark, not black, racial characteristics dresses well and is educated, he will be treated the same as a light person (question 8). Further evidence that racial characteristics are perceived as being of relatively minor importance in determining success is indicated by question 7, where practically no one felt that race is the most important factor in life. Finally, and perhaps most importantly, is the fact that to the extent that persons have knowledge of the Cartagena power structure, there is a recognition that the infused racial system is present in the area (see question 5). That is, there is an awareness that miscegenated persons can and have succeeded in Cartagena. Once again we find that the elite recognizes its miscegenated background, a factor conducive to reduce guilt feelings in racial matters, a condition that is propitious to reduce the effectiveness of racial movements.

To obtain a fuller picture of racial attitudes in Cartagena we explored the aspect of personal racial prejudice among the class groups. To this end we asked the four questions contained in Table 5.3.

As can be seen from the responses to question 22, at the least intimate-level personal prejudice is very low among all the social class groups in Cartagena. Only significant minorities of elite members and slum dwellers show a reticence always to work with colored (*de color*) people. The explanation for this at the elite level is clear; they are prejudiced and they do discriminate. As to the slum dwellers' attitude, our interviews revealed that a frequent reason for not wishing always to work with *personas de color* was their desire to improve their economic situation. As seen in the previous chapter, the probability of increasing one's economic position increases when working with the lighter racial types. Thus the response reflects the presence of the discrimination principle at this class level. Question 23, which placed the respondent in a subordinate status to a "colored" person, revealed a similar pattern, with the addition that a significant minority of the servants would be reticent to have a colored boss. Probably, the reason for this attitude is, once again, partly economic.

At the most intimate level—marriage in the family—we find a marked increase in prejudice, particularly at the elite level, in which, over 80 percent of this group manifested op-

TABLE 5.3   Personal Race Prejudice in Percentages

	Upper Class	Middle Class		Working Class			Lower Class
	Elite	Solid Middle Class	Middle-Class Aspirants	Labor Leaders	Solid Working Class	Servants	Slum Dwellers
Would it bother you always to work with colored people? (Q. 22):							
Yes	29	8	8	3	19		29
No	71	92	86	90	77	93	71
No information			6	7	4	7	
Total	100	100	100	100	100	100	100
Would it bother you if you had a colored boss? (Q. 23):							
Yes	25	8			2	20	15
No	75	92	96	97	94	73	85
No information			4	3	4	7	
Total	100	100	100	100	100	100	100
Would it bother you if a member of your immediate family married a colored person? (Q. 24):							
Yes	83	29	18	17	17	33	32
No	17	71	76	79	79	60	68
No information			6	3	4	7	
Total	100	100	100	100	100	100	100
Do persons here wish to have children whiter than themselves? (Q. 17):							
Yes	96	75	82	62	71	47	73
No	4	21	16	38	21	47	24
No information		4	2		8	7	2
Total	100	100	100	100	100	100	100

149

position to this type of liason. However, in contrast to findings in some non-Iberian contexts (5), the majority of all other class groups would accept mixed marriages within their own families. It should be noted here that the acceptance of these mixed marriages would be with "colored," not *negros*, for as some of our subjects responded after probing, they would oppose marriages with *palenqueros* (6). Obviously, as noted, although there is a tendency toward endogamy at the top pole of the class structure, miscegenation is highly legitimized in Cartagena, and this is a necessary condition for the infused racial system.

We now turn our attention to a most crucial mechanism of racial adaptation in the area—the bleaching process. It is clear from the answers to question 17—do persons here wish to have children whiter than themselves?—that with the exception of the servants large majorities of all class groups support this mechanism. There is awareness of the already-described process of movements toward miscegenated integration. It is very important to note that although the elites are the strongest proponents of bleaching, the middle-class aspirants are the next highest. That is, this group, highly sensitive to racial discrimination, projects feelings that bleaching is a most desirable process. In this respect, insofar as the bleaching process operates among upwardly mobile groups, the potential for racial conflict is diminished. Although the selectivity by which this mechanism works causes tension, as noted in Chapter 4, bleaching does occur in Cartagena. Our interviews revealed that this process is most conspicuously present in cases of highly successful Negroid individuals. This is easy to understand. In Cartagena, down to and including the working-class level, there are sufficient numbers of light persons to provide a bleaching "pool" for successful individuals. This mechanism, then, operating at the middle sectors of the class system, prevents the presence of significant numbers of highly Negroid persons attempting to penetrate the elite, a situation, of course, that reduces the probabilities of racial strife (7). A final note concerning the servants: the fact that almost half of this group did not indicate the desirability of lighter children can be explained in that these females can be in a sexually precarious position with regard to their employers. Under these conditions, having a lighter child could be interpreted as the outcome of sexual relations with the employer's family unit, a reason for dismissal. (See the discussion of question 12 in support of this interpretation.)

We now turn our attention to a discussion of perceptions of the structural location of discrimination in Cartagena, for in the preceding chapter, where we analyzed the racial composition of elite groups, we found that as one moved from the social through the economic to the political elite sectors of the city, there was an increase in Negroid racial types. Our task here is to determine if the population is aware of these racial differentials and are given in Table 5.4.

The first question (question 10) which deals with the political and economic elite sectors could not be answered effectively by the three lowest class groups whose knowledge of these areas was too limited. Of the remaining class groups who could answer the question, the elite and, to a lesser extent, the solid middle class correctly perceived that the political realm was more opened to Negroid persons than the economic realm. Surprisingly, the highly politicized labor leader group was not aware of the distinction that we had found present at the elite level.

It was to be expected that even more of our sample would be unaware of the social-racial discriminatory practices at the elite level. Indeed, this is true, for almost half of the labor leaders could not answer the question. However, the limited access of Negroid persons to the social elite sector was accurately perceived by the elite to a great extent and, to a lesser extent, by the middle class. This question also reveals that a substantial minority of the middle class was unaware of the racial discriminatory practices of the Cartagena "establishment." In this respect, it is apparent that the racial discrimina-

TABLE 5.4   Locations of Discrimination in Percentages

	Upper Class	Middle Class		Working Class			Lower Class
	Elite	Solid Middle Class	Middle-Class Aspirants	Labor Leaders	Solid Working Class	Servants	Slum Dwellers
Do you believe that in Cartagena a greater percentage of nonwhites are successful in political rather than economic elite activities? (Q. 10):							
Yes	58	46	44	38			
No	33	38	50	52			
Don't know	8	17	6	10			
Total	100	100	100	100			
Do you believe that in Cartagena a greater percentage of nonwhites are successful in political rather than social elite activities? (Q. 11):							
Yes	75	58	44	17			
No	8	17	26	34			
Don't know	17	25	30	48			
Total	100	100	100	100			
Is the Brazilian refrain "Money Whitens" true here? (Q. 9):							
Yes	75	75	68	55	62	93	80
No	25	21	20	34	27	7	17
No information		4	12	10	10		2
Total	100	100	100	100	100	100	100

tion practiced by elite *cartageneros* does not greatly affect the bulk of the population of the city. Further, the responses to these questions indicate that insofar as persons are aware of the power structure of Cartagena, they acknowledge the presence of the class-race structure inferred by us. Finally, the responses to question 9 (Is the Brazilian refrain "money whitens" true here?) which was intended to measure the importance of money (class) vis-à-vis race, shows clearly that *cartageneros* perceive race as a secondary determinant of social status; the great majority of all class groups agreed that "money whitens." Once again—see question 8—*cartageneros* assign a secondary importance to the racial factor.

We now turn to a discussion of attitudes toward race mixture and racial sexuality, as shown in Table 5.5. The unqualified acceptance by all social class groups of high levels of miscegenation in Cartagena (question 2) provides strong evidence for a climate of racial tolerance in the city and a recognition of the infused racial system. Our interviews revealed that most *cartageneros* acknowledge themselves and others as mixed bloods; thus the notion of racial purity that lies at the base of less-tolerant racial systems is rare in Cartagena. Additional evidence for this point is the widespread belief that passing is quite prevalent in Cartagena (see question 6), a situation that hardly exists where racial purity is an effectively implemented value. We might speculate here about a conservative or adaptive tendency among the solid middle and working classes. Their relatively lower acknowledgment of passing might indicate feelings that there is no need for pretending to be white. The theme of racial tolerance notwithstanding, we see the results of personal prejudice and discrimination in the area of differential treatment by sex (question 14). Here again we find that the majority of the discriminators—the elites—do not accord preferential treatment to "colored" women, and the discriminated against—the slum dwellers—also feel that women *de color* do not receive preferential treatment. The servant group, which as we have seen is not very aware of ra-

TABLE 5.5   Attitudes Toward Race Mixture and
Racial Sexuality in Percentages

	Upper Class	Middle Class		Working Class			Lower Class
	Elite	Solid Middle Class	Middle-Class Aspirants	Labor Leaders	Solid Working Class	Servants	Slum Dwellers
Is there a lot of race mixture in Cartagena? (Q. 2):							
Yes	92	96	90	100	94	100	93
No	8	4	10		2		5
Don't know					4		2
Total	100	100	100	100	100	100	100
Are there many persons here who pass for white but are not white? (Q. 6):							
Yes	88	67	80	72	65	93	90
No	8	29	16	24	25		7
Don't know	4	4	4	3	10	7	2
Total	100	100	100	100	100	100	100
Are colored women treated better than colored men in Cartagena? (Q. 14):							
Yes	38	67	44	48	48	13	10
No	62	29	50	52	48	73	73
Don't know		4	6		4	13	17
Total	100	100	100	100	100	100	100
In some societies there is the belief that mulatto women are sexually superior to white women. Is this the case in Cartagena? (Q. 15):							
Yes	71	58	46	76	60	40	76
No	29	38	44	21	27	33	24
Don't know		4	10	3	12	27	
Total	100	100	100	100	100	100	100

Upper Class	Middle Class		Working Class			Lower Class
Elite	Solid Middle Class	Middle-Class Aspi-rants	Labor Lead-ers	Solid Work-ing Class	Ser-vants	Slum Dwell-ers

In some societies there is the belief that *negros* are more virile than white men. Is this the case in Cartagena? (Q. 16):

	Elite	Solid Middle Class	Middle-Class Aspirants	Labor Leaders	Solid Working Class	Servants	Slum Dwellers
Yes	25	54	60	55	48	73	83
No	50	42	30	31	42	20	15
Don't know	25	4	10	14	10	7	2
Total	100	100	100	100	100	100	100

cial matters, also see little difference in treatment by sex. The theme of the sexual idealization of the mulatto women, which has been traced to the Moorish conquest (8) and is an integral part of the tolerance-miscegenation syndrome, is supported by our data; with the exception of the two entirely female groups—the middle-class aspirants and the servants—the majority of our respondents felt that indeed the *mulata* is sexually superior. The corollary of this theme is the greater virility of the black man. Here we find a somewhat different picture in that both female groups and the predominantly black slum dwellers subscribed strongly to this theme. All other class groups, with the exception of the elite, are fairly evenly split. Only a small minority of the discriminating, predominantly white elite accept the notion of black male virility.

In addition to the sexual interpretation of Iberian American race relations, there are two other themes found in the literature we surveyed. The first is the concept of paternalism, with its implications of benign treatment of subordinate groups and rigid racial boundaries. The responses to question 20 in Table 5.6 indicate once again that *cartageneros* do not believe this to be prevalent in the society. Only the elites maintain a relatively traditional outlook in racial matters. The second theme that we explored was that the Spanish cultural heritage was responsible for racial cordiality in the area. Our respondents generally felt that this is true. Of course, this possibly ethnocentric orientation is conducive to complacency in racial matters. We might note, however, that there is a direct relationship between the acceptance of this idea and social class position.

Finally we explored whether attitudes toward race relations were changing in the area. We did this by asking if there was a

TABLE 5.6   Cultural Sources of Racial "Cordiality" in Percentages *

	Upper Class	Middle Class		Working Class	
	Elite	Solid Middle Class	Middle-Class Aspirants	Labor Leaders	Solid Working Class
Do you think that race relations here are paternalistic in nature? (Q. 20):					
Yes	62	38	30	38	33
No	25	58	40	48	40
Don't know	12	4	30	14	27
Total	100	100	100	100	100
Do you believe that it is the Spanish cultural heritage that accounts for the better treatment of the colored people here than in the United States? (Q. 21):					
Yes	83	79	74	66	58
No	8	12	10	17	17
Don't know	8	8	16	17	26
Total	100	100	100	100	100

* These questions were not asked to the servants and slum dwellers because pretesting showed that they did not understand either of the concepts enough to answer the questions.

TABLE 5.7   Racial Attitudes and Social Change
in Percentages

	Upper Class	Middle Class		Working Class			Lower Class
	Elite	Solid Middle Class	Middle-Class Aspi-rants	Labor Lead-ers	Solid Work-ing Class	Ser-vants	Slum Dwell-ers

Do you believe that the younger generation has different racial attitudes than the older generation? (Q. 12):

No	25	25	14	17	19	27	17
Yes—they are more tolerant	75	71	82	76	73	27	76
Yes—they are more prejudiced					2	40	
Don't know		4	4	7	6	7	7
Total	100	100	100	100	100	100	100

difference in racial attitudes between the younger and the older generation (see Table 5.7). Overall we found that there is an optimism present in Cartagena because all but the servants felt that the younger generation was more racially tolerant than their elders. The reason for this exception appears to be linked to their occupation. In effect, these servant females must take orders from young persons, who because of their youth may be more demanding and less considerate than their elders, and who also may be more prone to making sexual advances toward the domestics.

CONCLUDING REMARKS

In this chapter we have surveyed the racial attitudes of several class groups of Cartagena. Our objective was to corroborate the class-race pyramid of the city and to probe more deeply into the sources of racial tension and adaptation within its class structure. In the previous chapter we had considered that two principles operate in the Cartagena eclectic racial system: the principle of discrimination by which class and race are directly related and the principle of integration whereby miscegenated persons are infused throughout the class structure and persons of different racial characteristics compete on equal terms and intermarry freely within the system. Our survey data confirm the operation of both principles. Evidence for the presence of the discrimination principle follows. First, the lighter elites hold feelings of racial prejudice and discriminate. A substantial majority of them uphold attitudinally the principle of endogamy. Second, the highly Negroid lower classes are aware of racial discrimination and feel discriminated against. Third, interclass upwardly mobile persons feel that racial factors can handicap their success. Finally, all groups are aware that discrimination is centered against the polar racial type, the *negros*.

Nevertheless, there is also evidence that the integration principle operates in Cartagena. First, even the prejudiced elites recognize their miscegenated background. Second, all class groups consider that there is substantial miscegenation in the system, (i.e., that there are very few racially "pure" individuals in the city) and that racial factors do not have an overriding importance in determining success in Cartagena. In short, *cartageneros* are aware that they live in an infused racial system in which racial boundaries are relatively fluid and can be overcome. Most *cartageneros* subscribe to the bleaching process and are tolerant of mixed marriages.

As expected from our structural analysis, the discrimination principle is most strongly manifested at the poles of the class pyramid. Furthermore, the integration principle is most conspicuous in the solid middle class; this predominantly miscegenated group does not consider the racial factor to be very important. Whereas interclass upwardly mobile persons are racially sensitive, it appears that intraclass mobility is conducive to racial complacency in the area. Finally, at the solid-working-class level the principle of integration balances the principle of discrimination to neutralize high levels of racial sensitivity.

Let us return now to the question of the potential for racial mobilization in Cartagena. Our data indicate that there are conditions favoring a coalition between emerging-middle-class groups and the lower classes to form a racial social movement. However, this has not occurred in the past and does not seem to be a very likely possibility in the near future because the factors of integration seem to outweigh those of discrimination. Indeed, the tolerance-miscegenation syndrome with the penetration of miscegenated persons at all class levels reduces the probability of such a movement. As the responses in Table 5.1 indicate, in Cartagena, except for the polar racial types, practically all other racial types are significantly present at all class levels. This is not a contention of the authors, for *cartageneros* themselves at the various class levels employ racial self-designations that connote mixed ancestry and cut across the class lines. That is, in Cartagena there are *mestizos* and *morenos* at every class level. Thus racial self-identities transcend class boundaries. This being the case, in Cartagena class boundaries and identifications are more salient than racial ones. The explanation for this lies in the complex racial terminology that characterizes the Iberian American infused system. It is to the analysis of this nomenclature that we now turn our attention.

NOTES

1. Harris, "Race in Minas Velhas," *op. cit.*
2. Pierson, *op. cit.*
3. See Chapter 4.
4. In this respect, our data does not confirm the hypothesis that Ibe-

rian Americans prefer dark skin color because dark was not a majority response for any class group. However, at the poles there is some support for the interpretation that there is a preference for one's own skin color. See Tumin with Feldman, *op. cit.*, pp. 207–208.

5. For the United States, see Hyman and Sheatsley, *op. cit.*, pp. 284–285; for Great Britain, see Banton, *op. cit.*, p. 70; for New Zealand, see Richard Thompson, "Race in New Zealand," in *Comparative Perspectives on Race Relations, op. cit.*, p. 181.

6. *Palenqueros* are almost pure blacks who live in isolation and maintain African customs.

7. For a similar interpretation, see Pierson, *op. cit.*

8. See Chapter 3.

Chapter Six

. . . .

RACIAL NOMENCLATURE AND
RACIAL CONFLICT IN
CARTAGENA

In the preceding chapter we saw that *cartageneros* employ a multiplicity of racial terms to define themselves and that the employment of these terms is partly related to class position. We also observed that the principles that characterize the infused racial system are manifested in its racial terminology because the poles of the class system tend to employ racially polar terms to define themselves (the discrimination principle) and because some terms are employed by members of all social classes to define themselves racially (the integration principle). That is, the complex racial terminology of Cartagena leads to a situation in which persons at the same class level employ different terms to define themselves racially, and these terms cut across class lines so that some persons at all class levels define themselves as being racially similar. Therefore, in terms of the potential for the generation of a racial social movement, the racial nomenclature of the infused system appears to be a fundamental barrier to its materialization, for the society cannot bifurcate itself into clear racial groups. Indeed, the bulk of the population does not define itself in terms of the poles—*blanco* and *negro*. Rather, several racial "subgroups" are infused throughout the entire social structure. As one black middle-class respondent told us, "in Cartagena it is very difficult to generate a racial movement because some *negros* call themselves *morenos,* others *trigueños,* and so on. Here there is a lot of confusion in racial matters." In short, the Cartagena racial nomenclature is characterized by a multiplicity of terms that are assigned subjectively and objectively in an unreliable fashion (1). This terminology is a direct reflection of the ideology of the infused racial system. Indeed, a complex racial nomenclature permits the employment of racial euphemisms to define the self and others, it allows latitude for racial manipulations, and it reflects relativism in race relations. As we show, rather than blindness in racial matters, Iberian Americans are flexible and tolerant in race relations, and this is permitted by their racial nomenclature.

In this chapter we present the nature of the Cartagena racial terminology within an experimental context—what main terms are employed, what their meaning is, how terms are manipulated by class groups, and, finally, what the conflict implications of the manipulation of racial terminology by *cartageneros* are.

THE RACIAL DEFINITIONS OF CARTAGENEROS

The literature has acknowledged the propensity of Iberian Americans to employ a multiplicity of racial terms. In contrast to the dichotomous system of the United States, where persons are white or Negro, Latin American racial nomenclature is quite extensive and complex. Persons are not only black or white but can be *moreno, mestizo, mulato,* and so on. In addition to specific terms, modifiers are also used with high frequency. Thus, a person could be a *moreno claro* (light *moreno*) or a *moreno oscuro* (dark *moreno*). In this respect, it can be argued that Latins are much more precise or "scientific" than Americans in their racial definitions, for the minuteness of the terminology has a relatively high descriptive function (2). The usage of multiple racial terms is a corollary to the ambiguous and fluid position of the miscegenated in the society and gives relativism to race relations. Indeed, an important feature of the multiplicity of terms is that the probability for "error" is much higher than where very few terms are used. For example, if, as in the United States, any sign of Negroid physical characteristics denotes a person who will be called Negro and the absence of any such signs determines that a person will be called white, there is little room for error. This produces a great degree of consensus on racial definitions, consequently, there is little room for a person to negotiate his race. In contrast, in the Iberian system, which uses many terms, there is considerable room for manipulating racial definitions to accommodate the self, with the exception of the very polar racial terms. Thus, paradoxically, the greater "precision" of the Iberian American system leads to a situation of greater ambiguity, relativism, and dissensus in racial definitions (3).

In this section we analyze how persons at different class levels define themselves and others racially. Emphasis is placed on the implications for racial conflict that derive from a system where fluidity and ambiguity in racial terminology or ideology predominate.

Racial Self-Designations and Class

In the preceding chapter we presented the racial self-designations of the surveyed class groups (see Table 5.1). Six racial terms predominated: *blanco, trigueño, moreno, mestizo, mulato,* and *negro.* Variations of these terms were subsumed under the general headings. For instance, a *moreno claro* response was placed in the *moreno* group. Further, in the few instances in which synonyms were employed, they were also subsumed under the major headings. For example, if a respondent called himself a Spaniard we placed him in the *blanco* category.

The reader will recall that the usage of polar racial terms predominated only at the extremes of the class pyramid, and that all class groups contained significant proportions of persons who defined themselves by using various terms. At the elite level, *blanco* predominated. At the middle sectors of the class pyramid down to the solid working class, *mestizo* was the most frequent response. The remaining sectors of the working class employed a majority of *moreno* response in self-designation. It was only at the lowest level of the class structure—the slum dwellers—where the term *negro* obtained a slight majority—only 51 percent.

It is important to note that in Cartagena terms connoting black ancestry, such as *negro* and *mulato*, are infrequently used to define the self (4). Indeed, persons acknowledging miscegenation prefer to employ the terms *mestizo, moreno,* and, to a lesser extent, *trigueño*. As noted, the Castillian meaning of *mestizo* is the mixture between whites and Indians, a mixture somatically closer to *blancos* than *mulato*. On the other hand, *moreno*—derived from Moor—is a highly ambiguous term, for it can describe white brunettes, miscegenated persons, and even, as a euphemism, *negro* (5). The term *trigueño* is derived from the Spanish word *trigo* (wheat). In Castillian, it denotes a light Iberian type, but in Cartagena it can also describe miscegenation. Therefore, it appears that the terminological manipulations of most class groups in Cartagena favor the prevalence of the integration principle, for these manipulations, in effect, lighten the population, particularly at the crucial middle-class level, and reduce identifications with the polar discriminated-against racial type.

The Racial Designations of Others by Class Groups

In addition to the analysis of how class groups in Cartagena define themselves racially, it is important to know how they define others, for this is the only way to assign a meaning to the racial nomenclature and to analyze the manipulation of racial terminology in the area. The meaning and manipulation of racial terms can have an important bearing on the adaptive or strain-producing aspects of the racial system; if, for example, a certain class group lightens the entire population, then this group will not be prone to racial polarization. If on the other hand, *cartageneros* of certain class groups do not assign lighter terms to persons who are well dressed and appear in high status positions, then "money does not whiten" in the area, and racial barriers cannot be overcome, a condition that is conducive to the generation of racial strife.

To determine how persons designate others racially we gave a picture test to a sample of respondents from our surveyed class groups. Fifty-two photographed individuals were presented to 62 respondents to obtain their racial definitions of the photographed subjects. The respondents consisted of 31 males and 31 females. We randomly selected 13 members of our elite sample, 15 from the solid middle class, 18 from the solid working class, and 16 from the slum dwellers to view our pictures. The photographed individuals covered a spectrum of racial types and patterns of dress so that some of the darkest racial types were very well dressed and some of the lightest were poorly dressed. To establish the racial nomenclature of the class groups we constructed an "objective" scale of racial type. With the assistance of two students, we applied to the pictures a scale from 0 to 9, where persons ranked by us as 0 were phenotypic Caucasians, and those ranked 9 were phenotypic Negroes. This index was compared with the racial classifications given by the respondents to the pictures.

Now, let us look at the data. In contrast to our 10-point racial classification, our respondents utilized no less than 62 different racial designations. Table 6.1 presents the terms. The highest number of terms employed by a respondent to describe the pictures was 11 and the lowest was 2.

We organized the terms employed around key terms, that is, those appearing most frequently. As in the case of the racial

TABLE 6.1   Racial Terms Employed

Term	Frequency	Term	Frequency
Negro	635	Puro español	1
Mestizo	351	Mestizo mesclado	1
Moreno	344	Más o menos blanco	1
Blanco	300	Mulato negro	1
Mulato	295	Chino y blanco	1
Claro	99	Negro azul	1
Moreno claro	72	Super negro	1
Moreno oscuro	29	Mono moreno	1
Trigueño	28	Chino puro	1
Criollo	16	Moreno trigueño	1
Indio	12	Blanco con negro	1
Amarillo	10	Blanco con poco negro	1
Chino	9	Mestizo moreno	1
Trigueño claro	8	Blanco con tinta	
Bastante claro	7	negroide	1
Blanco trigueño	5	No blanco del todo	1
Negrito	4	"Del color"	1
Rubio	4	Blanco con tinta	1
Negro puro	3	"Del color" pero castaño	1
Trigueño oscuro	3	mezcla clara	1
Moreno tostado	3	Por el pelo moreno	1
Moreno avanzado	3	Morenita acrespada	1
Asiático	3	Amonado	1
Blanco moreno	3	Mestiza clara	1
Negroide	2	Mono blanco	1
Indio y negro	2	Blanco y ñato	1
Arabe	2	Regular, moreno,	
Sambo	2	claro, mezcla	1
Mulato claro	2	Blanco rosado	1
Moreno o mestizo	2	Mulato lavado	1
Mezcla	2	Mulatona	1
Moreno subido	2	Mestizona	1
Negro claro	2	Moreno caliente	1
Moreno bastante	2	Negro o mulato	1

166

self-designations, the criteria employed was to group together clearly synonomous terms, for example, *español puro* (pure Spanish) and *blanco* (white). The same racial term modified by different adjectives were grouped under the main term. For example, *moreno oscuro* and *moreno claro* (dark and light *moreno,* respectively) were grouped under *moreno.* There were 21 infrequently used terms that we could not classify under the main terms. These were classified under a residual category. Table 6.2 presents the categories.

TABLE 6.2   Classification of Racial Terms

1. *Blanco*	*Mestizo claro*	*Regular, moreno*
Del color *	5. *Moreno*	*claro, mezcla*
Blanco rosado	*Moreno caliente*	*Mezcla*
Blanco trigueño	*Moreno bastante*	*Mezcla clara*
Mono blanco	*Morenita acrespada*	*Indio*
Puro español	*Por el pelo moreno*	*Indio y negro*
Arabe	*Moreno trigueno*	*Sambo*
Rubio	*Moreno claro*	*Blanco y ñato*
Criollo	*Moreno subido*	*Blanco con tinta*
2. *Negro*	*Moreno avanzado*	*No blanco del todo*
Negrito	*Moreno tostado*	*Blanco tinta negroide*
Negro puro	*Moreno oscuro*	*Blanco con poco*
Super negro	6. *Trigueño*	*negro*
Negro azul	*Trigueño oscuro*	*Blanco con negro*
Negro claro	*Trigueño claro*	*Más o menos blanco*
3. *Mulato*	7. *Claro*	*Negroide*
Mulatona	*Bastante claro*	*Amonado*
Mulato claro	8. *Chino*	*Blanco moreno*
Mulato lavado	*Chino puro*	*Negro o mulato*
Mulato negro	*Amarillo*	*Mono moreno*
4. *Mestizo*	*Asiático*	*Mestizo moreno*
Mestizona	9. *Miscellaneous*	*Chino y blanco*
Mestizo mesclado	*Del color pero castaño*	*Moreno o mestizo*

* *Del color* is a term employed by some lower-class segments to define a white person, whereas the more educated sectors of the population employ it to refer to nonwhites. We included it under *blanco* because in our sample it was only employed in its lower-class variant.

In contrast to racial self-designations, when defining others, *cartageneros* employed a greater multiplicity of terms. This is partly because although a respondent could use only one term (and its modifier) to describe himself, he had the option of using a different racial term for each of the pictures. However, with the exception of *claro* and *chino,* the majority of terms employed to describe others did cluster around the same terms used in self-description.

It is important to note here the minuteness of detail employed by some respondents and how this minuteness is linked to racial ambiguity and tolerance. For example, *más o menos blanco* (more-or-less white), *blanco con poco negro* (white with a little Negro), *no blanco del todo* (not completely white), and *blanco y ñato* (white with Negroid nose) are responses which combine racial awareness with a relativistic attitude; no "racist" society employs the term white with a modifier. Indeed, as noted by Harris for Brazil, in Cartagena too there is a tendency to view persons as being more-or-less white (6). Further, as also suggested by Hutchinson for Brazil, in Cartagena too there is a tendency for racial designations to convey the meaning of personal physical characteristics rather than simply racial categorizations (7). This is clearly the case of the *blanco y ñato* response. In addition to this, paternalistic or affective dimensions appeared in some racial designation in the form of diminutives, such as *negrito* and *morenita acrespada* (8). Finally, the already-noted sexual connotations given to some nonwhites types in the area find terminological expression in responses such as *morena caliente, mulatona,* and *mestizona.* Yet some responses, such as *mulato lavado* (washed *mulato*) and *"regular, moreno claro, mezcla"* (so so, not totally white) indicate the positive evaluation given to white characteristics in the area.

We now turn to an analysis of the relationships between social class position and the racial designation of others to determine the extent to which class affects perceptions of race.

Racial Nomenclature and Class

Overall, the average number of terms employed by each class was similar: upper, 6.1; middle, 5.7; working, 5.8; and lower, 6.5. However, as we show, there is a variation in the terms employed by the class groups. Although there was low consensus in the racial definitions of the subjects as a whole, the greatest consensus or agreement was found in defining the polar racial types, particularly Negroes, a characteristic suggesting the greater discrimination experienced by this racial type. We now present the patterns of racial nomenclature employed by the four class groups.

The Elite. There is little consensus among the elite on the racial designation of others; of the 51 photographed persons (9), only 8 photographs were classified by all elite respondents with a single term. The pattern that emerges from our elite sample is one in which most of our photographs received multiple racial designations. For example, a single photograph was designated as *mulato* by one respondent, *negro* by another, *blanco* by another, and *mestizo* by still another. See Table 6-3. As expected, consensus in racial designations is only found at the poles of the racial continuum, for only two persons were seen by all of the elites as white and only six as Negro. The elites then, perceive very few people to be white, relatively more to be *negro,* and the overwhelming majority to be miscegenated. This finding contrasts sharply with the thesis that Iberian Americans are relatively tolerant in racial matters because, given their darkness, they do not perceive racial mixture and do define large numbers of persons as being white. Our data show that the elites see very few people as *blanco.* However, a note should be entered here to the effect that we are dealing with an experimental situation in which subjects were asked to give racial definitions of anonymous photographs. For this reason, we are unable to register with this in-

TABLE 6.3   Patterns of Elite Racial Designations

Majority Response	Second Largest Response	Third Response	N (photo-graphs)
Blanco			
Blanco			2
Blanco	*Mulato*		2
Blanco	*Mestizo*		1
Blanco	*Moreno-mulato*		1
4 *blanco* patterns			6
Negro			
Negro			6
Negro	*Mulato*	*Moreno*	6
Negro	*Mulato*		4
Negro	*Mulato-mestizo-moreno*		1
Negro	*Mestizo*	*Mulato*	1
Negro	*Mulato*	*Mestizo*	1
Negro	*Mestizo*		1
7 *negro* patterns			20
Mestizo			
Mestizo	*Mulato*	*Blanco*	3
Mestizo	*Mulato*	*Moreno*	2
Mestizo	*Mulato*	*Blanco-negro*	1
3 *mestizo* patterns			6

strument the social-racial context of everyday life in Cartagena. Thus the mechanisms described, such as the tendency to suspend pejorative racial classifications when dealing with friends, to give them a *social blanco* definition, are not operative in this situation.

As indicated by Table 6.3, when defining others the elite predominantly used three terms *negro, mulato,* and *blanco.* This contrasts to their self-designations, where the terms *mulato* and *negro* were never used. Once again, the elite appears as a relatively prejudiced group because they apply to others

Majority Response	Second Largest Response	Third Response	N (photographs)
Mulato			
Mulato	*Negro*	*Moreno*	4
Mulato	*Negro*	*Mestizo*	2
Mulato	*Blanco-mestizo*		2
Mulato	*Mestizo*		1
Mulato	*Blanco*	*Trigueño-mestizo*	1
Mulato	*Negro*	*Mestizo-blanco*	1
Mulato	*Mestizo*	*Moreno-blanco*	1
Mulato	*Moreno-mestizo*		1
Mulato	*Moreno-negro*		1
Mulato	*Blanco*	*Moreno-mestizo*	1
Mulato	*Moreno-mestizo-negro*		1
Mulato	*Mestizo*	*Blanco-trigueño-moreno*	1
12 *mulato* patterns			17
26 Single-term majority patterns			49*

* Two photographs did not receive a single term as a majority response. In one case, the photograph was considered to be *negro* or *mulato* by an equal number of respondents. In the other case the terms were *mestizo* and *mulato*.

terms connoting black blood that they do not apply to themselves. However, this suppression of terms connoting blackness in their midst which is permitted by the terminological complexity is precisely the mechanism by which the miscegenated are accepted. The prevalent pattern of racial designations that emerges from our experimental situation, then, consists of the polar terms *blanco* and *negro* and the middle term *mulato*, which clearly denotes black ancestry.

On the basis of these data, it is not possible to establish clearly the relative positions of other terms connoting miscegenation because there is very low consensus on the use of these terms. A case in point is the term *mestizo* which is used predominantly with the term *mulato* but is employed as a second designation to persons both predominantly defined as *blanco* and *negro*. Nevertheless, the fact that miscegenated elite members prefer the term *mestizo* to *mulato* to define themselves suggests the lighter connotations of the former term among this group.

To get a more precise picture of the racial perceptions and use of racial terminology by the elites we compared their responses with our objective scale of racial type. Of the 51 pictures, we considered six subjects to be phenotypically pure white and six to be phenotypically pure black. The bulk of our pictures represented miscegenated persons with a large proportion of darker types. See Table 6.4.

When comparing elite racial designations with our objective scale, we find that the elites were in agreement with us in terms of the polar racial type Negro, but not with that of whites; although the six pictures that we considered pure white received a dominant *blanco* definition, in only two of the six was there total agreement with this classification. See Tables 6.3 and 6.4. Thus the elites tend to consider that there are fewer *blancos* or more miscegenation in Cartagena than we did.

With the aid of our objective scale we can establish that *mestizo* is a lighter term than *mulato* for the elites. In effect, our respondents gave a dominant *mestizo* classification to our second lightest category, and at the middle of our scale *mestizo* disappears and *mulato* becomes the predominant designation. Thus the elites—the discriminators—tend to darken people, for, as noted, they employ the term *mulato* more frequently than *mestizo* to designate others. Further, they employ the term *negro* in a majority response for persons we considered to be toward the middle of the racial scale (Table 6.4). The following diagram summarizes the hierarchy of racial nomenclature employed by the elite as it relates to our objective racial scale:

Nomenclature: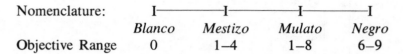
                   Blanco   Mestizo   Mulato   Negro
Objective Range   0   1–4   1–8   6–9

The Solid Middle Class. In contrast to the elite, there is even less consensus in the racial designations given by the solid middle class because total racial agreement is found in only two photographs. See Table 6.5. In this case, consensus was found only with *negros,* not *blancos.* Also, the middle class viewed even more persons as miscegenated than the elite; they saw fewer *blancos* and fewer *negros* (i.e., there was a relatively lower total agreement with polar racial types than that given by the elite). Thus the middle class darkened the *blancos* and lightened the *negros.* However, by the predominant use of the lighter term *mestizo* rather than *mulato,* this class group lightened the overall population in contrast to the elite. Evidence for the lighter connotation of *mestizo* over *mulato* at this class level is found in the fact that it is always the second-largest response for those pictures who were predominantly described as *blanco.* A *mestizo* connotation was rarely employed for persons considered to be *negro* by a majority of our middle-class respondents.

From our data it appears that under our experimental conditions, the middle-class racial scale shows a pattern of *blanco, mestizo,* and *negro,* with the terms *moreno* and *mulato* falling toward the Negroid end of the scale. Our inability to determine the relative position of the two latter terms from these data is based on the fact that both terms are most equally employed as the second-largest response when the term *negro* is dominant.

Overall, there is a congruency between the predominant racial self-designation of the middle class and their perceptions of others because, as noted, *mestizo* was very frequently employed for self and others. This congruency around a light racial term is consonant with the picture of relative compla-

TABLE 6.4 Objective Scale of Racial Type Compared with the Dominant Racial Designations by Class Groups

						Predominant Racial Response							
Class Group	Objective Scale Rank	Blanco	Mestizo	Claro	Mulato	Moreno	Negro	Blanco and Claro	Mestizo and Mulato	Moreno and Claro	Negro and Moreno	Claro and Mestizo	Negro and Mulato
Elite	0	6											
Middle class	(N=6)	5	1										
Working class		6											
Lower class		5						1					
Elite	1		3						1				
Middle class	(N=4)		4										
Working class		1				3							
Lower class						3				1			
Elite	2		1		1								
Middle class	(N=2)		2										
Working class		2											
Lower class				1		1							
Elite	3			1	2								
Middle class	(N=3)		3										
Working class		1	1					1					
Lower class		2				1							

		1	2	3	4	5	6
Elite	4			1			
Middle class	(N=2)	1	1				
Working class		1	2				
Lower class							1
Elite	5			5	1		
Middle class	(N=5)		4	1			
Working class		2			2	2	
Lower class		1			3		1
Elite	6			2		2	
Middle class	(N=4)		2			2	
Working class					4		
Lower class					4		
Elite	7			6		3	
Middle class	(N=9)		4		1	3	1
Working class		1			4	3	1
Lower class					9		
Elite	8					9	1
Middle class	(N=10)					9	1
Working class					3	6	1
Lower class					5	4	
Elite	9					6	
Middle class	(N=6)					6	
Working class						6	
Lower class						3	3

TABLE 6.5   Patterns of Middle-Class Racial Designations

Majority Response	Second Largest Response	Third Response	N (photographs)
Blanco			
Blanco	*Mestizo*	*Claro-mulato*	1
Blanco	*Mestizo*	*Claro*	1
Blanco	*Mestizo*	*Claro-moreno*	1
Blanco	*Mestizo*	*Moreno-negro*	1
Blanco	*Mestizo*	*Mulato*	1
5 *blanco* patterns			5
Negro			
Negro			2
Negro	*Mulato-moreno*		5
Negro	*Mulato*	*Moreno*	3
Negro	*Moreno*	*Mulato*	2
Negro	*Mestizo*	*Mulato*	2
Negro	*Moreno*		1
Negro	*Moreno*	*Mestizo*	1
Negro	*Moreno-mestizo*		1
Negro	*Moreno-mulato*		1
Negro	*Mulato*		1
Negro	*Mulato*	*Mestizo-moreno*	1
11 *negro* patterns			20
Moreno			
Moreno	*Mestizo-mulato-negro*		1
1 *moreno* pattern			1
Mulato			
Mulato	*Negro*	*Mestizo*	1
1 *mulato* pattern			1
Mestizo			
Mestizo	*Moreno*	*Negro*	3
Mestizo	*Moreno-blanco*		3
Mestizo	*Blanco*	*Moreno*	2
Mestizo	*Negro*	*Moreno-mulato*	1
Mestizo	*Blanco-claro-trigueño-moreno*		1
Mestizo	*Negro*	*Moreno*	1

Majority Response	Second Largest Response	Third Response	N (photographs)
Mestizo	*Moreno-negro*		1
Mestizo	*Moreno-mulato-negro*		1
Mestizo	*Blanco*	*Claro-trigueño-moreno*	1
Mestizo	*Blanco-trigueño*		1
Mestizo	*Moreno*	*Blanco-claro-mulato*	1
Mestizo	*Moreno*	*Blanco-trigueño*	1
Mestizo	*Mulato*	*Blanco-trigueño-moreno*	1
Mestizo	*Blanco*	*Trigueño*	1
Mestizo	*Negro*	*Trigueño-mulato-moreno*	1
Mestizo	*Trigueño*	*Moreno*	1
Mestizo	*Moreno-trigueño*		1
17 *mestizo* patterns			1
35 single-majority patterns			49*

* Two photographs did not receive a single term as a majority response. An equal number of respondents considered these two subjects to be *negro* or *moreno*.

cency in racial matters that we have seen to characterize this group. Obviously, if most persons are considered to be miscegenated and a light term is employed to define them, this is conducive to racial adaptation. Thus we see that at this class level the manipulation of racial terminology provides a mechanism of adaptation.

Again, we can complement the analysis by the use of the objective racial scale. In support of our contentions, the middle class darkens persons at the *blanco* extreme of the scale because they employ the term *mestizo* for persons we had considered to be pure white (Table 6.4). Secondly, they employ this term over a wide range of physical types thus lightening the overall population. Further evidence of this process is found in that, in contrast to the elite, they employ the darker *mulato* term much later in the objective scale. Also in contrast to the upper class, they lighten all but the darkest persons by using the term *moreno* toward the dark end of the continuum. The previous tendencies notwithstanding, the solid middle class follows the elite pattern of giving a majority *negro* definition to highly Negroid persons.

The following diagram summarizes the hierarchy of racial nomenclature employed by the middle class as it relates to our objective racial scale:

Nomenclature: I———I———I———I———I
                   Blanco *Mestizo* *Mulato* *Moreno* *Negro*
Objective range: 0   0–7   5   7–8   6–9

It is important to note that the middle-class racial nomenclature is more complex than that of the elite, a factor that supports our contention that a complex racial terminology has an adaptive racial function.

The Solid Working Class.   Thus far we have seen how, in support of the interpretations of the previous chapter, the analysis of the racial designations of others shows the elite as the group in which the principle of discrimination finds its greatest expression in an active form (i.e., they darken the population), and the solid middle class as an adaptive group where the principle of integration finds its greatest manifestation (i.e., they lighten the population). We now turn to the analysis of the racial designations of the solid working class.

As with the first two class groups, the solid working class shows little consensus in racial designations. See Table 6.6. The small consensus that exists resembles more the elite than the middle-class pattern in that in six cases all the respondents agreed that there were both *blanco* and *negro* subjects, that is, the two polar racial types. However, in contrast to the two other groups, the working class saw more white persons, evidenced by the relatively higher usage of the term *blanco*. In

TABLE 6.6   Patterns of Working-Class Racial Designations

Majority Response	Second Largest Response	Third Response	*N* (photographs)
Blanco			
Blanco			2
Blanco	*Claro*		5
Blanco	*Claro-moreno*		4
Blanco	*Moreno-mestizo*		1
Blanco	*Claro-mestizo-*		
	moreno-mulato	·	1
Blanco	*Claro-moreno-*		
	negro		1
6 *blanco* patterns			14
Negro			
Negro			4
Negro	*Moreno*		11
2 *negro* patterns			15
Claro			
Claro	*Blanco*	*Mestizo*	1
Claro	*Moreno-mulato*		1
2 *claro* patterns			2
Moreno			
Moreno	*Mestizo-mulato-*		
	negro		4
Moreno	*Negro*		3
Moreno	*Mestizo-mulato*		2
Moreno	*Blanco-negro*		2
Moreno	*Blanco*		2
Moreno	*Blanco-claro-*		
	mulato		1
Moreno	*Claro-negro*		1
Moreno	*Claro-blanco*		1
8 *moreno* patterns			16
18 single-majority patterns			47*

* Four photographs did not receive a single term as a majority response. In two cases *moreno* was tied to *negro* and in the remaining two, *claro* was tied with *blanco* and *mestizo*.

addition, at this class level the term *claro* is more extensively employed for the first time (10). *Claro*—literally, light—is a term used for racial designations but which has no biological or "racial" connotations. The innovation of the use of this nontraditional term is an example of the already-noted Iberian pattern of racial adaptation, which transforms racial characteristics into physical attributes. Another distinguishing feature of the solid-working-class terminology is that they rarely use—even less than the middle class—the term *mulato*, which has a clear Negroid connotation.

Now we come to a most interesting feature of the working-class terminology: the predominant use of the term *moreno*. It should be recalled that this term was the prevalent term of self-designation by the working class. Thus, much like the middle class, we also find a consistency within this group to use the same term to designate others as they do themselves.

From Table 6.6, the following racial scale appears: *blanco, claro, moreno,* and *negro*. The relative lightness of *claro* can be seen by its high usage with the *blanco* patterns. On the other hand, *moreno* is the only term that appears second to *negro*. Although *moreno* was predominantly employed at the Negroid end of the scale, it was also frequently employed at the lightest end. Thus we find that the predominant term for self-designation of the working class is highly ambiguous, even more so than the usage of *mestizo* or *blanco* by the middle and upper classes, respectively. In this respect, it is at the working-class level that the noted ambiguity of *moreno* finds its maximum expression under experimental conditions.

The terminological versatility of the solid working class is highlighted by looking at their racial definitions within the context of our objective racial scale (see Table 6.4). In effect, this class group loosely employed the term *blanco* to include persons of clearly mixed ancestry classified by us as 5. In fact, two of the respondents maintained the definition of *blanco* up to point 7 on the scale. In addition to this, versatility is also indicated in the usage of *moreno* at the second-lightest and darkest levels of the continuum. It is also important to note that this relatively Negroid group employs the term *negro* slightly more restrictively than the two higher class groups, and never uses the term *mulato* as a predominant response (see Table 6.9). Finally, the working class employs the term *claro* toward the middle of the objective scale where *mestizo* is also found. The following diagram summarizes the racial nomenclature of the working class:

Nomenclature:	I————I————I————I			
	Blanco	*Claro*	*Moreno*	*Negro*
Objective Range:	0–5	3–5	1, 6–8	7–9

In the preceding chapter, we saw that of all class groups the solid working class was quite evenly split on the questions of racial prejudice and discrimination in Cartagena. This contrast with the other class groups who showed a greater tendency toward beliefs of discrimination or the lack of it. Thus we have argued that there are two forces impinging on this group: (a) an awareness of the whiteness of the top of the social structure, and (b) a relative absence of racial discrimination in their personal occupational experiences. We can now see that their usage of racial terminology complements their attitudinal outlook. In effect, the awareness of whiteness at the top is suggested by the fact that the working class saw relatively more white photographs than the other higher class groups. (11) At the same time, the employment of the racially neutral term *claro* and of *moreno* within a highly ambiguous semantical context, indicates the presence of mechanisms for racial adaptation among the working class. In effect, the term preferred for racial self-designation connotes both darkness and lightness.

The Lower Class. In contrast to the solid working class, the slum dwellers perceive fewer *negros* (and *blancos*). See Table 6.7. It is particularly interesting to note that as one descends

TABLE 6.7   Patterns of Lower Class Racial Designations

Majority Response	Second Largest Response	Third Response	N (photo- graphs)
Blanco			
Blanco	*Claro*		4
Blanco	*Claro-moreno*		2
Blanco	*Claro*	*Moreno*	2
Blanco	*Claro*	*Moreno-mestizo*	1
4 *blanco* patterns			9
Negro			
Negro			2
Negro	*Moreno*		5
2 *negro* patterns			7
Moreno			
Moreno			1
Moreno	*Negro*		10
Moreno	*Claro*	*Blanco*	3
Moreno	*Claro*		2
Moreno	*Negro-claro- trigueño*		1
Moreno	*Blanco-claro- trigueño-mestizo*		1

the class structure, persons perceive fewer Negroes. Whereas both the elite and the solid middle class gave a majority of *negro* designation to 20 photographs, the working class and the lower class gave this response only to 15 and 7 pictures, respectively. However, although the lower class defined fewer *blancos* than the working class, they still considered more persons as *blanco* than the middle and upper classes.

The slum dwellers employ *claro* more frequently than the working class, and *mulato* and *mestizo* are less used by them. Nevertheless, as with the working class, *moreno* is the most prevalent term employed, and their racial scale is similar to that of the working class; the pattern is *blanco, claro, moreno,*

Majority Response	Second Largest Response	Third Response	N (photo-graphs)
Moreno	*Claro*	*Trigueño-mestizo*	1
Moreno	*Blanco-claro-trigueño*		1
Moreno	*Claro-mulato*		1
Moreno	*Claro*	*Blanco-mestizo*	1
Moreno	*Claro*	*Negro*	1
Moreno	*Blanco-claro-mestizo*		1
Moreno	*Blanco*	*Claro-trigueño*	1
Moreno	*Blanco-claro-mulato*		1
14 *moreno* patterns			26
Claro			
Claro	*Blanco*	*Moreno*	1
1 *claro* pattern			1
21 Single-term majority response patterns			43*

* Eight photographs did not receive a single term as a majority response. In four cases *moreno* was tied with *negro*, in three cases *moreno* was tied with *claro*, and in one case *blanco* was tied with *claro*.

and *negro*. Once again *moreno* is used ambiguously, because although it predominates with the term *negro*, it also appears frequently in the *blanco* and *claro* patterns.

The previous analysis is supported by employing our objective racial scale (see Table 6.4). The tendency to employ restrictively the term *negro* among this class group is confirmed by the fact that, in contrast to the other class groups, a predominant *negro* response is found only at the two darkest points on our scale. Furthermore, the slum dwellers employ the terms *blanco* (and *claro*) for clearly racially mixed persons and shy away from the term *mulato*. For this group, the term *moreno* is an all-purpose designation. It is used to cover a range from virtually white to Negro. Thus we see again a tendency to equalize all people racially. The following diagram summarizes the racial scale and nomenclature of the lower class:

Nomenclature: I ————— I ————— I ————— I
                 Blanco   *Claro*   *Moreno*   *Negro*
Objective Range: 0, 3–5   1–2, 4   1–9   8–9

In the preceding chapter we saw that the slum dwellers are one of the groups who perceive racial discrimination in Cartagena. This racial outlook appears to be consistent to their manipulation of racial terminology. The lower class perceives a relatively high number of *blancos* and *claros;* thus they are aware of the presence of light persons at the top of the class pyramid. On the other hand, a majority of the slum dwellers defined themselves as *negros,* and yet defined most other darker persons as *moreno.* This lack of congruency between self-designation and racial designation of others suggests feelings that they are truly the bottom of Cartagena's social pyramid. Nevertheless, even at this class level, we find mechanisms of racial adaption because only a slight majority of the slum dwellers called themselves *negro,* whereas most of them would be called *negro* by others. Thus, as with all other class groups, the lower class also lightens itself, and like the working and middle classes above them, they also tend to homogenize the population by employing a non-Negroid racial term over a long range of the racial continuum.

Dress, Context, and Racial Definitions

Before concluding this section on the racial designations of others by *cartageneros,* we must address ourselves to the question of what the effect of patterns of dress, physical location, and proximity to others on racial designations was. These factors are measures for the proposition that "money whitens." We first addressed ourselves to those cases where there was the greatest lack of congruency between the term of racial designation and our objective ranking. Because the working and lower classes showed the greatest variability, we begin with these groups.

First, dress does have an effect on lightening people, particularly for the working and lower classes. An outstanding example was a case where a clearly mulatto man who was extremely well dressed—suit, white shirt, tie, and glasses—classified by us as 5, received from the working and lower classes a *blanco* definition. Conversely, an individual who was defined as pure white by us but who was unkempt in his appearance was not defined as a *blanco* by many of these respondents. However, the effect of dress is restricted by other factors, even at this class level, as illustrated by the following cases. In one photograph of a group of men, a very well dressed man—suit, white shirt, tie, with a camera in his hand —whom we had defined as 8 (i.e., virtually Negro) was termed *negro* by the working class and *moreno* by the lower class. In contrast, another man in this same photograph dressed only casually, whom we rated 5, was termed *claro* by the working class and *blanco* by the slum dwellers. In this case, because he was a light type with only slight Negroid characteristics and was in the company of well-dressed individuals he was given a light classification—but he was not well dressed. Lightness and context prevailed here. The impact of dress, physical characteristics, and context are also present in the elite and the middle classes. Again, an unkempt pure white male received the lowest consensus of *blanco* definitions and a *mestizo* classification by the upper and middle classes, respectively. On the other hand, a very-light slum dweller pictured in front of his shack received a *mestizo* classification by the elite and the middle classes. In this case, physical type prevailed over dress and the situational context.

There also appears to be an interaction between class and physical type. In one photograph, a man who works as a waiter—dressed in a typical waiter dress, white shirt, black pants, and black bow tie—was classified by us as 1, only after very close scrutiny. He is virtually white. In contrast to the working class that defined this man as *blanco*, the elites designated him a *mestizo*. In this case, it appears that the absence of a class prejudice by the former group led to their lighter definition. Conversely, the elites seem to have reacted to the man's clearly working-class attire (12).

In addition to the factors of class, dress, context, and physical characteristics, there is another factor that influences the use of racial terminology. For want of a better term, we call it generosity toward children. In two pictures, where two mothers and three children are present, all class groups, except the slum dwellers, who employed the term *moreno* for all, gave a lighter designation to the children. These responses may also indicate that there is a feeling that racial flexibility permits producing lighter children in Cartagena. In any case, the rule of "hypodescent" does not prevail in the area.

Let us recapitulate. It is at the darkest pole of the racial scale—points 8 and 9—where physical characteristics prevail in influencing racial terminology in that at this level the influence of dress and other status characteristics have a minimal effect. Indeed, as noted, there was substantial consensus among all class groups at the Negroid, not white, pole of the continuum. The presence of very dark pigmentation is the overwhelming determinant of racial designation in Cartagena, for subjects rated by us as 8 were individuals with black pigmentation who did not have Negroid facial or hair characteristics. Yet, these types were generally defined as *negros* by our respondents (13). It is when we move away from extreme pigmentation that facial and hair characteristics become the salient physical determinants of race. However, at this level of the physical continuum, social factors, such as dress and context (i.e., class), play a role. Yet, our data suggest that except for the very-polar Negroid types, racial designations of others are largely determined by the racial ideologies of the class groups. These ideologies are, of course, somewhat related to the racial composition of the class groups. It is to this topic that we now turn our attention.

RACIAL SELF-DESIGNATIONS AND RACIAL ATTITUDES

Thus far we have related racial attitudes and perceptions to class position in Cartagena and have found that awareness of discrimination is relatively high at the poles of the class pyramid. Furthermore, we have considered that interclass upward mobility at the middle-class level and intraclass mobility among the working class increases and reduces the feelings of racial discrimination, respectively (14). We have also considered that the complex and ambiguous Iberian American racial terminology permits the manipulation of racial identity to the extent that, for example, only a slight majority of the highly Negroid slum dwellers call themselves *negro*. Obviously, racial perceptions and attitudes should be also influenced by the racial characteristics of individuals (15). Specifically, these perceptions and attitudes should be influenced by racial self-identities.

Within the Iberian American infused context the role of racial self-identity acquires particular importance because of the social fact that racial self-identity is highly negotiable. Indeed, although it would be incongruent for a highly Negroid person to call himself *blanco,* he has available a variety of terms with which to designate himself, and as we have seen, racial terms in Cartagena cover such a wide range of racial types that subjective racial preferences need not be highly incongruent with physical type. Thus we must address ourselves now to the relationship between racial self-identity and racial attitudes in Cartagena.

To explore this relationship we selected a few questions on racial attitudes that were presented to our class groups (see

TABLE 6.8   Racial Self-Designation
and Racial Attitudes (in Percentages)

	Blanco	Mestizo	Trigueño	Moreno	Mulato	Negro
Is there racial discrimination in Cartagena? (Q. 1):						
Yes	63	47	50	49	33	65
No	37	51	50	46	67	35
No information		2		5		
Total	100	100	100	100	100	100
Are persons treated differently because of racial characteristics? (Q. 4):						
Yes	69	51	50	51	33	68
No	29	46	46	42	58	27
No information	3	4	4	8	8	5
Total	100	100	100	100	100	100
In the life cycle of a person, as he grows older, are friendships lost for racial reasons? (Q. 13):						
Yes	71	60	54	52	25	38
No	29	39	46	45	75	62
No information		2		3		
Total	100	100	100	100	100	100

Chapter 5) and cross-tabulated the responses by racial self-designations. Table 6.8 contains the results.

An analysis of the first two general questions on discrimination indicates that it is at the poles of the racial self-designation scale that perceptions of discrimination are relatively
high. This was to be expected, given the noted high correlation between the polar racial types and the class structure.
Persons defining themselves as miscegenated perceived relatively lower levels of discrimination than the polar racial
types. It is particularly important to note that among the miscegenated group, those individuals who defined themselves as

	Blanco	Mestizo	Trigueño	Moreno	Mulato	Negro
Are there places here where Negroes are not admitted? (Q. 19):						
Yes	57	46	54	57	33	62
No	43	51	41	38	58	35
No information		4	4	5	8	3
Total	100	100	100	100	100	100
If a person with dark racial characteristics dresses well and is educated, is he treated the same as a light person? (Q. 8):						
Yes	77	75	77	78	83	84
No	23	25	23	22	17	14
No information						3
Total	100	100	100	100	100	100
N	35	57	22	65	12	37

Note: The column totals by racial self-designation are lower than for the class groups because 18 respondents would not give their racial self-designations.

mulato were the most complacent in racial matters. This is not difficult to understand because, as we have seen, these individuals live in a society in which miscegenated persons can employ a racial self-designation that does not have a Negroid connotation, and yet they have chosen to define themselves as Negroids.

Turning to question 13 (In the life cycle of a person, as he grows older are friendships lost for racial reasons?) again we see that *mulatos* were the most racially complacent. In addition, a substantial majority of the *negros* rejected the presence of this type of discrimination. This was to be expected for, as noted in Chapter 5, the bulk of our *negros* are slum dwellers who live in a relatively homogeneous racial context where friendships are rarely lost for racial reasons.

In terms of physical discriminatory barriers—see question 19—*mulatos* are again racially complacent, whereas *negros* are particularly aware of this type of discrimination. Finally, in response to question 8, which probes the notion that the racial factor is not the most important consideration for success in Cartagena, we find a general racial optimism among all racial "groups." This adaptive outlook is also present among all the class groups of Cartagena.

The previous analysis is somewhat contaminated by the class factor, for over half of the persons who called themselves *negro* in our sample are slum dwellers who are at the bottom of the class pyramid of Cartagena. Thus it is difficult when analyzing the attitudes of the *negro* group to determine whether their economic position or their racial identity determines their racial attitudes. Because the purpose of this section is to explore the impact of racial self-identity on attitudes, we next analyze the racial perceptions of Negroes who are not found at the bottom of the class structure. This is a very important group to analyze because the literature has considered that upwardly mobile Negroid individuals are most likely to be sensitive toward racial prejudice. Table 6.9 contains the relationships between racial self-identity and attitudes for all but the lower class.

An analysis of the first two general questions on discrimination—questions 1 and 4—indicates that the majority of nonlower-class *negros* consider that there is no racial discrimination in Cartagena. The pattern that emerges is similar to the previously described *mulato* pattern. Indeed, given the ambiguity and flexibility of the infused racial terminology, the fact that a person chooses to call himself *negro* (or *mulato*) indicates that he is relatively complacent in racial matters.

In terms of question 13 (In the life cycle of a person, as he grows older, are friendships lost for racial reasons?) we find a similar pattern of complacency by nonlower-class *negros* and *mulatos*. However, there is a slightly higher *negro* response now because, as noted, slum dwellers who live in racially homogeneous settlements are not prone to experience this type of discrimination. In sharp reversal of the lower-class *negro*

TABLE 6.9   Racial Self-Designation and Racial
Attitudes, Slum Dwellers Omitted, (in Percentages)

	Blanco	Mestizo	Trigueño	Moreno	Mulato	Negro
Is there racial discrimination in Cartagena? (Q. 1):						
Yes	63	41	45	52	27	39
No	37	57	55	43	73	61
No information		2		5		
Total	100	100	100	100	100	100
Are persons treated differently because of racial characteristics? (Q. 4):						
Yes	69	53	55	52	18	33
No	29	43	40	41	73	61
No information	3	4	5	7	9	6
Total	100	100	100	100	100	100
In the life cycle of a person, as he grows older, are friendships lost for racial reasons? (Q. 13):						
Yes	71	59	55	52	36	44
No	29	39	45	46	64	56
No information		2		2		
Total	100	100	100	100	100	100
Are there places where Negroes are not admitted? (Q. 19):						
Yes	57	43	60	59	36	44
No	43	53	35	36	54	50
No information		4	4	4	9	6
Total	100	100	100	100	100	100
If a person with dark racial characteristics dresses well and is educated, is he treated the same as a light person? (Q. 8):						
Yes	77	78	75	79	82	83
No	23	22	25	21	18	11
No information						6
Total	100	100	100	100	100	100
N =	35	51	20	56	11	18

pattern, the majority of nonlower-class *negros* do not feel that there are places in Cartagena where Negroes are not admitted (question 19). Finally, although once again all racial "groups" feel that the racial factor can be overcome in Cartagena (question 8) nonlower-class *negros* and *mulatos* are particularly optimistic in this respect.

Let us recapitulate. The infused racial nomenclature is characterized by a multiplicity of terms that are ambiguous, that can be manipulated to accommodate the self. We have seen that with the exception of persons at the poles of the class pyramid, most *cartageneros* define themselves as miscegenated and avoid terms with a Negroid connotation. The ambiguity and flexibility of this racial nomenclature lends itself to a unique phenomenon which we have called terminological miscegenation. That is, in Cartagena it is possible to manipulate racial identities terminologically to transcend actual biological miscegenation. For example, *negros* can and do call themselves *morenos*. Of course, this terminological miscegenation reduces identifications with the discriminated polar racial type.

We have already seen that the Cartagena racial nomenclature reflects a vital cultural feature of the infused racial system because it leads to a situation in which the principle of integration prevails. In effect, the terminology not only permits the reduction of the discriminated polar racial type—the bleaching process—but it also produces a structural situation in which individuals with different racial self-identities compete and intermarry freely at each class level, a situation in which persons with the same racial identity are found at every class level. Of course, these conditions reduce the probability for racial polarization and conflict.

There is one final potent effect of this system of racial nomenclature which directly inhibits the development of a racial social movement. As we have seen, nonlower-class persons who are relatively sensitive to discrimination tend to have non-Negroid self-identities. With the exception of the lowest class, where the skills for articulating racial leadership are absent, to the extent that individuals have Negroid self-identities, they are complacent in race relations. Thus we are left with a situation in which feelings of "Negritude" are adaptive. Of course, this is just the opposite case of societies where the infused racial system is absent.

CONCLUDING REMARKS

In this chapter we have explored the implications for conflict of the racial nomenclature found in Cartagena. This nomenclature, the basic characteristics of which were begun during the colonial period, is characterized by both its minuteness and its ambiguity. That is, on the one hand, the terminology reflects a cultural orientation that is highly descriptive of physical traits found in individuals. To this extent, it is "scientific" or "precise" and transcends the function of simply conceived racist categorizations. On the other hand, its multiplicity of terms provides ambiguity in racial matters, because in addition to the polar terms, there are various terms that define miscegenated individuals. This multiplicity reflects an ideology that recognizes miscegenation and attempts to provide terms that describe various types of racial mixture. However, given the large number of different racial types, that is, extensive miscegenation, present in the area, the terminology cannot serve its descriptive function and produces, instead, ambiguous racial categorizations. This is clearly seen in the relative consensus found in defining polar racial types and the very high dissensus found when defining other types.

In the final analysis, the Iberian American racial terminology is a direct reflection of tolerance toward the miscegenated because terms that define simple physical characteristics, such as *moreno* (i.e., brunette) have been employed since the colonial period as euphemisms for Negroid individuals. Thus from the outset the racial nomenclature was a hybrid of physical descriptions and racial categorizations. Furthermore, it has also reflected the ideology of the tolerance-miscegenation syndrome with its affective, paternalistic, and sexual aspects. In short, a system of racial nomenclature is an integral part of the racial ideology of a society.

There are two aspects to the usage of racial terminology: how people define themselves racially and how they define others. These definitions reflect the principles of racial stratification of the society. Let us now recapitulate the latter aspect. When classifying others, the class groups of Cartagena revealed a relatively higher consensus in defining the Negroid polar type. In this respect, it appears that there is less ambiguity and greater discrimination against Negroes. Second, all class groups are highly aware of miscegenation, as evidenced by the fact that they recognized very few pure whites. Third, a common characteristic of all class groups is their low consensus when defining others racially. In terms of the principles of racial stratification found in Cartagena, then, the first-outlined characteristic supports discrimination and the other two integration. However, there were differences between class groups in their racial definitions of others. The elites showed a tendency to darken people; the middle class tended to darken *blancos* but to lighten the overall population; the working and lower classes lightened the population, particularly persons with high status, and were relatively imprecise in their racial definitions. Thus it appears that the principles of discrimination and integration prevail at the elite and middle class levels, respectively. From these data we do not obtain a clear picture for the other class groups.

The complex terminology of the infused racial system produces a situation in Cartagena in which only at the poles of the class pyramid do we find a majority of persons identifying themselves as polar racial types. Thus it is at the class extremes where the principle of discrimination is relatively predominant. However, in terms of the entire system, the principle of integration prevails. Indeed, in Cartagena we find a situation in which persons with different racial self-identities compete and intermarry freely at each class level, and a significant number of persons with the same racial self-identity is found infused at all class levels. That is, racial self-identities transcend class boundaries in Cartagena's nonfeudalistic racial system. Further, the complex and ambiguous racial nomenclature permits processes of terminological miscegenation by which the bulk of the population at all but the lowest-class level avoids Negroid self-identities.

We have seen that the elites are the discriminators and that the middle classes are racially complacent in Cartagena. From a structural point of view, the principles of discrimination and integration appear to operate simultaneously at the working-class level. On the one hand, they are aware that light individuals are found at the top of the class system, and, on the other, there is an absence of occupational racial discrimination at their own class level. These processes are reflected in their racial definitions of others, for, as we have seen, the working class tends to define as *blanco* persons with high-status characteristics, but, at the same time, they employ the term *moreno* for self-designation and for designations of others over a very great range of physical types. At the lowest-class level the principle of discrimination is heightened, for it is here that a majority of persons define themselves as *negro* and, at the same time, lighten others and define successful individuals as *blanco*. Thus we are left with a picture of racial polarization at the extremes of the class-race pyramid.

Although we have depicted pockets of racial tension in Cartagena, the overall racial system is adaptive. A most important determinant of this characteristic is the system of racial nomenclature that leads to a situation in which class is a more salient and rigid factor than race. Indeed, our analysis of the relationship between racial self-identity and perceptions of discrimination showed that to the extent that persons perceived relatively high levels of racial discrimination in the society, they identified themselves as non-Negroids. The exception to this pattern is found mainly at the lowest-class level where feelings of economic deprivation are equated to a polar racial identity. Thus, to the extent that Negroid individuals are economically successful in Cartagena, they either disassociate themselves with "Negritude," or if they maintain a Negroid identification, they perceive little racial discrimination in the society. In short, the process of terminological miscegenation permitted by the racial nomenclature of the infused racial system practically negates the possibility of a national racial movement. But before making a final statement on the dual Colombian experience of high levels of political and class, rather than racial strife and violence, we must explore the impact of social change on race relations in Cartagena, for, as noted in Chapter 4, this city has and is experiencing rapid social change.

NOTES

1. This case is forcefully made for Brazil in Charles Wagley, "From Caste to Class in North Brazil," *Comparative Perspectives on Race Relations, op. cit.,* p. 47.

2. Hutchinson, *op. cit.,* p. 27.

3. For a recent discussion on this topic see Marvin Harris, "Referential Ambiguity in the Calculus of Brazial Racial Identity," *Southwestern Journal of Anthropology, 26,* 1970, pp. 1—14 and Roger Sanjek, "Brazilian Racial Terms: Some Aspects of Meaning," *American Anthropologist, 73,* 1971, pp. 1126–1143.

4. A parallel case has been made by Pierson for Bahia, Brazil. See Pierson, *op. cit.,* pp. 138–139. Of course, in Cartagena the only exception was the slum dwellers.

5. The ambiguity of the term *moreno* has been widely acknowledged in the Brazilian literature.

6. Harris, "Race in Minas Velhas," *op. cit.,* p. 61.

7. See Hutchinson, *op. cit.,* p. 27.

8. In this sense, for Brazil see for instance, *ibid.,* p. 28.

9. For the sake of economy we have dropped one of the pictures because it was clearly that of an Oriental.

10. No elite respondent employed this term. The middle class used it 10 times, and here it was used in 25 cases.
11. This point is supported by our findings on the impact of dress on racial definitions presented later on in this chapter.
12. Zimmerman has noted a similar class effect in Brazil. See Zimmerman, *op. cit.*, p. 104.
13. These findings contrast to those of Brazil. See, for instance, Pierson, *op. cit.*, p. 140; Zimmerman, *op. cit.*, p. 94; and Wagley, *op. cit.*, p. 121.
14. See Chapter 5.
15. Indeed, Tumin and Feldman consider that skin color is more important than class in determining racial attitudes in Puerto Rico. See Tumin with Feldman, *op. cit.*, p. 210.

Chapter Seven

. . . .

SOCIAL CHANGE AND RACIAL
CONFLICT IN CARTAGENA

At the outset of this monograph we introduced two main interpretations concerning the absence of racial strife in Iberian
America: the pessimistic and the optimistic. Pessimists argue
that low levels of racial violence in the area are the product of
a feudalistic, static equilibrium that maintains effective racial
subordination. This interpretation considers that processes of
social change, such as class and geographical mobility and urbanization and industrialization, will produce the breakdown
of traditional racial integration and lead to conflict and violence in the future. In sharp contrast, the optimistic interpretation stresses that the traditional racial equilibrium found in
Latin America is based on the presence of relatively fluid racial boundaries and the absorption or full integration of miscegenated individuals into white society. They perceive the
tolerance-miscegenation syndrome as being highly operative in
the presence of social change—upward and geographical mobility.

Examples of these contradictory interpretations are readily
found in the literature. For instance, Harris considers that the
upward class mobility of Negroid individuals increases racial

tension (1). On the other hand, Pierson has linked upward class mobility to miscegenation (2). Concerning the topic of geographical mobility, here again we find contrasting interpretations. For instance, Whitten traces the occupational subordination and displacement of blacks to *mestizo* migrations (3), whereas Mörner relates them to miscegenation (4), and Zimmerman considers migrations as a mechanism for successful miscegenation, particularly for polar racial types (5).

The reader is aware by now that our position is close to that of the optimists. Although we have acknowledged that interclass, not intraclass upward mobility increases awareness of prejudice in Cartagena, we have also seen that interclass upwardly mobile groups project feelings about the desirability of the bleaching process and that this process is, in fact, operative in the city. There is also evidence that the upward mobility of Negroid individuals produces racial adaptation in Cartagena. In effect, we have seen that except for the lowest-class group—by definition, nonmobile within the Cartagena context—insofar as persons perceive racial discrimination, they have (adopt) a non-Negroid self-identity, and conversely, those individuals who have (maintain) a Negroid identity are relatively complacent with the racial situation in Cartagena. In short, the mechanisms of adaptation provided by the infused racial system appear to prevail in the city.

In this chapter we address ourselves to geographical mobility, another aspect of social change, as it affects relations in Cartagena. We begin with a brief analysis of the structural and attitudinal components of race and class at one of the sources of migration, small towns surrounding Cartagena.

RACE IN THE RURAL AREAS

As with any large city, Cartagena is surrounded by villages and towns of varying sizes. Toward the coast, settlements are predominantly Negroid, but as one moves inland *mestizo* elements dominate. To obtain a picture of rural racial patterns we investigated structural and attitudinal racial aspects in four villages—populations range from 1500 to 7000—and in a town of approximately 20,000 inhabitants. Given our interest in black-white relations, all our sites had significant proportions of Negroes.

The structure of class and race found in areas that surround Cartagena can be seen as forming a continuum, from relative homogeneity of class and race to more differentiated structures. That is, in the smallest villages a subsistence economy prevails, and economic differences between individuals are small. From the perspective of the differentiated national society, the most successful persons in these villages fall into a lower-class category. In racial terms, these villages tend to be relatively homogeneous. The population is highly Negroid, and whites are rarely found there.

As community size and wealth increase, we find more differentiated structures with greater economic differences between individuals. In our town of 20,000 it is possible to speak of at least two clear classes: the upper-middle class, composed of professionals, businessmen, and white collar workers; and, the working-lower class, composed of skilled and unskilled manual laborers (6). In terms of the national society, the bulk of successful individuals in these communities appear to belong to the middle class. At this level of class differentiation racial heterogeneity increases to the point of finding *blancos*, miscegenated individuals of various characteristics, and *negros*.

If we were to look for parallels in the Cartagena society to the rural structures, the small villages would be represented by the poverty-stricken, highly Negroid slums. However, the racially heterogeneous towns already reflect the Cartagena infused racial system, for here it is rare to find heavily Negroid persons at the highest economic level, the bulk of the blacks live in poverty and in relatively segregated ecological locations, and the top of the class pyramid is *blanco*-miscegenated. In this respect, as hypothesized, it appears that the infused racial system manifests itself in the area when significant proportions of racial groups enter into contact.

To explore the racial attitudes that accompany the described rural structural characteristics we surveyed attitudes in these areas. Our preliminary explorations revealed very low levels of racial awareness in the small villages. Thus we concentrated our attention in the larger town. To this effect we interviewed 78 persons, 26 belonging to the upper-middle category and 52 to the working-lower group. The upper-middle group considered itself predominantly *blanco* (approximately 60 percent). The remainder considered that they were miscegenated, not *negros,* and employed various terms to define this condition. Approximately 40 percent of the working-lower sample defined itself as *negro,* and none as *blanco.* Our respondents were predominantly male, and practically all of them were born in small towns or villages. Table 7.1 presents the class patterns of racial attitudes for the two groups.

The overall pattern that emerges from our sample is one of low levels of racial awareness. This is particularly the case of the working-lower class group (see questions 1 and 13). Within this relatively traditional context we find practically no physical color bar, nor the fear for the potential for violence in "slum areas" that we had found in Cartagena (see questions 18 and 19). Most persons in our town believe that there is a lot of race mixture in the area and that the racial factor can be overcome (see questions 2, 7, 8, and 9). In this respect, the response patterns are similar to those found in Cartagena. Also, as in Cartagena, preference for skin color follows the physical characteristics of the respondents; light persons preferred light skin color, and dark ones, dark skin (see question 3). Further, both class groups indicated a preference for the bleaching process (see question 17). However, in contrast to Cartagena, we found feelings of lesser racial distance in the

TABLE 7.1   Racial Attitudes of Rural Class Groups
(in Percentages)

	Upper-Middle Class	Lower-Working Class
Is there racial discrimination here? (Q. 1):		
Yes	42	40
No	58	60
No information	—	—
Total	100	100
In the life cycle of a person as he grows older, are friendships lost for racial reasons? (Q. 13):		
Yes	42	19
No	58	81
No information	—	—
Total	100	100
Are there places here where Negroes are not admitted? (Q. 19):		
Yes	12	4
No	88	96
No information	—	—
Total	100	100
Is there a sector here where only colored people live where it is dangerous for a white person to visit? (Q. 18):		
Yes	—	4
No	100	96
No information	—	—
Total	100	100
Is there a lot of race mixture here? (Q. 2):		
Yes	65	75
No	35	21
No information	—	4
Total	100	100

	Upper-Middle Class	Lower-Working Class
Is it better to have white or dark skin here? (Q. 3):		
White	69	40
Dark	23	58
No information	8	2
Total	100	100
Is the Brazilian refrain "money whitens" true here? (Q. 9):		
Yes	81	69
No	12	19
No information	8	12
Total	100	100
What is most important in life, money, education or racial characteristics? (Q. 7):		
Money	15	12
Education	73	81
Racial characteristics	12	6
No information	—	2
Total	100	100
If a person with dark racial characteristics dresses well and is educated, is he treated the same as a light person? (Q. 8):		
Yes	69	75
No	12	21
No information	19	4
Total	100	100
Would it bother you to have a colored boss? (Q. 23):		
Yes	23	6
No	77	94
No information	—	—
Total	100	100

TABLE 7.1   Racial Attitudes of Rural Class Groups
(in percentages) (*Continued*)

	Upper-Middle Class	Lower-Working Class
Would it bother you if a member of your immediate family married a colored person? (Q. 24):		
Yes	46	19
No	54	81
No information	—	—
Total	100	100
Do persons here wish to have children whiter than themselves? (Q. 17):		
Yes	96	77
No	—	23
No information	4	—
Total	100	100
N	26	52

town, because even the light group did not manifest a strong concern against mixed marriages in their own families (see questions 23 and 24).

In sum, in contrast to Cartagena, we found in our town a relatively lower awareness of racial prejudice and discrimination. Further, the Cartagena-rural differences appear to be concentrated among the relatively poor groups, for we have seen that in Cartagena the middle class is also relatively complacent in racial matters, the opposite being the case for persons of a low economic position found in the slums. Thus it appears that the process of urbanization has an impact on racial attitudes, at least among some class groups. It is to this question that we must address ourselves now.

URBANIZATION AND RACIAL ATTITUDES

To explore the plausible impact of urbanization on race relations in Cartagena we first analyzed the racial attitudes of the various class groups according to whether persons were born in Cartagena or had migrated there from rural areas. We could not analyze the elite and servant groups because very few elites were not born in Cartagena and only a slight proportion of the servants were not born in small towns. Table 7.2 presents the resulting patterns.

The analysis of question 1 (Is there racial discrimination in Cartagena?) indicates that with the exception of the solid middle class—persons who are relatively successful in Cartagena —those individuals who migrated to the city perceived slightly more discrimination. This is understandable because, as we have seen, there is relatively less awareness of discrimination in the outlying areas of Cartagena. However, the responses to question 4, a more specific question dealing with racial discrimination, showed a reversal in the pattern. These weak patterns that neutralize themselves suggest that whether a person was born in Cartagena or migrated from a small town does not highly affect his racial attitudes. But before we conclude our analysis let us proceed with the investigation of Table 7.2.

When asked about racial discrimination in terms of friendships lost during the life cycle (question 13) we find that there is a slightly greater awareness of discrimination on the part of native *cartageneros*. However, with the exception of the slum dwellers, native *cartageneros* of most of the other class groups perceive less of a color bar against Negroes than migrants. On the other hand, and this is understandable, migrants are more likely to feel that there are sections of Cartagena where it is dangerous for whites to go (see question 18).

The analysis of the remaining questions contained in our table indicate that the factor of place of birth (e.g., migration)

TABLE 7.2 Urban-Rural Attitudes by Class Groups (in Percentages)

| | Middle Class | | | | Working Class | | | | Lower Class | |
| | Solid Middle Class | | Middle-Class Aspirants | | Labor Leaders | | Solid Working Class | | Slum Dwellers | |
	Cartagena	Town	Cartagena	Town	Cartagena	Town	Cartagena	Town	Cartagena	Town
Is there racial discrimination in Cartagena? (Q. 1)										
Yes	25	17	58	68	17	31	46	50	68	70
No	75	83	39	26	83	69	46	46	32	30
No information	—	—	3	5	—	—	9	4	—	—
Total	100	100	100	100	100	100	100	100	100	100
Are persons treated differently here because of racial characteristics? (Q. 4)										
Yes	25	50	61	58	58	46	50	46	63	60
No	75	50	29	32	25	46	41	31	32	35
No information	—	—	10	10	17	8	9	23	5	5
Total	100	100	100	100	100	100	100	100	100	100
In the life cycle of a person, are friendships lost for racial reasons? (Q. 13)										
Yes	67	50	81	63	50	38	41	38	37	35
No	33	50	19	32	50	62	55	58	63	60
No information	—	—	—	5	—	—	4	4	—	5
Total	100	100	100	100	100	100	100	100	100	100

Are there places in Cartagena where Negroes are not admitted? (Q. 18)

Yes	50	50	52	58	50	54	50	65	74	60
No	50	50	39	37	42	46	46	23	26	40
No information	—	—	10	5	8	—	4	12	—	—
Total	100	100	100	100	100	100	100	100	100	100

Is there a sector in the city where only colored people live where it is dangerous for a white person to visit? (Q. 18)

Yes	50	42	39	58	25	54	36	50		
No	50	50	55	42	67	46	59	42		
No information	—	8	6	—	8	—	4	8		
Total	100	100	100	100	100	100	100	100		

Is there a lot of race mixture in Cartagena? (Q. 2)

Yes	92	100	94	84	100	100	100	88	100	85
No	8	—	6	16	—	—	—	4	—	10
No information	—	—	—	—	—	—	—	8	—	5
Total	100	100	100	100	100	100	100	100	100	100

Is it better to have white or dark skin in Cartagena? (Q. 3)

White	50	42	39	32	42	23	23	23	21	35
Dark	17	—	16	47	42	31	32	46	63	40
No difference	33	58	36	21	17	46	36	27	16	20
No information	—	—	10	—	—	—	9	4	—	5
Total	100	100	100	100	100	100	100	100	100	100

TABLE 7.2 Urban-Rural Attitudes by Class Groups (in Percentages) *(continued)*

	Middle Class				Working Class				Lower Class	
	Solid Middle Class		Middle-Class Aspirants		Labor Leaders		Solid Working Class		Slum Dwellers	
	Cartagena	Town	Cartagena	Town	Cartagena	Town	Cartagena	Town	Cartagena	Town
Is the Brazilian refrain "money whitens" true here? (Q. 9)										
Yes	75	75	74	58	58	46	64	62	79	80
No	17	25	19	21	33	38	32	23	21	15
No information	8	—	6	21	8	15	4	15	—	5
Total	100	100	100	100	100	100	100	100	100	100
What is most important in life: money, education, or racial characteristics? (Q. 7)										
Money	8	—	3	5	17	8	4	12	—	—
Education	67	100	90	90	58	85	91	69	84	85
Racial characteristics	—	—	—	5	—	—	—	—	10	10
Don't know, other	25	—	6	—	25	8	4	19	5	5
Total	100	100	100	100	100	100	100	100	100	100
If a person with dark racial characteristics dresses well and is educated, is he treated the same as a light person? (Q. 8)										
Yes	92	75	81	74	67	85	82	69	84	75
No	8	17	19	26	33	15	14	31	16	25
No information	—	8	—	—	—	—	4	—	—	—
Total	100	100	100	100	100	100	100	100	100	100

Would it bother you to have a colored boss? (Q. 23)

Yes	—	17	—	—	—	—	—	4	16	10
No	100	83	94	100	100	92	100	88	84	90
No information	—	—	6	—	—	8	—	8	—	—
Total	100	100	100	100	100	100	100	100	100	100

Would it bother you if a member of your immediate family married a colored person? (Q. 24)

Yes	17	42	16	21	17	15	18	15	26	40
No	83	58	74	79	83	77	82	77	74	60
No information	—	—	10	—	—	8	—	8	—	—
Total	100	100	100	100	100	100	100	100	100	100

Do persons here wish to have children lighter than themselves? (Q. 17)

Yes	75	75	81	84	67	54	68	73	68	75
No	17	25	19	10	33	46	23	19	26	25
No information	8	—	—	5	—	—	9	8	5	—
Total	100	100	100	100	100	100	100	100	100	100
N	12	12	31	19	12	13	22	26	19	20

Note: Information on place of birth was lacking on 4 labor leaders and 2 slum dwellers.

TABLE 7.3   Racial Attitudes and Place of Birth
by Racial Identity (in Percentages)

	Blanco		Mixed		Negro	
	Carta-gena	Town	Carta-gena	Town	Carta-gena	Town
Is there racial discrimination in Cartagena? (Q. 1):						
Yes	64	62	48	47	68	67
No	36	38	49	50	32	33
No information	—	—	3	3	—	—
Total	100	100	100	100	100	100
Are persons treated differently here because of racial characteristics? (Q. 4):						
Yes	73	62	55	50	74	53
No	27	31	44	40	21	40
No information	—	8	1	10	5	7
Total	100	100	100	100	100	100
In the life cycle of a person, are friendships lost for racial reasons? (Q. 13):						
Yes	82	54	63	43	32	40
No	18	46	37	53	68	60
No information	—	—	—	4	—	—
Total	100	100	100	100	100	100
Are there places in Cartagena where Negroes are not admitted? (Q. 19):						
Yes	46	77	52	51	74	60
No	54	23	44	43	26	33
No information	—	—	4	5	—	7
Total	100	100	100	100	100	100

	Blanco		Mixed		Negro	
	Carta-gena	Town	Carta-gena	Town	Carta-gena	Town

Is there a sector in the city where only colored people live where it is dangerous for a white person to visit? (Q. 18):

	Carta-gena	Town	Carta-gena	Town	Carta-gena	Town
Yes	46	54	48	54	30	38
No	54	38	49	42	70	62
No information	—	8	3	4	—	—
Total	100	100	100	100	100	100

Is there a lot of race mixture in Cartagena? (Q. 2):

	Carta-gena	Town	Carta-gena	Town	Carta-gena	Town
Yes	96	92	96	93	100	80
No	4	8	4	4	—	13
No information	—	—	—	3	—	7
Total	100	100	100	100	100	100

Is it better to have white or dark skin in Cartagena? (Q. 3):

	Carta-gena	Town	Carta-gena	Town	Carta-gena	Town
White	68	46	35	24	26	40
Dark	—	15	30	40	53	40
No difference	27	38	32	35	21	7
No information	4	—	3	—	—	13
Total	100	100	100	100	100	100

Is the Brazilian refrain "money whitens" true here? (Q. 9):

	Carta-gena	Town	Carta-gena	Town	Carta-gena	Town
Yes	73	69	69	69	84	67
No	27	23	24	23	16	13
No information	—	8	7	8	—	20
Total	100	100	100	100	100	100

TABLE 7.3   Racial Attitudes and Place of Birth
by Racial Identity (in Percentages) (*Continued*)

	Blanco		Mixed		Negro	
	Carta-gena	Town	Carta-gena	Town	Carta-gena	Town
What is most important in life, money, education, or racial characteristics? (Q. 7):						
Money	9	—	6	8	—	—
Education	59	92	79	81	95	87
Racial characteristics	—	8	3	4	—	7
Don't know, other	32	—	13	7	5	7
Total	100	100	100	100	100	100
If a person with dark racial characteristics dresses well and is educated is he treated the same as a light person? (Q. 8):						
Yes	73	85	78	76	90	80
No	27	15	22	24	10	20
No information	—	—	—	—	—	—
Total	100	100	100	100	100	100
Would it bother you to have a colored boss? (Q. 23):						
Yes	23	8	1	7	16	13
No	77	92	96	89	84	80
No information	—	—	3	4	—	7
Total	100	100	100	100	100	100
Would it bother you if a member of your immediate family married a colored person? (Q. 24):						
Yes	59	23	18	20	32	40
No	41	77	78	76	68	53
No information	—	—	4	4	—	7
Total	100	100	100	100	100	100

	Blanco		Mixed		Negro	
	Carta-gena	Town	Carta-gena	Town	Carta-gena	Town
Do persons here wish to have children lighter than themselves? (Q. 17):						
Yes	91	69	70	70	84	87
No	9	31	25	26	10	7
No information	—	—	4	4	5	7
Total	100	100	100	100	100	100
N	22	13	71	74	19	15

Notes: Information on place of birth was lacking for 11 mixed and 3 *negros*. The number of cases for question 19 is lower because the slum dwellers were not asked this question.

does not determine in a significant manner the racial attitudes of our respondents. Of course, this contrasts sharply to our findings about the role of class and racial self-identity in the determination of racial patterns.

Let us now turn our attention to the relationship between place of birth and racial self-identity as it affects racial attitudes. Table 7.3 presents this relationship.

The analysis of the first two questions on racial discrimination (see questions 1 and 4) indicates that a slightly higher proportion of native *cartageneros*, regardless of their racial self-identity, perceive higher levels of discrimination than the migrants. Yet we must stress that this relationship is very weak. In reference to the next two questions, which deal with the loss of friendships for racial reasons and the presence of a physical color bar, questions 13 and 19, once again we see that no clear pattern emerges. Furthermore, migrants are again more prone to perceive the existence of areas of Cartagena that are dangerous for whites (question 18) than native-born *cartageneros*. Finally, the urban-rural place of birth factor does not produce a consistent pattern in terms of the remaining questions that were analyzed.

Let us recapitulate. In this chapter we have attempted to bring our data to bear on the controversy between optimists and pessimists on the role of one of the processes of social change—rural-urban migration—on race relation in Cartagena, a city which has and is experiencing rapid urban change. Our exploration of the rural areas that surround Cartagena suggested the presence of a relatively low awareness of prejudice and discrimination in these areas. This finding, coupled with that of the awareness found in the racially quasi-homogeneous, quasi-rural, economically deprived slums of Cartagena, led us to consider that urbanization heightens perceptions of discrimination. Yet we have seen that the attitudes of persons living in Cartagena are not affected by migration in a consistent or significant way. This basically means that class position and racial self-identity are more powerful determinants of the racial outlook of individuals than migration.

We must avoid the fallacy of composition, that is, attributing properties of the parts to the whole. Although the urbanization experience does not significantly affect the racial attitudes of persons of the same class group *currently* living in Cartagena, this is not to say that urbanization has no effect on race relations, for it certainly does. Obviously, to the extent that urbanization affects the overall class structure of the society, it has racial consequences. Thus far in the history of Cartagena the mechanisms of adaptation we have described have prevailed to produce more conspicuous and higher levels of class prejudice and tension than racial conflict and strife. However, to the extent that social change leads to increases in the size of a Negroid *lumpenproletariat*, the potential for racial conflict increases, for we know that there is racial "discontent" in Cartagena's slums. Nevertheless, given the described mechanisms of the infused racial system, the probability that grievances will take racial, rather than class, overtones appear to be low in the near future. It is our opinion that the structural characteristics of the infused racial system that is traditional in Cartagena are resilient enough to minimize the development of substantial, overt racial strife in the forseeable future.

NOTES

1. Harris, "Race in Minas Velhas," *op. cit.* Also see Mörner, *op. cit.* pp. 66–67.
2. Pierson, *op. cit.*
3. Whitten, *op. cit.* For a similar interpretation for white migrations see Fernandes, *op. cit.*
4. Mörner, *op. cit.*, p. 75.
5. Zimmerman, *op. cit.*, p. 109.
6. The reader should be aware that we are not denying that the surveyed structures are much more complex than presented here. Our objective is simply to establish characteristics that are pertinent for our investigation.

Chapter Eight

. . . .

RACIAL DISCRIMINATION
WITHOUT VIOLENCE:
AN INTERPRETATION

In this monograph we have attempted to explain the historical phenomenon found in Latin America of relative high levels of political and class conflict and low levels of overt racial conflict. We focused our investigation on the infused racial system primarily because its compositional properties of sufficient proportions of whites and blacks provide the most probable setting for the generation of racial conflict. The potential for conflict is not nearly as strong in more racial homogeneous areas such as in the European and *mestizo* national complexes. It is in the relatively heterogeneous infused system, which combines the historical dominance of whites with substantial proportions of the most *racially* discriminated-against blacks, that the potential for conflict is greatest, for in Iberian America regions with a highly homogeneous black population are uncommon. Thus the analysis of this system is crucial for the understanding of our research problem.

Several reasons led us to select Cartagena. First, there are no studies of the infused racial system in Colombia. By selecting a research site in this country we were able to broaden the base of the empirical investigation of race relations in Iberian America. Cartagena was chosen in particular because it is a city with a long-established aristocratic tradition, and it is experiencing rapid social change manifested in class, not racial, conflict in the support given to antisystem political forces. This setting seemed propitious to explore whether the absence of racial conflict in the area is the product of a paternalistic, feudalistic system of racial control that is breaking down with the sociopolitical mobilization of nonwhites that accompanies social change.

The race-class structure of Cartagena is typical of racially heterogeneous areas in Negroid Iberian America and is characterized by the presence of two principles: the principle of discrimination and the principle of integration. The first principle finds its ultimate expression in the closed racial system which is characterized by endogamy, hierarchical race relations, and a lack of acceptance of miscegenation. On the other hand, the second principle underlies the ideal-type, open racial system with exogamy, racial homogeneity—total miscegenation or a single racial group—and nonhierarchical race relationships. We have defined the eclectic racial system of Cartagena in which both principles coexist simultaneously as the infused racial system. The principle of discrimination finds expression in this system in that endogamous relationships prevail among the polar racial types and there is a direct relationship between color and class. However, integration is also present because persons with different racial characteristics intermarry freely and relate to each other in a nonhierarchical manner. The integration principle is the direct result of the acceptance of the miscegenated, not blacks, which leads to a situation in which *blancos* and miscegenated persons of the same class intermarry freely, and in which mixed bloods are found infused and competing throughout the entire class pyramid.

Our investigaton indicates the eclectic nature of the Cartagena racial system. In effect, we found predominantly *blanco* and *negro* upper and lower classes, respectively. The upper class consistently appeared as the discriminators, and the lower class felt discriminated against. In addition, the upper class verbally upheld endogamy and maintained hierarchical race relations by blocking the access to its ranks of upwardly mobile Negroid individuals. However, the principle of integration also operates in Cartagena. Indeed, even at the elite level there is a recognition of exogamy and nonhierarchical race relations, for our respondents recognized substantial miscegenation within their own intimate elite circles. Many persons of the highest standing in the community freely acknowledged their mixed ancestry. Second, with the exception of the upper class, the majority of *cartageneros* verbally upheld exogamy. In addition to these factors, the overall pattern of response in the area was that race is not a paramount deterrent to success in the city. There is firm support for the ideology that "money whitens." *Cartageneros* are aware of the infused racial system in which they live, with discrimination centered against *negros,* but with the existence of very high levels of miscegenation and the full integration of miscegenated individuals at all levels of the social class structure.

Up to this point we have briefly recapitulated the static characteristics of the closed, open, and infused racial systems. We must now turn to the dynamic aspects of the three systems. In the closed system, "equilibrium" is maintained by enforcement of endogamy, hierarchical group relationships, and the myth of racial purity, either by normative acceptance or coercion. However, this equilibrium is unstable because the system is prone to break down when the subordinated group no longer accepts its inferior position. The acceptance of miscegenation breaks down the closed system because, in the long run, this condition brings about racial equalization, the direct opposite of the fundamental principle of the closed system. The closed system also enters a state of disequilibrium, when through mechanisms of social change racial ascription is eroded and racial groups engage in competition with another. These processes are tied to racial strife, violence, and the generation of racist national movements. The open racial system, on the other hand, finds itself in a situation of stable equilibrium in that it is impervious to change because race is not a factor in social relations. The dynamic element of this system is that individuals with different physical characteristics intermarry and compete freely with each other without forming groups along different physical or racial lines. Thus in this system conflict develops in spheres other than race.

Where does the infused system fit within the outlined framework? This system was the product of a pigmentocracy that included slavery and coexisted with high levels of miscegenation and the acceptance of mixed bloods into white society. It is not biological miscegenation per se but its acceptance under the cultural mechanism of terminological miscegenation that typifies the infused system. In terms of equilibrium, the infused system has been characterized as a condition of an evolutionary, long-run, dynamic equilibrium. That is, the tensions produced by discrimination have been more than offset by the adaptive mechanisms of the system whereby overt racial protest is minimized. As recognized by *cartageneros,* the dynamics of the infused racial system consist of the tolerance-miscegenation syndrome by which the miscegenated are accepted, miscegenation is high, and there is a belief in the racial mobility of individuals, not aggregates.

The main sources of racial tension found in the infused system are related to the imperfect operation of the tolerance-miscegenation syndrome which is exacerbated by social change. First, given the preference for lightness, there is little sexual contact between the racial poles. The poor in the black community have little opportunity to miscegenate—economic and ethnic factors compound physical ones to block this process—and these aggregates grow as the result of rural-urban migration. Second, there are the upwardly mobile Negroid persons who in the process of achieving interclass mobility are discriminated against and become racially sensitive prior to the fulfillment of the mechanisms by which "money whitens." However, our data indicate that these tensions are outweighed by the tolerance-miscegenation syndrome. In effect, successful *negros* can and do miscegenate in Cartagena. They accomplish this in two ways: biologically and terminologically. The first process—which reduces the number of highly Negroid persons as one ascends the socioeconomic ladder, thus reducing the potential for racial conflict—is facilitated by the structural characteristic of the infused system that provides an adequate marriage pool of relatively poor light individuals available to successful blacks for miscegenation. In the second process, the complex and ambiguous racial nomenclature of Iberian America permits the manipulation of racial self-identity to accommodate racial sensitivities, for, as we have seen, relatively successful Negroid individuals who are racially self-conscious tend to change their identity by utilizing terms that do not connote black ancestry. Conversely, those persons who are not racially sensitive maintain a Negroid self-identity. Thus, in the infused system overt feelings of Negritude are adaptive.

In Cartagena the class factor is more potent than the racial one, producing a situation of greater class partisanship or conflict. When we "control" for the class factor, we find the effects of race highly attenuated. First, it is the *fusion* of poverty with blackness that produces relatively high levels of racial sensitivity among slum-dwellers. Second, to the extent that persons belong to the same social class, there is a tendency to transform racial characteristics into physical attributes. Thus, when interclass mobility is successful, the above-mentioned racial tensions are reduced. Finally, the relatively low salience of the racial factor is found in that some *cartageneros* of all social classes share the same racial self-identity. For example, there are persons who call themselves *mestizos, morenos,* and *trigeños* who live in the best and worst social sectors of the city; that is, they are found in the elite social club and in the slums. Obviously, class distinctions are far more clear than racial ones in Cartagena, and from a political science perspective it is very difficult to form effective, nonaggregative, political movements representing polar racial groups.

We must address ourselves now to the question of what the factors were that contributed to the development of the infused racial system in Iberian America, a system where the essential adaptive ingredient was the *cultural* tolerance toward the miscegenated, which furthered miscegenation, which in turn furthered tolerance—that is, the tolerance-miscegenation syndrome. One of the major factors purported to explain different racial systems has been population proportions. Proportions do have an impact on racial patterns. Indeed, the volume of biological miscegenation found in the society is dependent on proportions. Nevertheless, the Anglo-Saxon lack of acceptance of the miscegenated had led in the Western Hemisphere to white-dominated caste relationships regardless of population proportions. In contrast, in the Iberian American variant the tolerance toward the miscegenated had led to relatively racially homogeneous societies; cultural factors outweighed structural ones. At one end of the continuum heavy European migration and a residual Indian population have produced basically European societies. In those societies with an overwhelming Indian presence, the *racial* result has been *mestizo* or miscegenated societies. As we have seen, even the relatively heterogeneous infused racial sysem is much more homogeneous than their Anglo-Saxon counterparts. The racial adaptability of Iberian American societies is domonstrated by the relatively historical absence of racial conflict. In Latin America there was an adequate level of European migration during the colonial period that, linked with racial tolerance, produced racial compositions at the elite level which reflected sufficiently the racial compositions of the societies such that the wars of independence were not racial in nature.

Another major interpretation of racial systems is the *Gemeinschaft-Gesellschaft* sociological model with its emphasis on the competitive variable. Briefly, the former envisions a society characterized by paternalism, ascription, and elitist rule.

In the absence of racial competition relations between the races are "intimate." The latter is characterized by an ideology of achievement and equalitarianism, where racial contacts are of a threatening nature because racial groups are prone to compete in the stratification system. Under such a dynamic system the propensity is toward racial avoidance and competitive strife. The main weakness of this ahistorical, macrosociological explanation is its failure to account for the transition from an alleged noncompetitive, quasi-feudal order, with high levels of miscegenation, to the actual high levels of interpersonal competition between persons of different racial characteristics that, as we have seen, typifies the Latin American infused racial system. Another case in point is the attempt to explain contemporary racial systems in terms of restrictive, economic deterministic interpretations such as the effort to link them to specific systems of slavery, for, as we have discussed, similar contemporary racial patterns have developed from a variety of slave systems. In sum, the construction of interpretative general models that attempt to explain variations in contemporary racial patterns without taking into account the unique historical phenomena that produced them are erroneous. On the other hand, historically biased interpretations that rely excessively on a particular historical phenomenon to explain current racial systems also leave much to be desired. From our point of view, to explain contemporary racial systems and to make adequate projections of their future development, it is necessary to analyze current racial patterns in the context of their historical trends. That is, we subscribe to the strategy of the historical sociologist.

To return to the question of the factors that produced the Iberian American infused racial system under adequate proportions of whites and blacks, we believe that the major determinant of this system was the ideology of acceptance of the miscegenated manifested during the colonial period, coexisting with the harsh institution of slavery. From a historical-sociological perspective, we see that the current system of racial terminology is the fundamental indicator of this ideology of racial tolerance and that this nomenclature can be traced to the precolonial period in the Iberian peninsula. The racial nomenclature of contemporary Cartagena is the most important feature of racial tolerance and adaptation in the area because its complex ambiguity leads to a situation in which racial definitions are highly unreliable and racial self-identities are achieved rather than ascribed. Further, the current employment of Moorish-derived terms in Cartagena and in Latin America to designate whites and nonwhites, and sexual symbols, indicates the important role of precolonial Iberian historical experiences in the development of the infused racial system. In addition to the Moorish conquest, there is another interpretation that transcends the *Gemeinschaft-Gesellschaft* model and restrictive economic interpretations, which can be linked to the acceptance toward the miscegenated: the somatic likeness. We have seen that this factor operated during the colonial period to facilitate racial mobility.

With the conspicuous exceptions of the Moorish conquest, with its impact on the *acceptance* of darker individuals and the somatic or physical determinist interpretation, most of the factors that scholars have considered to produce the tolerance-miscegenation syndrome and its resultant infused racial system can be seen to exemplify paternalistic themes. Indeed, the tradition with slavery; a relatively unproductive "colonial" economy characterized by low levels of social mobilization; a colonial political structure heavily influenced by the hierarchical, ecumenical, and benevolent orientations of the Catholic Church; and the traditional cultural ethos of *personalismo-machismo*, all can be linked to paternalistic orientations. Of course, these sociohistorical factors can be seen to be congruent with some of the characteristics of the highly abstract, sociological *Gemeinschaft* ideal type. However, they transcend such a conceptualization. For example, a tradition with slavery is not a necessary condition for the emergence of *Gemeinschaft* societies. Further, in historical or empirical terms,

tensions are found between the abstract sociological concep-
tualizations and some of the factors. Such is the case of the
role of Catholicism with its "universalistic" ecumenism,
on the one hand, and its "particularistic" traditional hierarchical conceptualization of the social order.

We have already discussed at length the ways in which particular variables appear to have most probably affected the
relative racial openness of Iberian American racial patterns.
Both the acceptance of the miscegenated and adequate population proportions are necessary conditions for the emergence
of the infused racial system, although the latter is not a sufficient cause. Given the dearth of empirical studies addressed to
the answering of the problem of population proportions
we deal with this variable as a given. In addition to the
Moorish conquest and the somatic interpretation, we have
acknowledged that although racial adaptation in Latin America cannot be equated with the absence of interpersonal racial
competition, the cultural orientations associated with a capitalistic-competitive system—and we must emphasize, puritanical orientations—appear to pose a cultural stress on the type
of racial acceptance that characterizes the infused system. Indeed, these orientations can be linked to *Herrenvolk* democracies. In addition, we have considered Catholicism as a reinforcer of the tradition with slavery and have related the role
of the Catholic church, with its corporate sociopolitical
philosophy—as opposed to Protestant individualistic pluralism—to a mild racial system. Finally, we have linked the
preindustrial, precapitalist economy to the traditional, personalistic, cultural ethos and to the racial tolerance syndrome.

We are now left with two alternative ways of explaining the
development of the infused racial system. The first and easiest
is to say that it was the combination of all the factors that can
be linked logically to the emergence of the system that produced it. The second alternative is far more difficult, and that
would be to assign relative weights to each of the factors. In
order to do this in an adequate fashion we would need a suffi-

cient number of cases so that we could assign values to the variables. Unfortunately, in the Western Hemisphere we find too few cases for this systematic type of analysis.

There are three factors unique to Iberian American civilization that can be linked to the infused racial system: the Moorish conquest, the tradition with slavery, and the ethos of *personalismo-machismo* of the dominant group. Consequently, these factors cannot be rejected. There are three other factors —the church, the somatic, and the economy—that can be linked to racial tolerance but have not produced the infused system in other contexts. The French colonization and the case of Guyana are exceptions that undermine the power of these three variables. A simplistic way of dealing with this problem is to reject these factors. However, many crucial sociological variables, although necessary for the emergence of important social institutions, are not sufficient; that is, their effects are conditioned by the presence of other variables. Thus we prefer not to exclude them from the constellation of factors that led to the infused system. We hope that by our formalization of the infused racial system, and the mode of analysis followed in the monograph, a direction has been given to students of the comparative study of race relations for the eventual determination of the sociohistorical variables that produced it. Only by the investigation of societies with different historical and cultural contexts can a more valid theory of the infused system materialize.

Our analysis of the current racial situation in Cartagena reveals the predominance of mechanisms of racial adaption over those of tension. The history of the city appears to have witnessed an early materialization of the infused racial system that has prevailed throughout periods of social change. The changes in the class-race pyramid of Cartagena have basically been an expansion of the middle class within the context of evolutionary processes of miscegenation. The infused racial system was institutionalized in Cartagena during an early period and has been highly resilient. There are reasons to believe that the path toward a more open racial system in Cartagena will take the form of interclass conflict, as in Cuba, with only lesser racial undertones, and that this process of class mobilization will most likely lead to a more homogeneous, miscegenated, open racial system.

Appendix A

. . . .

THE QUESTIONNAIRE

a. Age
b. Sex
c. Place of birth
d. Time in Cartagena
e. Race

Question
1. Is there racial discrimination in Cartagena?
2. Is there a lot of race mixture in Cartagena?
3. Is it better to have white or dark skin in Cartagena?
4. Are persons treated differently because of racial characteristics?
5. Are there many important people here who have nonwhite ancestors?
6. Are there many persons here who pass for white who are not white?
7. What is most important in life, money, education, or racial characteristics?
8. If a person with dark racial characteristics dresses well and is educated, is he treated the same as a light person?
9. Is the Brazilian refrain "money whitens" true here?
10. Do you believe that in Cartagena a greater percentage of

nonwhites are successful in political rather than in economic-elite activities?

11. Do you believe that in Cartagena a greater percentage of nonwhites are successful in political rather than in social-elite activities?

12. Do you believe that the younger generation has different racial attitudes than the older generation?

13. In the life cycle of a person, as he grows older, are friendships lost for racial reasons?

14. Are colored women treated better than colored men in Cartagena?

15. In some societies there is the belief that mulatto women are sexually superior to white women. Is this the case in Cartagena?

16. In some societies there is the belief that *negros* are more virile than white men. Is this the case in Cartagena?

17. Do persons here wish to have children whiter than themselves?

18. Is there a sector in the city where only colored people live, where it is dangerous for a white person to visit?

19. Are there places here where Negroes are not admitted?

20. Do you think that race relations here are paternalistic in nature?

21. Do you believe that it is the Spanish cultural heritage that accounts for the better treatment of the colored people here than in the United States?

22. Would it bother you always to work with colored people?

23. Would it bother you if you had a colored boss?

24. Would it bother you if a member of your immediate family married a colored person?

BIBLIOGRAPHY

Abshire, David M. "The Portuguese Racial Legacy," in David M. Abshire and Michael A. Samuels, Eds., *Portuguese Africa, A Handbook*. New York: Praeger, 1969.

———, and Norman A. Bailey. "Current Racial Character," in David M. Abshire and Michael A. Samuels, Eds., *Portuguese Africa, A Handbook*. New York: Praeger, 1969.

Adams, Romanzo. "The Unorthodox Race Doctrine of Hawaii," in Melvin M. Tumin, Ed., *Comparative Perspectives on Race Relations*. Boston: Little, Brown, 1969.

Almanch de Gotha pour l'anné, 1810.

Almanch de Gotha pour l'anné, 1889.

Alonzo Pinzón, Martín. "Zaguán," in Donaldo Bossa Herazo, *Cartagena Independiente: Tradición y Desarrollo*. Bogota: Tercer Mundo, 1967.

Anuario Estadístico de Colombia, 1943, 1953.

Ashton, Guy T. *The Differential Socio-Economic Adaptation of Two Slum Groups and The Working Class To A Housing Project in Cali, Colombia*. Unpublished Ph.D. dissertation, Department of Anthropology, University of Illinois, Urbana, 1972.

Baker, Ray Stannard. *Following the Color Line: American Negro Citizenship in the Progressive Era*. New York: Doubleday, 1908.

Banton, Michael. *Race Relations*. New York: Basic Books, 1967.

———. "White and Coloured in Britain," in Melvin M. Tumin, Ed., *Comparative Perspectives on Race Relations*. Boston: Little, Brown, 1969.

Beals, Ralph L. "Indian-Mestizo-White Relations in Spanish America,"

229

in Melvin M. Tumin, Ed., *Comparative Perspectives on Race Relations*. Boston: Little, Brown, 1969.

Blalock, Hubert M., Jr. *Toward a Theory of Minority-Group Relations*. New York: Wiley, 1967.

Blumer, Herbert. "Industrialization and Race Relations," in Guy Hunter, Ed., *Industrialization and Race Relations*. London: Oxford University Press, 1965.

Boletín Estadístico de Bolívar, Enero y Febrero, 1969.

Campos, Mons. Germán Guzmán, et al. *La Violencia en Colombia.* Bogota: Ediciones Tercer Mundo, 1962.

Camacho Leyva, Ernesto. *Quick Colombian Facts.* Bogota: Editorial Argra, 1962.

de Castellanos, Juan. *Historia de Cartagena.* Bogota: Biblioteca Popular de Cultura Colombiana, 1942.

The Chicago Commission on Race Relations. *The Negro in Chicago: A Study of Race Relations and a Race Riot.* Chicago: University of Chicago Press, 1922.

Davie, Maurice R. *Negroes in American Society.* New York: McGraw-Hill, 1949.

Departamento Administrativo Nacional de Estadística. *XIII Censo Nacional de Población (1964), Resumen General.* Bogota: Imprenta Nacional, 1967.

Dix, Robert H. *Colombia: The Political Dimensions of Change.* New Haven: Yale University Press, 1967.

El Tiempo. Bogota: January 30 and February 1, 1970.

Escalante, Aquiles. *El Negro en Colombia.* Bogota: Facultad de Sociología, Universidad Nacional de Colombia, 1964.

Fernandes, Florestan. "Relaciones de Raza en Brasil: Realidad y Mito," in Celso Furtado et al., *Brasil: Hoy.* Mexico: Siglo XXI Editores, S. A., 1968.

Freeling, William W. "Slavery and the Nullification Crisis," in Allen Weinstein and Frank Otto Gatell, Eds., *American Negro Slavery.* New York: Oxford University Press, 1968.

Freyre, Gilberto. *Brazil: An Interpretation.* New York: Knopf, 1945.

———. *The Masters and the Slaves.* New York: Knopf, 1946.

Genovese, Eugene D. *The World the Slaveholders Made.* New York: Vintage Books, 1971.

Gillin, John P. "Some Signposts for Policy," in Richard N. Adams et al., *Social Change in Latin America Today.* New York: Vintage Books, 1960.

Goldstein, Sidney, and Calvin Goldscheider. *Jewish Americans: Three Generations in a Jewish Community*. Englewood Cliffs, N.J.: Prentice-Hall, 1968.

Gordon, Milton M. *Assimilation in American Life*. New York: Oxford University Press, 1964.

Gutiérrez, José. *De La Pseudo-Aristocracia a la Autenticidad*. Bogota: Tercer Mundo, 1961.

Gutiérrez de Pineda, Virginia. *Familia y Cultura en Colombia*. Bogota: Coediciones de Tercer Mundo y Departamento de Sociología (Sección Investigaciones), Universidad Nacional de Colombia, 1968.

Harris, Marvin. *Patterns of Race in the Americas*. New York: Walker and Company, 1964.

————. "Race Relations in Minas Velhas, A Community in the Mountain Region of Central Brazil," in Charles Wagley, Ed., *Race and Class in Rural Brazil*. Paris: Unesco, 1952.

————. "Referential Ambiguity in the Calculus of Brazilian Racial Identity." *Southwestern Journal of Anthropology*. 26, Spring 1970.

Hoetink, Herman. *The Two Variants in Caribbean Race Relations, A Contribution to the Sociology of Segmented Societies*. London: Institute of Race Relations, Oxford University Press, 1967.

Hutchinson, Harry W. "Race Relations in a Rural Community of the Bahian Recôncavo," in Charles Wagley, Ed., *Race and Class in Rural Brazil*. Paris: Unesco, 1952.

Hyman, Herbert H., and Paul B. Sheatsley. "Attitudes toward Desegregation," in Melvin M. Tumin, Ed., *Comparative Perspectives on Race Relations*. Boston: Little, Brown, 1969.

Instituto De Crédito Territorial. *Desarrollo en Cartagena: Filosofía y Criterios*. Cartagena: Oficina de Rehabilitación de Tugurios, Mayo, 1969.

Jaramillo Uribe, Jaime. *Ensayos Sobre Historia Social Colombiana*. Bogota: Universidad Nacional de Colombia, 1968.

————. "Esclavos y Señores en la Sociedad Colombiana del Siglo XVIII," *Annuario Colombiano de Historia y de la Cultura*, 1963.

Juan, Jorge and Antonio de Ulloa. *Noticias Secretas de América*. Buenos Aires: Ediciones Mar Océano, 1953.

Kerner, Otto, et al. *Report of the National Advisory Commission on Civil Disorders*. New York: Bantam Books, 1968.

King, James Ferguson. "Negro Slavery in New Granada," in James

Ferguson King, Ed., *Greater America, Essays in Honor of Herbert Eugene Bolton.* Freeport, N.Y.: Books for Libraries Press, 1945.

Klein, Herbert S. *Slavery in the Americas, A Comparative Study of Virginia and Cuba.* Chicago: University of Chicago Press, 1967.

Kling, Merle. "Toward a Theory of Power and Political Instability in Latin America," *Western Political Quarterly, 9,* 1956.

Kottak, Conrad Phillip. "Race Relations in a Bahian Fishing Village," *Luso-Brazilian Review, 4,* 1967.

Lee, Alfred McClung. *Race Riot.* New York: Dryden Press, 1943.

Lemaitre, Daniel. *Flor de Corralitos de Piedra.* Cartagena: Ediciones Corralito de Piedra, 1961.

Lemaitre, Eduardo. *Antecedentes y Consecuencias del Once de 1811. Testimonios y documentos relacionados con la gloriosa gesta de la independencia absoluta de Cartagena de Indias.* Cartagena, 1961.

Leo XIII. *Libertas* and *Rerum Novarum.*

Linz, Juan. "The Party System of Spain: Past and Future," in Seymour M. Lipset and Stein Rokkan, Eds., *Party Systems and Voter Alignments.* New York: The Free Press, 1967.

Love, Joseph L. "Commentary [on Henry H. Keith's 'The nonviolent tradition in Brazilian history: a myth in need of explosion?'']," in Henry H. Keith and S. F. Edwards, Eds., *Conflict and Continuity in Brazilian Society.* Columbia: University of South Carolina Press, 1969.

Lowenthal, David. "Race and Color in the West Indies," in Melvin M. Tumin, Ed., *Comparative Perspectives on Race Relations.* Boston: Little, Brown, 1969.

Mörner, Magnus. *Race Mixture in the History of Latin America.* Boston: Little, Brown, 1967.

Morse, R. "Toward a Theory of Spanish American Government," *Journal of the History of Ideas, 15,* 1954.

Moskos, Charles C., and Wendell Bell. "Emerging Nations and Ideologies of American Social Scientists," *The American Sociologist, II,* 1965.

Myrdal, Gunnar. *An American Dilemma.* New York: McGraw-Hill, 1944.

Needler, Martin C. *Political Development in Latin America: Instability, Violence and Evolutionary Change.* New York: Random House, 1968.

Payne, James L. *Patterns of Conflict in Colombia.* New Haven: Yale University Press, 1968.

Pius IX. *Quadragessimo Anno.*

Pierson, Donald. *Negroes in Brazil, A Study of Race Contact at Bahia.* Chicago: University of Chicago Press, 1942.

Poppino, Rollie E. *Brazil, The Land and People.* New York: Oxford University Press, 1968.

Restrepo, Félix, S. J. *Colombia en la Encrucijada.* Bogota: Biblioteca Popular de Cultura Colombiana, 1951.

Reuter, Edward Byron. *Race Mixture: Studies in Intermarriage and Miscegenation.* New York: Whittlesey House, McGraw-Hill, 1931.

Rudwick, Elliot M. *Race Riot in East St. Louis.* Carbondale, Ill.: Southern Illinois Press, 1964.

Sanjek, Roger. "Brazilian Racial Terms: Some Aspects of Meaning and Learning," *American Anthropologist, 73,* 1971.

Segovia, Rodolfo. "Teoría de Cartagena: Por qué se Pierde un Siglo," in Donaldo Bossa Herazo, *Cartagena Independiente: Tradición y Desarrollo.* Bogota: Tercer Mundo, 1967.

Sellers, Charles Grier. "The Travail of Slavery," in Allen Weinstein and Frank Otto Gatell, Eds., *American Negro Slavery.* New York: Oxford University Press, 1968.

Smith, T. Lynn. *Brazil: People and Institutions.* Baton Rouge: Louisiana State University Press, 1946.

————. "The Racial Composition of the Population of Colombia," in T. Lynn Smith, Ed., *Studies of Latin American Societies.* New York: Anchor Books, 1970.

Solaún, Mauricio. *Sociología de los Golpes de Estado Latinoamericanos.* Bogota: Universidad de los Andes, 1969.

————. *Political Violence in Colombia.* Unpublished Ph.D. dissertation, Department of Sociology, University of Chicago, Chicago, 1971.

————, and Michael Quinn. *Sinners and Heretics: Patterns of Military Intervention in Latin America.* Urbana, Ill.: University of Illinois Press, 1973.

Tannenbaum, Frank. *Slave and Citizen: The Negro in the Americas.* New York: Knopf, 1947.

XIII Censo Nacional de Población, 1964, Resumen General.

Thompson, Richard. "Race in New Zealand," in Melvin M. Tumin,

Ed., *Comparative Perspectives on Race Relations*. Boston: Little, Brown, 1969.

Tumin, Melvin, M., with Arnold Feldman. "Social Class and Skin Color in Puerto Rico," in Melvin M. Tumin, Ed., *Comparative Perspectives on Race Relations*. Boston: Little, Brown, 1969.

Valtierra, Angel, S. J. *San Pedro Claver, El Santo Que Libertó Una Raza*. Cartagena: Santuario de San Pedro Claver, 1964.

van den Berghe, Pierre. *Race and Racism, A Comparative Perspective*. New York: Wiley, 1967.

———. "South Africa: The Culture and Politics of Race," in Melvin M. Tumin, Ed., *Comparative Perspectives on Race Relations*. Boston: Little, Brown, 1969.

Vasconcelos, José. *La Raza Cósmica*. Paris: Agencia Mundial de Librería, 1925.

———. "La Raza Cósmica, Misión de la Raza Latinoamerica," in Carlos Ripoll, Ed., *Conciencia Intelectual de América, Antología del Ensayo Hispanoamericano (1836–1959)*. New York: Las Americas Publishing Company, 1966.

Wagley, Charles. *Amazon Town, A Study of Man in the Tropics*. New York: Macmillan, 1967.

———. "From Caste to Class in North Brazil," in Melvin M. Tumin, Ed., *Comparative Perspectives on Race Relations*. Boston: Little, Brown, 1969.

———, Ed. *Race and Class in Rural Brazil*. Paris: Unesco, 1952.

Weber, Max. *The Theory of Social and Economic Organization*. New York: Oxford University Press, 1947.

West, Robert C. *Colonial Placer Mining in Colombia*. Baton Rouge: University of Louisiana Press, 1952.

Whitten, Norman E., Jr. "The Ecology of Race Relations in Northwest Ecuador," paper presented in the annual Meeting of the American Anthropological Association, New Orleans, Louisiana, 1969.

Williamson, Robert C. *El Estudiante Colombiano y Sus Actitudes*. Bogota: Facultad de Sociología, Universidad Nacional de Colombia, 1962.

Zimmerman, Ben. "Race Relation in the Arid Sertão," in Charles Wagley, Ed., *Race and Class in Rural Brazil*. Paris: Unesco, 1952.

INDEX

Adaptation, *see* Racial adaptation
Ambiguity, of terms, 1, 9, 18, 52,
    190, 193, 194, 223
Amerindians, 2, 3, 52
Awareness, of prejudice, 199, 204,
    214
    racial, 26, 27, 31, 39, 130, 137,
    168

Blacks, 1, 2, 3, 4, 6, 7, 8, 9, 10, 17,
    20, 21, 23, 24, 26, 27, 30, 32,
    34, 35, 36, 38, 50, 51, 54, 56,
    61, 63, 64, 68, 71, 77, 81, 82,
    84, 85, 86, 87, 90, 101, 102,
    106, 108, 109, 130, 131, 139,
    161, 162, 163, 164, 169, 170,
    171, 172, 173, 178, 180, 181,
    182, 183, 184, 185, 187, 189,
    190, 192, 195, 198, 199, 200,
    201, 205, 216, 217, 218, 219,
    220, 222
    ancestry, 7, 33, 36, 164, 220
Blancos, see Whites
Bleaching process, 7-8, 36, 62, 85,
    124, 125, 126, 143, 150, 158,
    201
Brazil, 2, 5, 6, 22, 25, 59, 60, 61, 62,

72, 79, 168

Cartagena, 3, 4, 5, 9, 10, 16, 24, 25,
    27, 30, 31, 36, 40, 51, 53, 55,
    61, 77, 78, 81, 102, 103, 105,
    106, 108, 109, 110, 112, 113,
    114, 116, 118, 119, 120, 121,
    123, 124, 127, 128, 130, 131,
    132, 137, 138, 141, 142, 143,
    146, 147, 148, 150, 151, 157,
    158, 159, 161, 162, 164, 168,
    170, 172, 181, 184, 187, 190,
    192, 193, 194, 195, 196, 199,
    200, 201, 204, 205, 213, 214,
    215, 216, 217, 218, 220, 223,
    225
    infused racial system of, 22, 24,
    25, 49, 54, 90, 101, 126, 131,
    136, 148, 153, 158, 194, 196,
    200, 215, 217, 226
    lower class, 24, 106, 107, 117-18,
    119, 125-26, 130, 131, 137, 138,
    140, 141, 143, 148, 158, 159,
    181-84, 185, 190, 192-93, 194,
    195, 199, 200, 201, 205, 217,
    220
    middle class, 24, 77, 106, 107, 115,

235

DATE DUE

2/22/74			